ROME, 16 OCTOBER 1943
HISTORY, MEMORY, LITERATURE

LEGENDA

LEGENDA is the Modern Humanities Research Association's book imprint for new research in the Humanities. Founded in 1995 by Malcolm Bowie and others within the University of Oxford, Legenda has always been a collaborative publishing enterprise, directly governed by scholars. The Modern Humanities Research Association (MHRA) joined this collaboration in 1998, became half-owner in 2004, in partnership with Maney Publishing and then Routledge, and has since 2016 been sole owner. Titles range from medieval texts to contemporary cinema and form a widely comparative view of the modern humanities, including works on Arabic, Catalan, English, French, German, Greek, Italian, Portuguese, Russian, Spanish, and Yiddish literature. Editorial boards and committees of more than 60 leading academic specialists work in collaboration with bodies such as the Society for French Studies, the British Comparative Literature Association and the Association of Hispanists of Great Britain & Ireland.

The MHRA encourages and promotes advanced study and research in the field of the modern humanities, especially modern European languages and literature, including English, and also cinema. It aims to break down the barriers between scholars working in different disciplines and to maintain the unity of humanistic scholarship. The Association fulfils this purpose through the publication of journals, bibliographies, monographs, critical editions, and the MHRA Style Guide, and by making grants in support of research. Membership is open to all who work in the Humanities, whether independent or in a University post, and the participation of younger colleagues entering the field is especially welcomed.

ALSO PUBLISHED BY THE ASSOCIATION

Critical Texts
Tudor and Stuart Translations • *New Translations* • *European Translations*
MHRA Library of Medieval Welsh Literature

MHRA Bibliographies
Publications of the Modern Humanities Research Association

The Annual Bibliography of English Language & Literature
Austrian Studies
Modern Language Review
Portuguese Studies
The Slavonic and East European Review
Working Papers in the Humanities
The Yearbook of English Studies

www.mhra.org.uk
www.legendabooks.com

ITALIAN PERSPECTIVES

Editorial Committee

Professor Simon Gilson, University of Oxford (General Editor)
Professor Francesca Billiani, University of Manchester
Professor Manuele Gragnolati, Université Paris-Sorbonne
Professor Catherine Keen, University College London
Professor Martin McLaughlin, Magdalen College, Oxford

Founding Editors

Professor Zygmunt Barański and Professor Anna Laura Lepschy

In the light of growing academic interest in Italy and the reorganization of many university courses in Italian along interdisciplinary lines, this book series, founded by Maney Publishing under the imprint of the Northern Universities Press and now continuing under the Legenda imprint, aims to bring together different scholarly perspectives on Italy and its culture. *Italian Perspectives* publishes books and collections of essays on any period of Italian literature, language, history, culture, politics, art, and media, as well as studies which take an interdisciplinary approach and are methodologically innovative.

Managing Editor
Dr Graham Nelson, 41 Wellington Square, Oxford OX1 2JF, UK
www.legendabooks.com

Rome, 16 October 1943

History, Memory, Literature

❖

Mara Josi

l

LEGENDA

Italian Perspectives 60
Modern Humanities Research Association
2023

Published by Legenda
an imprint of the Modern Humanities Research Association
Salisbury House, Station Road, Cambridge CB1 2LA

ISBN 978-1-83954-211-4 (HB)
ISBN 978-1-83954-212-1 (PB)

First published 2023

Copy-Editor: Charlotte Wathey

CONTENTS

❖

To my parents and to my grandparents

ACKNOWLEDGEMENTS

❖

This book is the outcome of an almost decade-long engagement with Italian Holocaust literature and the literary writings devoted to the Roman round-up. For this reason, there are many people I want to thank for their support, advice, and patience as well as many institutions that hosted me throughout this process. I am grateful to the University of Turin, from where my interest in academic research and specifically Holocaust culture stemmed. I thank the scholars that guided me and supported my choice to leave Italy, Pietro Adamo, Alberto Cavaglion, Enrica Culasso, Fabio Levi, Beatrice Manetti, and Enrico Mattioda, and my first readers, supporters, and colleagues, Federica Jacobsen and Elena Matassa.

I am deeply grateful to Gonville and Caius College for being such a welcoming home ever since I first arrived in Cambridge. My sincerest thanks go to the people in the Italian Department at the University of Cambridge for providing such a vibrant, enriching, and supportive community in which to work and grow: Pierpaolo Antonello, Abigail Brundin, J. D. Rhodes, Helena Sanson, and Heather Webb. I thank my PhD examiners, Stefania Lucamante and Katia Pizzi, for their careful reading of my doctoral thesis and for their perceptive suggestions. My gratitude and my heart go to my Cantabrigian family, Erica Bellia, Alessia Carrai, Tommaso Forni, Serena Laiena, and Nicole Maniero.

I am truly grateful to the Irish Research Council for supporting my Postdoctoral Fellowship at University College Dublin. At UCD, I had fruitful dialogues with a heterogenous group of scholars who provided me with thought-provoking insights on my research. Thanks to Paolo Acquaviva, Manu Braganca, Marc Jones, William Mulligan, and Síofra Pierce.

In Cambridge and Dublin, I had the privilege to be supervised and mentored respectively by Robert S. C. Gordon and Ursula Fanning, whom I sincerely thank for their intellectual and human generosity, constant encouragement, and unfailing kindness and patience. They taught me a lot, if not what I know.

I proofread the manuscript of this book at the University of Manchester, where I found a group of colleagues that supported me in every possible way with challenging and stimulating conversations, chocolate, coffee, and dinners. My heartfelt thanks to Guyda Armstrong, Jeff Barda, Francesca Billiani, Monica Boria, Jean-Marc Dreyfus, and Stephen J. Milner.

I am very grateful to Legenda for accepting my manuscript and for smoothly and quickly organising the publication. Thanks to Simon Gilson for his generosity and enthusiasm, to Graham Nelson for his patience and accuracy, to Charlotte Wathey for her precise comments, and to the two anonymous readers who endorsed my work and provided me with attentive intuitions for a better publication.

Many warm thanks to the scholars who spent time reasoning with me, read various drafts of my work, supported my choices, and guided me: Richard Cook, Guido Furci, Francesco Lucioli, Vittorio Montemaggi, Martina Piperno, Sue Vice, and Katrin Wehling-Giorgi.

Finally, my appreciation goes to the staff and librarians of the Cambridge University Library, the Archivio contemporaneo 'Alessandro Bonsanti' in Florence, the Biblioteca Nazionale Centrale in Rome, the Fondazione Centro Documentazione Ebraica and Fondazione Arnoldo e Alberto Mondadori in Milan, and the Centro Primo Levi in Turin for their support. My gratitude goes to the British School at Rome and the Centre for War Studies at UCD where I presented work-in-progress and received precious feedback that I collated in the final version of this book.

⋆   ⋆   ⋆   ⋆   ⋆

This book would have not been possible without my loved ones, the old and the new, and I do not need to call you by your name. I am sure that all of you know how precious you are to me and how grateful I am to have found you on my way. You are all treasured in my heart.

I dedicate this book to my parents and grandparents for their support, sacrifices, and love.

ABBREVIATIONS

❖

The following abbreviations are used for references to the primary texts discussed in Chapters 3 to 6.

CE   Giacomo Debenedetti, 'Campo di ebrei', in *Saggi* (Milan: Mondadori, 1999), pp. 858–65

D   Anna Foa, *Diaspora: storia degli ebrei nel Novecento* (Rome: Laterza, 2009)

FW   Rosetta Loy, *First Words: A Childhood in Fascist Italy*, trans. by Gregory Conti (New York: Metropolitan Books/ Henry Holt, 2000)

H   Elsa Morante, *History: A Novel*, trans. by William Weaver (New York: Aventura, 1984)

OE   Giacomo Debenedetti, *Otto ebrei*, in *Saggi* (Milan: Mondadori, 1999), pp. 25–63

OS   Giacomo Debenedetti, *October 16, 1943; Eight Jews*, trans. by Estelle Gilson (Notre Dame, IN: University of Notre Dame Press, 2001)

PE   Rosetta Loy, *La parola ebreo* (Turin: Einaudi, 1997)

PO13 Anna Foa, *Portico d'Ottavia 13: una casa del ghetto nel lungo inverno del '43* (Rome: Laterza, 2013)

PO   Anna Foa, *Portico d'Ottavia*, illus. by Matteo Berton (Rome: Laterza, 2015)

S   Elsa Morante, *La Storia: romanzo*, in *Opere*, 2 vols (Milan: Mondadori, 1990), II, 255–1036

SO   Giacomo Debenedetti, *16 ottobre 1943*, in *Saggi* (Milan: Mondadori, 1999), pp. 25–63

SS   Elsa Morante, 'Il soldato siciliano', in *Opere*, 2 vols (Milan: Mondadori, 1990), I, 1509–15

INTRODUCTION

❖

Imagine a prism. Observe it from afar. You have a general, supranational perception of the Holocaust.[1] Get closer. You recognise different facets, different national perspectives on it. Countries have a particular history to recollect, come to terms with, and represent. Each one influences and is influenced by the others. Through fluid and migratory ways, national histories and perspectives of the Holocaust cross national boundaries, cultural borders, the facets of the prism. The perception of the Holocaust, therefore, is not only supranational but also transnational. Now, draw closer to one facet of the prism, to Italy, to Rome, to one day in October during the German occupation of 1943–45, to the largest single round-up and deportation of Jews from Italy.

In 1943 one of the most populous Italian Jewish communities was located in Rome. On Saturday 16 October 1943, 1259 people were arrested by the German occupiers and gathered in a temporary detention centre for two days. On 17 October, 252 of 1259 were freed because they had been recognised as what the Germans defined as 'non-Jews'. The rest were deported on 18 October from a local railway station, Stazione Tiburtina, to Auschwitz-Birkenau, where they arrived on the night of Friday 22 October. Sixteen people survived and returned to Rome after the end of the Second World War.[2]

The round-up and deportation of the Roman Jews took place after Rome had been declared an 'open city' in August 1943, in what was then the southernmost city in the Italian Social Republic (RSI) after the Allies had reached Naples on 21 September. It was perpetrated in the heart of the Roman Catholic world, in a city of international as well as national significance. The Roman round-up is notable in its own right and in relation to the deportations that occurred elsewhere in Italy and in Europe, and it is also notable for its subsequent complicated and fluctuating phases of memory which influence and are influenced by the perception of the Holocaust at national, supranational, and transnational levels.

In the months after October 1943, there was a vague awareness among the Allies and in the occupied Italian territories of what had happened in Rome. In Italy, initially, the process of discovery and then recall was undefined and it was complicated by rapid political and social developments. Public and collective commemoration of the event only started about ten years later. It was only during the 1960s that the episode started to be commemorated beyond the Roman Jewish community. In the 1970s and 1980s commemoration and recollection became strained in the context of ongoing Arab-Israeli conflicts and new forms of anti-Semitism in Europe and Italy. In the 1990s, with a new international interest in the Holocaust, there were new commemorative programmes, including some with the participation of Israel. In the 2000s, commemorations of 16 October grew both in Rome and across the country, especially following the establishment of International Holocaust Remembrance Day, 'Giorno della memoria', in 2001. In fact, on that occasion, some people had hoped that the 'Giorno della memoria' in Italy could be commemorated on 16 October, so as to guarantee a national perspective on the supranational remembrance of the Holocaust. Today, 16 October stands as an emblem of the persecution of Italian Jews. It represents a powerful case study of how such emblematic events move from being local and little-known or understood to becoming sites and sources of cultural memory.

In both national and international terms, little was written about the Roman round-up until the 2000s, when there was a peak in historical research projects and publications.[3] Few research projects, however, have been dedicated to discourse on the cultural and collective memory of the Roman round-up.[4] Even fewer have been devoted to the literary texts that have been written about it.[5] And yet literary texts have emerged as a major medium of the production of its memory.

Building on the research conducted so far, this bi-partite book intends to broaden the scholarship on 16 October by focusing on the literary corpus and providing an updated overview of literary texts devoted to the round-up.[6] Part I offers the introductory, newly articulated theoretical framework which lays the ground for the entire investigation and is at the core of the textual analysis of Part II which provides alternative paths of exegesis of the four most influential texts about the Roman round-up: a chronicle-narrative-essay published in book form in 1945 by Giacomo Debenedetti, *16 ottobre 1943*; an historical novel published in 1974 by Elsa Morante, *La Storia*; an autobiographical novel-essay published in 1997 by Rosetta Loy, *La parola ebreo*; and a work of popular history published in 2013 by Anna Foa, *Portico d'Ottavia 13*.[7] As a whole, the book analyses these four works in relation to the hybrid forms through which each one links history, memory, and literature. It examines the ways in which these four literary interpretations and narrativisations of this historical event have facilitated a national and international understanding and recollection of 16 October 1943.

16 ottobre 1943 was published while Italy was still at war and Italian Jews were hiding in order to avoid deportation to Nazi extermination and concentration camps; *La Storia* while the persecution and the deportation of the Italian Jews were commonly seen only as death mechanisms perpetrated by the Nazi occupiers; *La parola ebreo* when the resurgence of the far right wing in Italian politics involved a new interest in the Holocaust and a return of Holocaust-related publications; *Portico d'Ottavia 13* on the seventieth anniversary of the Roman round-up when in Rome and in Italy more broadly the numerous and various commemorations of 16 October — books, plays, exhibitions, for example — increased the interest in the Holocaust and Holocaust-related events in Italian society. Through the analysis of these four texts, this book maps changes and developments in Italian cultural memory of the Holocaust over the last eighty years. It considers how these four works were influenced by, and at the same time have influenced, the collective memory of the times in which they were published and how they left their mark on Italian cultural memory of the Holocaust. For this reason, the last section of each chapter of Part II captures the impact of each book as a form of bequests from each author to later texts and to readers of their own generation and beyond.

This book shares the idea of cultural memory as a product of personal memories which are told in different media and which are both influenced by a collective framework and, at the same time, constitute it. It agrees with the view of literature as one of the media which most fruitfully explores and explains what cultural memory is and, indeed, enacts it.[8] It, therefore, presents *16 ottobre 1943*, *La Storia*, *La parola ebreo*, and *Portico d'Ottavia 13* as both key ingredients in the process of constructing the cultural memory of the Roman round-up and a means for observing it. Through an interdisciplinary framework which combines theories of cultural memory studies, it shows how these texts have operated on the personal and on the collective level: in other words, on the reader and on society. It demonstrates how they have created images of the episode which are part of both the conscious mechanisms of recollection and the unconscious process of remembering. It discusses how they have shaped awareness of the Roman round-up by framing it as the representative event of discrimination and persecution in the Italian territories under German occupation and how they have engaged in an enduring dialogue with historians regarding the interpretation of 16 October 1943. It presents them as bearers of historical knowledge and channels of memory; not only outcomes of remembrance but also active ingredients in the process of forging cultural memory.

The four works are also examined in relation to their authors, who are characterised by various shared and distinctive factors: by their Jewish or non-Jewish background, both in its own right and in relation to the persecution and the risk of deportation during the war; by the extent of their first- or second-hand experience of persecution; by their generational framework. Marianne Hirsch's generational approach to Holocaust studies is applied here to analyse the works and to read their authors' commitment to narrating the Roman round-up.[9] However, it is not my intention to define the notion and/or the evolution of *impegno* [commitment] in relation to the Holocaust within the career of Debenedetti, Morante, Loy, and Foa. My interest is in tracing plausible reasons that the authors had for choosing to write about 16 October. I believe that Debenedetti, Morante, Loy, and Foa each perceived their process of writing not only as inextricably related to the world but also inscribed in it and addressed to it. Thus, the second section of each chapter of Part II considers their choice to write about the Roman round-up as their willingness, or commitment, to represent different shades of an event that was either ignored, as in the case of Debenedetti writing in 1945, or else going through different stages of recollection, as in the case of the later writers.

In their works, Debenedetti, Morante, Loy, and Foa all interweave various genres and combine in many ways historical elements and sources with literary re-elaborations of individual memories. In this regard, *La Storia*, *La parola ebreo*, and *Portico d'Ottavia 13* are also read in relation to some of the notions explored by new historicist and feminist perspectives in Italy in the early 1990s which suggest a re-evaluation of both the method of historical research and the writing of and about history.[10] I look at three women writers' similar methods of re-working personal testimonies, exploring ego–documents, and adapting sources, as well as their willingness to bring 16 October to a critical communal awareness by elevating the private, the silenced, and the neglected to public consciousness, to collective memory.

Despite the differences in genre, personal experience, and combination of historical sources and personal memories, the four authors share recurrent themes in their treatment of the Roman round-up and develop similar literary strategies and techniques. They combine historical facts and personal stories in narrative forms which transmit the past in and through lived experience. They use a range of techniques such as elaborate first-person narratives, detailed descriptions of everyday life, and present-tense voice to convey embodied and seemingly immediate experiences. They address readers in intimate ways, typical of direct, personal, and informal communication. These and other strategies involve readers in their stories and create collective affective bonds within and across generations. In this sense, by combining notions of cultural memory studies and theories of emotion, the book shows that these texts reactivate and re-embody distant individual and social memories, represent them in familiar forms of mediation and aesthetic expression, and create a sense of shared social space and historical time in readers, thus facilitating their understanding and recollection of the Roman round-up.

★   ★   ★   ★   ★

Part I of this book consists of two chapters. It examines the triangular relationship between history, memory, and literature, investigates how cultures manage the recollection of their own history, and considers the role of literature in cultural memory, calling upon the more traditional field of Holocaust studies and notions of cultural memory studies and theories of emotions.[11]

Chapter 1, 'History, Memory, Literature: A Triangular Relationship', explores how the bond between history and memory has changed in many ways in the last hundred years, especially after the impact of the Holocaust, and shows how the transmission of memory through literature has become an authoritative medium for the representation of the past. It provides an account of the evolution of the concept of collective memory and examines the idea of cultural memory by looking at the role literary texts play in the transmission of past memories in Holocaust writing. It lays, therefore, the grounds for the methodological approach that will be used for the re-reading of the literary texts analysed in Part II. Chapter 2, '16 October 1943: The Roman Round-up', provides an overview of the perception of the Holocaust and of the Roman round-up within Italian culture from 1944 to date; it shows how certain works of literature, along with historiography and other cultural forms of expression, have influenced the perception and memory of 16 October at a national level; it recapitulates the phases which preceded the round-up and explores the transmission of this event in Italian cultural memory.

Part II is composed of four chapters, each dedicated to one of the four core texts. On the basis of the theoretical framework provided in Part I, the chapters develop detailed textual analyses of the works in question, looking also at their genesis, composition, and position in their respective author's biography and work. They locate their different elements of genre, their structure and style, and their specific relation to the events of 16 October 1943 in the context of Italian literary and cultural history. Finally, they explore the relationship of each text to Italian cultural memory of the Holocaust, or, rather, the hybrid of its history, memory, and literature as explored in Part I.

Chapter 3, 'Giacomo Debenedetti, *16 ottobre 1943*', considers Debenedetti's proximity to the events described and his willingness to record them. It analyses *16 ottobre 1943*, its genesis, its moment of publication, and its mode of constructing its testimonial voice and narrative; it looks at the influence of the text in both the historical and the literary fields, and proposes a re-reading of *16 ottobre 1943* in light of cultural memory.

Chapter 4, 'Elsa Morante, *La Storia*', examines Morante's literary re-elaboration of the Roman round-up. Although the round-up itself constitutes only a small part, the description of 16 and 18 October in the chapter '1943' has become a channel of transmission for the cultural memory of the event. The chapter considers Morante's Jewish origins and her public commitment to writing a novel about the Second World War. It links her description of the Roman round-up to that of Debenedetti and begins to build the chain of transmission of literary memory. Morante's literary representation of the events of 16 and 18 October is read through the lens of her depiction of the sensory perceptions of the main characters, thus showing a link between theories of emotion and cultural memory studies.

Chapter 5, 'Rosetta Loy, *La parola ebreo*', considers Loy's commitment to the subject of the Holocaust as a vicarious Catholic witness of the Roman round-up. It proposes three lenses through which to examine *La parola ebreo* and her description of 16 October in relation to discrimination and persecution in Italy: otherness, oblivion, and responsibility. In terms of cultural memory, it investigates the strategies she used to merge historical data, personal memories, and literary techniques to make the Roman round-up more shareable and memorable, and it draws comparisons with the strategies proposed by Debenedetti and Morante.

Chapter 6, 'Anna Foa, *Portico d'Ottavia 13*', considers Foa's work of narrative history dedicated to the Roman round-up and its subsequent adaptation as a picture book for children. It considers this text, or texts, as a work of postmemory and examines Foa's will to represent 16 October through places and microhistories. It reads her text in relation to *16 ottobre 1943*, *La Storia*, and *La parola ebreo*, thus drawing to a close the survey and analysis of literary works as a medium of memory of the Roman round-up from 1945 to 2013.

The concluding pages of the book offer an overview of the wealth of works created for cinema, television, and theatre about the Roman round-up produced over the last twenty years.[12] They broaden the close textual focus of the analysis and contribute to further consideration of the memory of the Roman round-up addressed through other media. The cluster of twenty-first-century screen and stage adaptations and representations of the Roman round-up demonstrates that cinema, television, and theatre follow paths similar to those of literature, and, at times, precisely the path of the four works examined in this book, in their attempts to share the past and transmit it into cultural memory. It shows that we can establish direct and indirect intertextual references to our four texts in multiple media, and it proves once more the foundational and leading role that all four have had in the Italian cultural memory of the Roman round-up and of the Holocaust in Italy. The concluding pages confirm that the trajectory of the memory of the Roman round-up is continually growing and traversing facets of the abovementioned prism, thus contributing to a deeper perspective of the Holocaust at national, supranational, and transnational levels.

Notes to the Introduction

1. Every possible term for naming the genocide of Europe's Jews and other Nazi genocides brings with it problems and limitations. I have opted for the most common term in English and in Israel in its English-language publications: 'Holocaust'. On the terminology of the Holocaust see for example: Anna Vera Sullam Calimani, 'A Name for Extermination (Hurban, Auschwitz, Genocide, Holocaust, Shoah)', *Modern Language Review*, 94.4 (1999), 978–99, and, *I nomi dello sterminio* (Turin: Einaudi, 2001); Robert S. C. Gordon, 'The Holocaust in Italian Collective Memory: "Il giorno della memoria", 27 January 2001', *Modern Italy*, 2.2 (2006), 167-88, and *The Holocaust in Italian Culture, 1944–2010* (Stanford, CA: Stanford University Press, 2012), pp. 157-87. Also, I acknowledge the persecution of Romani people and homosexuals in Italy. In this book, however, I will specifically consider the Holocaust from the perspective of Jewish persecution and deportation.
2. For the most accurate number of people deported see Gabriele Rigano, '16 ottobre 1943: accadono a Roma cose incredibili', in *Roma, 16 ottobre 1943: anatomia di una deportazione*, ed. by Silvia Haia Antonucci and others (Milan: Guerini, 2006), pp. 63-85 (p. 51).
3. The earliest examples of historiography that refer to 16 October include Renzo De Felice, *Storia degli ebrei italiani sotto il fascismo* (Turin: Einaudi, 1961); *Gli ebrei in Italia durante il fascismo*, ed. by Paolo Foa (vol. 1) and Guido Valabrega, 3 vols (Milan: CDEC, 1961-63); Robert Katz, *Black Sabbath* (London: Barker, 1969). Major recent publications on the subject include *Roma, 16 ottobre 1943*, ed. by Haia Antonucci and others; Marcello Pezzetti, *16 ottobre 1943: la razzia degli ebrei di Roma* (Rome: Gameni, 2013); *Dopo il 16 ottobre: gli ebrei a Roma tra occupazione, resistenza, accoglienza e delazioni*, ed. by Silvia Haia Antonucci and Claudio Procaccia (Rome: Viella, 2017); Liliana Picciotto, 'The Decision-making Process of the Roundup of the Jews of Rome (October 1943): A Historiographic Revisitation Based on OSS (Office of Strategic Services) Documents', *Yad Vashem Studies*, 48.1-2 (2020), 1-36.
4. See for example *16 ottobre 1943: la deportazione degli ebrei romani tra storia e memoria*, ed. by Martin Baumeister, Amedeo Osti Guerrazzi, and Claudio Procaccia (Rome: Viella, 2016).
5. On the subject see, for example: Gordon, *The Holocaust in Italian Culture*, pp. 86-138; Alberto Cavaglion, 'Il grembo della Shoah: 16 ottobre 1943 di Umberto Saba, Giacomo Debenedetti, Elsa Morante', in *Dopo i testimoni: memorie, storiografie e narrazioni della deportazione razziale*, ed. by Marta Baiardi and Alberto Cavaglion (Rome: Viella, 2014), pp. 245-61; Stefania Lucamante, *Forging Shoah Memories: Italian Women Writers, Jewish Identity, and the Holocaust* (New York: Palgrave MacMillan, 2014), pp. 153-97.
6. This volume considers the works published up to 2022 and, in the Conclusion, film, television series, and plays produced up to 2022.
7. Giacomo Debenedetti, '16 ottobre 1943', *Mercurio*, 1 (1944), 75-97 (subsequently published as a book, *16 ottobre 1943* (Rome: OET, 1945)); Elsa Morante, *La Storia* (Turin: Einaudi, 1974); Rosetta Loy, *La parola ebreo* (Turin: Einaudi, 1997); Anna Foa, *Portico d'Ottavia 13: una casa del*

ghetto nel lungo inverno del '43 (Rome: Laterza, 2013).

8. On cultural memory and its relation to literature see for example: Ann Rigney, *Imperfect Histories: The Elusive Past and the Legacy of Romantic Historicism* (Ithaca, NY: Cornell University Press, 2001); Renate Lachmann, 'Cultural Memory and the Role of Literature', *European Review*, 12.2 (2004), 165–78; Astrid Erll and Ann Rigney, 'Literature and the Production of Cultural Memory', *European Journal of English Studies*, 10.2 (2006), 11–115; Marianne Hirsch and Leo Spitzer, 'Testimonial Objects: Memory, Gender and Transmission', *Poetic Today*, 27.2 (2006), 353–83; Marianne Hirsch, 'The Generation of Postmemory', *Poetics Today*, 29.1 (2008), 103–28; *A Companion to Cultural Memory Studies*, ed. by Astrid Erll, Ansgar Nünning, and Sara Young (New York: De Gruyter, 2010); Astrid Erll, *Memory in Culture* (New York: Palgrave Macmillan, 2011).

9. Hirsch, 'The Generation of Postmemory'.

10. On this see, for example: *Discutendo di storia: soggettività, ricerca, biografia*, ed. by Società Italiana delle Storiche (Turin: Rosenberg & Sellier, 1990); *Donne tra memoria e storia*, ed. by Laura Capobianco (Naples: Liguori, 1993); Carol Lazzaro-Weiss, *From Margins to Mainstream: Feminism and Fictional Modes in Italian Women's Writing* (Philadelphia: University of Pennsylvania Press, 1993); *Generazioni: trasmissione della storia e tradizione delle donne*, ed. by Società Italiana delle Storiche (Turin: Rosenberg & Sellier, 1993); *The Lonely Mirror*, ed. by Paola Bono and Sandra Kemp (London: Routledge, 1993); *Le donne e la storia: problemi di metodo e confronti storiografici*, ed. by Maria Rosaria Pellizzari (Naples: Edizioni Scientifiche Italiane, 1995); Maria Ornella Marotti, 'Literary Historicism and Women's Tradition', *Italian Culture*, 13 (1995), 261–72, and 'Feminist Historians/ Historical Fictions', *Italian Culture*, 14 (1996), 147–60.

11. In the larger field of Holocaust studies, the following works have been especially useful: Lawrence Langer, *Holocaust Testimonies. The Ruins of Memory* (New Haven, CT: Yale University Press, 1991); Berel Lang, 'Holocaust Genres and the Turn to History', in *The Holocaust and the Text: Speaking the Unspeakable*, ed. by Andrew Leak and George Paizis (Basingstoke: Macmillan, 2000), pp. 17–31; Erlud Ibsch, 'Memory, History, Imagination: How Time Affects the Perspective on Holocaust Literature', in *Contemporary Jewish Writers in Italy: A Generational Approach*, ed. by Raniero Speelman, Monica Jansen, and Silvia Gaiga (Utrecht: Igitur, 2007), pp. 1–13. On theory of emotion see for example: Dolf Zillmann, 'Mechanisms of Emotional Involvement with Drama', *Poetics*, 23 (1994), 33–51; Patrick Colm Hogan, 'Simulation and the Structure of Emotional Memory Learning From Arthur Miller's *After the Fall*', in *Cognitive Literary Science: Dialogues between Literature and Cognition,* ed. by Michael Burke and Emily T. Troscianko (New York: Oxford University Press, 2017), pp. 113–34, and 'What Literature Teaches Us About Emotion: Synthesizing Affective Science and Literary Study', in *The Oxford Handbook of Cognitive Literary Studies*, ed. by Lisa Zunshine (New York: Oxford University Press, 2015), pp. 273–90.

12. A complete list, with summaries, of the films, television series, and plays which deal with the round-up is to be found in the Appendix to this volume.

PART I

CHAPTER 1

❖

❖

History, Memory, Literature:
A Triangular Relationship

From Collective to Cultural Memory

The relationship between history and memory has changed in many ways over the past century. From being seen as unreliable and distorting sources, individual memories have become the partners of historiography, documents in the reconstruction of the recent past. This kinship deepens and evolves with the inclusion of literature as a third element. Especially after the impact of the Holocaust, the transmission of memory through literature has become an authoritative medium for the representation of that past. This triangular relationship between history, memory, and literature helps us to reconsider the role of literature in cultural memory on both a personal and a collective level.

Investigation into the process of collective recollection finds its roots in the mid-1920s in France. In 1925, the French sociologist Maurice Halbwachs established that there is a connection between a social group and a collective memory and started systematically using the concept of collective memory in his work *Les Cadres sociaux de la mémoire*, in which he argued that individual memories are socially constructed and that 'there are no recollections which can be said to be purely interior'.[1] According to Halbwachs, individual memories are triggered and shaped by external factors. They are perceivable and verifiable only within a social framework and they are carried by a specific social group, limited in space and in time.

In the last seventy years, scholarly discussions on collective memory have greatly developed, teasing out multiple connections and innovative methods, and proposing interdisciplinary research on the memory, the recollection, and the remembrance of the past in contemporary societies and cultures. The concept of collective memory has, in other words, influenced and has been influenced by many fields of study including history, sociology, anthropology, philosophy, psychology, linguistics, literature, theory of narrative, media studies, and cognitive studies.

In this book, the term 'collective memory' refers not only to Halbwachs's original concept but also to the linked notion of collected memory which was developed in the 1990s. Scholars offered a new paradigm: they redefined the concept of 'collective memory', what a given society remembers, and supplemented it with the idea of 'collected memory', that is the set of individual memories that people of a given society share.[2] Elena Esposito, for example, suggests that the reference points of collective memory are not anchored to society, but to the consciousness of the individuals in it.[3] Similarly, Jeffrey K. Olick stated that 'the fundamental presumption [...] is that individuals are central: only individuals remember [...] and any publicly available commemorative symbols are interpretable only to the degree to which they elicit a reaction in some group of individuals'.[4] Specifically referring to the Holocaust, to its memory and public art, James E. Young, too, discusses the difference between 'collective' and 'collected' memory, and preferably uses the syntagm 'collected memory'. 'If societies remember,' he says, 'it is only insofar as their institutions and rituals organize, shape, even inspire their constituents' memories'.[5] In this sense, the personal and the collectivity come together.

Every nation remembers, or forgets, the past according to its own tradition, ideals, and experiences. The memory of an event is therefore a mixture of collected memories, a mixture engendered by radically different contemporary and later experiences of the people involved. In this respect, Richard Terdiman and Wulf Kansteiner, for example, agree that collective memory resides in the perceiving consciousness of each individual as well as in the practices and the institutions of the society to which it refers.[6] There are therefore two constituents of memory: one is biological memory; the other is composed of the symbolic institutions, practices, and media by which social groups construct a shared past.[7] The two, the cognitive and the social, are inextricably bound and interact continuously. The syntagm 'collective memory' is used here to illustrate and design a collectivity made up of numerous individuals whose memories assume relevance when they are structured, represented, and used in a social setting.

Aleida Assmann is among the scholars who most widely explored the concept of collective memory. She theoretically elaborated it into strands of social, political, and cultural memory. These strands respectively refer to the past as experienced and transmitted within a given society, to the role of memory for the formation of national identities, and to the memories transmitted via different media and re-elaborated in these. According to Assmann, cultural memory exists across generations. It translates 'the transient into the permanent, that is, [it invents] techniques of transmitting and storing information deemed vital for the constitution and continuation of a specific group'.[8] It has active and archival dimensions and reconfigures itself in the process of remembering. It is built on informal face-to-face exchanges of lived experiences and on the transmission of experiences that have been entirely recast in the media. Cultural memory, therefore, has no temporal horizon. It refers to the memories maintained across generations by social practices and institutions such as media, monuments, and commemorations.[9] It is the product of personal memories which are influenced by a collective framework and which, at the same time, constitute it. The individual and the social convene. Personal stories, told in different media — literary texts, films, plays, etc. — enrich the heterogeneous, changing, and continuous image of the past which a group of people shares. 'We are presented,' to cite Assmann, 'with a dynamic model of continuous reconstruction and elastic adaptability to the demands of an ever-changing present'.[10]

Cultural memory can be explored through different disciplines depending on whether individuals, groups, networks, or communities, each using different media, are examined. By looking at the transmission of the past through the medium of literary texts, this book proposes to analyse the idea of cultural memory in light of the triangular relationship between history, memory, and literature.

Literature and Cultural Memory

The idea of a triangular relationship between history, memory, and literature has its roots in the first decades of the twentieth century, specifically in Marc Bloch and Lucien Febvre's theories of history. They are linked to the Annales school of historiography and the corresponding journal, *Annales d'histoire économique et sociale*, which was founded by Bloch and Febvre in 1929 and of whose editorial board Halbwachs became a member.[11]

According to Bloch and Febvre, the past can be traced in documents which have not traditionally been assumed to transmit historical data, providing different but also foundational insights into the past through collective representations, myths, and images. They see a recalibration of the authority traditionally vested in historical sources and, in fact, a collaboration between disciplines — geography, sociology, psychology, economics, linguistics, social anthropology, and so on — contributing to historical research and understanding. Literary texts can take facts, stories, and experiences which had been neglected, dismissed, overlooked, forgotten, or ignored and transform them into something that is memorable.

What follows is a newly articulated theoretical framework which merges notions of cultural memory studies with theories of emotions. This framework is indebted to Astrid Erll's modes of writing the past, Ann Rigney's five ways of interaction between literature and cultural memory, Alison Landsberg's prosthetic memory, and theories of emotions applied to literature by Terence Cave and by Caroline Pirlet and Andreas Wirag. It will be applied for the first time here to corroborate the literary analysis in Part II.

Astrid Erll, Ann Rigney, and Alison Landsberg have in their different ways fruitfully investigated the relationship between history, memory, and literature.[12] Literary texts re-elaborate different kinds of knowledge and ideological viewpoints and they come to be etched into memory spaces. They can display and juxtapose divergent and contested memories and give different insights into past societies and cultures. They can adapt and allude to manifold documents, including historical sources, which they can quote, rephrase, incorporate, and discuss; they create intertextual bonds with previous or contemporary literary and non-literary texts. Renate Lachmann, more broadly, notes that literature 'sketches out a memory space into which earlier texts are gradually absorbed and transformed'.[13]

This reciprocal influence suggests that literature is both a channel for perpetuating traditions and a source of new perceptions of the past. It is a vehicle for envisioning the past and thus for facilitating the understanding and the recollection of historical data through engaging and therefore memorable literary re-elaborations. In this sense, throughout this book, I refer to literature as one of the media which most effectively investigates, explains, and even enacts cultural memory. I look at it as both a key ingredient in the process of constructing cultural memory and a means for observing it. I consider the extent to which literature allows us to reflect on the use and the value of personal and collective memory, thus prompting a dialogue with historians about the transmission and the interpretation of the past in a given society. I believe literature can turn into a medium of memory and a bearer of historical knowledge.

Erll, Rigney, and Landsberg have variously looked at narrative forms of writing to carry out research on the transmission and recollection of historical knowledge through and in literature. They see the boundaries between history and narrative as ill-defined: historical sources and their literary re-elaborations can integrate and support each other. Erll looks at literary texts and concentrates on particular modes of writing. She reflects on the ways in which some narrative strategies and techniques engage and address the reader. Rigney examines the influence literary texts have on cultural memory. Landsberg explores the reasons why individual stories are more easily understood, interiorised, and then remembered than historical accounts of facts. These three lines of investigation are here intertwined to build a lens through which to read the literary texts considered in this volume. More specifically, Erll's textual analysis is conducted in relation to the influence that texts have on a collective and on a personal level. Rigney's approach is linked to a close reading of the text and to the relations the text establishes with readers. Similarly, Landsberg's theories are to be analysed in relation to the modes of representing the past and to the different ways of transmitting and recollecting past events and memories in cultural memory.

According to Erll, there are five modes of writing the past: the 'experiential', the 'monumental', the 'antagonistic', the 'historicising', and the 'reflexive'. The 'experiential' mode transmits the past as a lived-through experience; here Erll broadly refers to soldiers' tales. The 'monumental' envisages the past as mythical. The 'historicising' conveys literary events and people as if they were objects of scholarly historiography. The 'antagonistic' helps to promote interpretation of a past coming from specific group identities; here Erll cites feminist or post-colonial writings. The 'reflexive' simultaneously observes how the past is remembered and offers new ways for its recollection, and here Erll cites present-day historiographic metafictions.[14] She assumes that, by combining these modes of writing, literary texts establish different mnemonic strategies and therefore some narrative strategies and techniques can be re-read through the lenses of cultural memory study. The personal voice is used, she notes, 'to convey embodied, seemingly immediate experience'; similarly, the circumstantial realism gives the idea of 'everyday life in the past'.[15] Through different strategies and techniques, literary representations engage readers in reflections on particular aspects of an event and influence the perception they have of the past. Literary texts are, therefore, a formative medium that contributes to the recollection of historical facts. But they are also performative when they influence the readership beyond the passing moment of reading.

'Literature,' as Brigit Neumann suggests, 'is endowed with a (memory-)cultural effectiveness and can contribute to a new perspectivization of extra-textual orders of knowledge and hierarchies of values'.[16] It can change readers' approach to the past and make them aware of the mechanisms behind the processes of recollection, remembrance, and neglect.

Rigney constructs a model of five distinct ways in which literature interacts with cultural memory and transmits historical knowledge. She suggests that a piece of writing may be defined as a 'relay station' when it conveys earlier forms of recollection of historical facts; as a 'stabilizer' when it succeeds in representing particular periods in a memorable way and becomes a stabilising factor in cultural memory; as a 'catalyst' when it draws attention to historical events hitherto neglected; as an 'object of recollection' when it is recalled in other media or other forms of expression; and as a 'calibrator' when it represents a benchmark for critical reflection on a dominant memorial practice.[17] According to Rigney, *Notre-Dame de Paris* by Victor Hugo can be seen as an example of a 'relay station' in that Hugo provided the first vivid description of the Cathedral of Notre-Dame; *Old Morality* by Walter Scott as a 'stabilizer' for its depiction of the seventeenth-century Scottish civil war which became a foundational cultural frame for later recollections; *Captain Corelli's Mandolin* by Louis de Bernières as a 'catalyst' for the re-elaboration of neglected events of the Italian experience in Greece during the Second World War and therefore for its commemoration; *Ulysses* by James Joyce as an 'object of recollection' in its extensive celebration in Dublin in 2004 for the one hundredth anniversary of the fictional story set in 1904 and, I might add, in 2022 for the one hundredth anniversary of its first publication; *Foe* by J. M. Coetzee as a 'calibrator' for its critical reflections on Daniel Defoe's *Robinson Crusoe* in light of post-colonial studies.[18]

These theories of Erll and Rigney stand in interesting relation to Landsberg's concept of prosthetic memory. In *Prosthetic Memory*, Landsberg examines those memories that derive from a deep engagement with a mediated representation of events and that are perceived as lived by viewers. She studies the extent to which the mass media influence the way in which members of a community remember their past and argues that they have the potential to instil a personal and communal sense of belonging, civic engagement, and political responsibility. She points out that:

> Prosthetic memory emerges at the interface between a person and a historical narrative about the past [...]. The person does not simply apprehend a historical narrative but takes on a more personal, deeply felt memory of a past event through which he or she did not live [...]. The resulting prosthetic memory has the ability to shape that person's subjectivity and politics.[19]

Literature, too, can be re-read and re-interpreted in light of prosthetic memory, as more broadly and recently argued by Jessica Ortener, Tea Sindbæk Andersen, and Fedja Wierød Borčak.[20] Literature influences both individual and collective memory. It can steer emotions, engage people, motivate them to act, and thus become a socio-cultural mode of action. It can lead to new social involvement by having an impact on readers' perception, knowledge, and everyday communication.

I believe that the concept of prosthetic memory can furthermore be usefully linked to theories which have developed in the last fifteen years in the areas of cognitive literary studies, especially theories of emotion.[21] As we have seen, culture and memory intersect on two levels: that of the individual, or cognitive memory, and that of society, or collective memory. Theories of emotion especially and cognitive studies more broadly can help us understand the formative influence that narrative texts have on readers, and therefore the mechanisms behind the process of prosthetic memory and more broadly behind cultural memory.[22]

Cognitive literary studies aim at a wide variety of theoretical paradigms in literary and cultural studies.[23] As Terence Cave commented:

> Literature offers a virtually limitless archive of the ways in which human beings think, how they imagine themselves and their world [...]. Literature in the broad sense is the most far-reaching and enduring vehicle and instrument of human thought, the most revealing product and symptom of human cognition, an outgrowth of one of the most fundamental of human cognitive instruments, namely language itself.[24]

Following these indications, I propose to look at the process by which an individual remembers, link the process to the emotional framework fostered in the narrative text, and re-read it through the cognitive literary approach. Literature has aesthetic and affective dimensions, which help readers remember the events they have read about. Although emotional evaluations of readers change according to the culture or society in which they live, there exists a basic emotional repertoire that anyone, from any culture, is capable of experiencing.[25] 'The universal aspects of emotion,' Caroline Pirlet and Andreas Wirag write, 'can, at least partially, account for why readers can agree on certain interpretations in the first place and why they are able to recuperate narrativity from texts beyond their own restricted historical period or culture'.[26] This fact allows literature to bridge both spatial and temporal frontiers. Readers become involved not merely rationally but also emotionally so that they feel for characters, fictional or not, and suffer with them. They are brought into intimate contact with a set of experiences which may fall well outside their own lives. They are asked to look through someone else's eyes and thus to empathise with characters.

Once re-read through the cognitive literary lens, the emotional framework and the consequent process of identification recall and deepen some aspects of Landsberg's prosthetic memory. Landsberg believes that 'empathy requires an act of imagination — one must leave oneself and attempt to imagine what it was like for that other person given what he or she went through'.[27] Literary narratives provide aesthetically-modelled experiences which engage readers with the lives and perspectives of their characters. They foster the formation of new behavioural and cognitive patterns; they enrich and possibly alter the response of readers to their own lives.[28] This is because the emotional experiences that literature transmits are similar to those that readers experience in life. Literature involves aspirations, frustrations, and conflicts. Literary writings favour readers' emotional involvements with characters, involvements which underscore readers' understanding of the self and of others and their evaluation of both real-life and fictional worlds. This most often entails an empathetic response to characters, their lives, goals, conditions, their successes and failures, and their fate.

In the field of literature, cultural memory and cognitive approaches are intertwined especially through empathy and theories of emotions. As Rigney notes, literature 'involves a memory which is not based in autobiographical experience but on exposure to vivid mediation [...] generating empathy with actors in the past with whom one has hitherto not been affiliated'.[29] The emotions within the literary text build an imaginative and empathetic bridge between past actors and present readers by making the stories of others accessible and therefore memorable. 'By selecting and establishing a hierarchy among given pieces of information,' Pirlet and Wirag write, 'emotions *ipso facto* shape readers' understanding of what the text is about'.[30] Going a little further, I believe that emotions and the sense of empathy and identification not only influence the perception of the historical data re-elaborated, narrated, and discussed within a literary text, but also foster their recollection and engender forms of prosthetic memory. Emotions are, indeed, an indestructible core of the process of memorisation.[31]

Part I of this book lays the ground for the analysis in Part II. Through the newly-articulated theoretical framework developed in this chapter, Part II shows how literary texts have helped with the recollection of the Roman round-up on a personal and on a collective level and how they have turned into distinct sources of information. While acknowledging, of course, that their representation of the round-up is imperfect, it considers how literary texts have shown the past from a different perspective and how they have helped produce shared past memories and contribute to the larger discussion devoted to the influence of narrative texts on the understanding of historical events and on their recollection.

Notes to Chapter 1

1. Maurice Halbwachs, *Les Cadres sociaux de la mémoire* (Paris: Alcan, 1925); *On Collective Memory*, trans. by Lewis A. Coser (Chicago: Chicago University Press, 1980), p. 167.
2. See: James E. Young, *The Texture of Memory* (New Haven, CT: Yale University Press, 1993); Jeffrey K. Olick and Daniel Levy, 'Collective Memory and Cultural Constraint: Holocaust Myth and Rationality in German Politics', *American Sociological Review*, 62.6 (1997), 921–36; Jeffrey K. Olick, 'Collective Memory: The Two Cultures', *Sociological Theory*, 17.3 (1999), 333–48; Howard Schuman, Robert F. Belli, and Katherine Bischoping, 'The Generational Basis of Historical Knowledge', in *Collective Memory of Political Events: Social Psychological Perspectives*, ed. by James W. Pennebaker, Darío Paez, and Bernard Rimé (Mahwah, NJ: Lawrence Erlbaum Associates, 1997), pp. 47–77; Astrid Erll, 'Narratology and Cultural Memory Studies', in *Narratology in the Age of Cross-disciplinary Narrative Research*, ed. by Sandra Heinen and Roy Sommer (Berlin: De Gruyter, 2009), pp. 212–27; Cristina Demaria, *Il trauma, l'archivio e il testimone: la semiotica, il documentario e la rappresentazione del reale* (Bologna: Bononia University Press, 2012).
3. Elena Esposito, 'Social Forgetting: A Systems-theory Approach', in *A Companion to Cultural Memory Studies*, ed. by Erll, Nünning, and Young, pp. 181–89.
4. Olick, 'Collective Memory', p. 338.
5. Young, *The Texture of Memory*, p. xi.
6. Richard Terdiman, *Present Past: Modernity and the Memory Crisis* (Ithaca, NY: Cornell University Press, 1993), p. 34; Wulf Kansteiner, 'Finding Meaning in Memory: A Methodological Critique of Collective Memory Studies', *History and Theory*, 41.2 (2002), 179–97 (p. 188).

7. On this see, for example, Astrid Erll, 'Cultural Memory Studies: An Introduction', in *A Companion to Cultural Memory Studies*, ed. by Erll, Nünning, and Young, pp. 1-17.

8. Aleida Assmann, 'Re-framing Memory: Between Individual and Collective Forms of Constructing the Past', in *Performing the Past: Memory, History, and Identity in Modern Europe*, ed. by Karin Tilmans, Frank van Vree, and Jay M. Winter (Amsterdam: Amsterdam University Press, 2010), pp. 35-49 (p. 43).

9. On this see, for example, the work by Jan Assmann who sees a distinction between what he calls 'communicative memory' and 'cultural memory'. Communicative memory is located within a generation and has a limited temporal horizon of four generations. Cultural memory is transgenerational and has no temporal horizon. Jan Assmann, 'Communicative and Cultural Memory', in *A Companion to Cultural Memory Studies*, ed. by Erll, Nünning, and Young, pp. 109-18.

10. Aleida Assmann, 'Three Stabilizers of Memory: Affect - Symbols - Trauma', in *Sites of Memory in American Literatures and Culture*, ed. by Udo J. Hebl (Heidelberg: Universitätsverlag C. Winter, 2003), pp. 15-30 (p. 15).

11. On this see: Peter Burke, *The French Historical Revolution: The Annales School 1929–89* (Cambridge: Polity Press, 1990); Jean-Pierre V. M. Herubel, 'Historiography's Horizon and Imperative: Febvrian Annales Legacy and Library History as Cultural History', *Libraries & Culture*, 39.3 (2004), 293-312.

12. Erll, *Memory in Culture*; Ann Rigney, 'The Dynamics of Remembrance: Texts Between Monumentality and Morphing', in *A Companion to Cultural Memory Studies*, ed. by Erll, Nünning, and Young, pp. 345-56; Alison Landsberg, *Prosthetic Memory: The Transformation of American Remembrance in the Age of Mass Culture* (New York: Columbia University Press, 2004).

13. Renate Lachmann, *Memory and Literature* (Minneapolis: University of Minnesota Press, 1997), p. 15.

14. Erll, *Memory in Culture*, pp. 158-59.

15. Ibid., p. 158.

16. See, for example: Brigit Neumann, 'The Literary Representation of Memory', in *A Companion to Cultural Memory Studies*, ed. by Erll, Nünning, and Young, pp. 333-43 (p. 341).

17. Rigney, 'The Dynamics of Remembrance', pp. 350-51.

18. Ibid., pp. 350-52.

19. Landsberg, *Prosthetic Memory*, p. 2.

20. Jessica Ortener, Tea Sindbæk Andersen, and Fedja Wierød Borčak, '"Fiction Keeps Memory About the War Alive": Mnemonic Migration and Literary Representations of the War in Bosnia', *Memory Studies*, 15.4 (2022), 918–34.

21. See: *Narrative Theory and the Cognitive Sciences*, ed. by David Herman (Stanford, CA: CSLI Publications, 2005); *Stories and Minds: Cognitive Approaches to Literary Narrative*, ed. by Lars Bernaerts and others (Lincoln: University of Nebraska Press, 2013); *The Oxford Handbook of Cognitive Literary Studies*, ed. by Lisa Zunshine (New York: Oxford University Press, 2015); *Cognitive Literary Science: Dialogues Between Literature and Cognition*, ed. by Michael Burke and Emily T. Troscianko (New York: Oxford University Press, 2017).

22. See: Zillmann, 'Mechanisms of Emotional Involvement with Drama'; Colm Hogan, 'Simulation and the Structure of Emotional Memory Learning From Arthur Miller's *After the Fall*' and 'What Literature Teaches Us About Emotion'.

23. See, for example, Lisa Zunshine, 'What is Cognitive Cultural Studies?', in *Introduction to Cognitive Cultural Studies*, ed. by Lisa Zunshine (Baltimore, MD: Johns Hopkins University Press, 2010).

24. Terence Cave, *Thinking with Literature: Towards a Cognitive Criticism* (Oxford: Oxford University Press, 2016), p. 15.

25. Contexts determine emotional life. 'Emotionology' is the umbrella term spanning the collective emotional standards of a given culture: Peter N. Stearns and Carol Z. Stearns, 'Emotionology: Clarifying the History of Emotions and Emotional Standards', *The American Historical Review*, 90.4 (1985), 813-36.

26. Caroline Pirlet and Andreas Wirag, 'Towards a "Natural" Bond of Cognitive and Affective Narratology', in *Cognitive Literary Science*, ed. by Burke and Troscianko, pp. 35-53 (p. 49).

27. Alison Landsberg, 'Memory, Empathy, and the Politics of Identification', *International Journal of Politics, Culture and Society*, 22.2 (2009), 221–29 (p. 223).
28. See: Colm Hogan, 'What Literature Teaches Us About Emotion'; Pirlet and Wirag, 'Towards a "Natural" Bond of Cognitive and Affective Narratology'.
29. Ann Rigney, 'Cultural Memory Studies: Mediation, Narrative, and the Aesthetic', in *Routledge International Handbook of Memory Studies*, ed. by Anna Lisa Tota and Trevor Hagen (London: Routledge, 2015), pp. 65–75 (p. 73).
30. Pirlet and Wirag, 'Towards a "Natural" Bond of Cognitive and Affective Narratology', p. 38.
31. Similar conclusions are drawn by Assmann in 'Three Stabilizers of Memory', p. 17.

CHAPTER 2

16 October 1943:
The Roman Round-up

Fluctuating Memory

Literary re-elaborations have played a foundational role in the discourse concerning the Roman round-up of 16 October 1943. By observing the perception of the Holocaust and of the Roman round-up within Italian culture from 1944 to date, in this chapter I show how certain works of literature, along with historiography and other cultural forms of expression, have influenced the perception and memory of 16 October, and recapitulate the phases which preceded the round-up by exploring the transmission of this event in Italian cultural memory.

The body of Italian literary works dedicated to the Holocaust can be divided into cultural phases which correspond to socio-historical changes from the end of the Second World War to the building of a democratic, republican Italy, to the Cold War and the cultural Americanisation of the economic boom, to the Years of Lead, to globalisation and multiculturalism, and to the present day.[1] Interest in the Holocaust has evolved in diverse and sometimes conflicting ways during these phases.

The first pictures of extermination camps and corpses appeared in newspapers while in Italy there was a war between anti-Fascists, Fascists, and Nazi occupiers. Upon their return, when they began to bear witness to their experiences, Jewish survivors of concentration and extermination camps were not listened to; their early testimonies did not gain a wide readership.[2] From the late 1940s to the late 1950s, there was relatively little interest in the Holocaust. The trial of Adolf Eichmann in 1961 marked a turning-point. It was widely covered in the press and became the core of numerous books written and published very quickly in Italy.[3] The period after 1961 registered a shift from widespread indifference to increasing interest in the Holocaust, which, however, was perceived as a crime committed solely by the Nazis. In literary terms, Holocaust or Holocaust-related experiences began to be re-elaborated in works of fiction, autofiction, and autobiography.[4] Still into the 1970s and 1980s, the persecution and deportation of the Italian Jews were commonly presented as a consequence of German occupation, violence, and brutality. These perspectives coincided with the adoption of selective forms of memory, which transmitted the idea that the Italian Holocaust was carried out by foreigners and that Italians, broadly speaking, resisted.[5] This perception began to be contested during the 1980s when new forms of anti-Semitism appeared and the Racial Laws of 1938 began to be studied and commemorated more frequently. From that time onwards, there was a growing awareness of Italian complicity in the discrimination against Italian Jews, their persecution, and their deportation.[6] The national narrative of Fascism and the Second World War began to include the Holocaust, and national and local memorialisation grew especially following the establishment of International Holocaust Remembrance Day, 'Giorno della memoria', in 2001.[7] In very recent years, the exploration of the process of collective and cultural memory of the Holocaust has been strictly linked to the spread of both nationalist parties and anti-Semitic attacks.[8] In 2018, Liliana Segre, an Italian survivor of the Holocaust, was named Senator for Life. Recently, she has found herself at the centre of one of the most intense national debates about anti-Semitism and intolerance in Italy. She has been the direct target of anti-Semitic messages online and has been assigned a police escort because of the threats against her.[9]

The transmission of an idea and a network of memories of the Italian Holocaust has inevitably included transmission of the memory and recollection of specific events within it. The round-up that occurred in Rome in October 1943 is particularly interesting both in relation to the deportations that occurred elsewhere in Italy and in Europe and because of the complex and fluctuating phases in which the event has been recalled. This event, 'the Roman round-up', was the largest single deportation from Italy during the German occupation. At the time, one of the most populous Italian Jewish communities was in Rome, and the majority of it was still living in the neighbourhood that had been the former Jewish ghetto.

In the months following October 1943, there was little knowledge of what had happened in Rome. Rapid political and social change in post-war Italy made the process of discovery and remembrance of the Roman round-up difficult.[10] In the 1950s, public and societal commemorations of 16 October eventually began, but it wasn't until ten years later that the episode started to be remembered beyond the Jewish community. Due to the Arab-Israeli wars in the 1970s and 1980s, the remembrance and memory of 16 October went through strained phases of recollection. In those years, new forms of anti-Semitism arose and culminated in the attack on the great synagogue in Rome on Saturday 9 October 1982 in which a three-year-old boy died and thirty-seven people were badly injured.[11] In the 1990s, there were new forms of commemoration: for example, olive trees from Israel were planted in front of the synagogue and an increasing number of witnesses and historians were invited to talk to young people in schools.[12] In 2018, its seventy-fifth anniversary, documentaries, television programmes, and stage plays dedicated to the Roman round-up were broadcast and performed for the first time on Holocaust Remembrance Day. Today, the Roman round-up embodies the persecution of Jews in Italy between 1943 and 1945.

The cultural memory of 16 October has arisen from communal, collective, and literary representations of the event, as much if not more than from historiography. I, therefore, now turn to analyse how literary texts emerged as a major medium for the production of memory of the Roman round-up and in the evolving panorama of the Italian Holocaust.

Literary Perspectives

The reflections in Chapter 1 on the modalities of literature and its role in transmitting memory and historical knowledge are used here as a useful lens for
examining the field of literature on the Roman round-up, both in terms of cultural
memory and in the context of Holocaust literature. The study of the literary
transmission of 16 October throws light on the strong influence that texts on the
edge between literature and history have had on this field of Italian collective
and cultural memory. As noted in the Introduction, I look in detail at four texts
that appeared over a time span of seventy years: *16 ottobre 1943* (1945) by Giacomo
Debenedetti, *La Storia* (1974) by Elsa Morante, *La parola ebreo* (1997) by Rosetta Loy,
and *Portico d'Ottavia 13* (2013) by Anna Foa.

In his essay 'Il grembo della Shoah', Alberto Cavaglion divides Italian Holocaust
literary production into two main currents. On the one hand, there are the texts
which re-elaborate personal, first-hand memories of deportation. They describe
life in extermination or other Nazi camps, represent the ways in which the victims
were dehumanised, and prompt reflections on the processes of bestialisation and
reification. On the other, there are literary works which describe the round-up
and the deportation of the Roman Jews in October 1943. Cavaglion defines these
texts as 'choral' (he talks of a 'coralità di voci'): descriptions that combine multiple
testimonies and multiple perspectives. These texts belong to Italian Holocaust
writing because they describe how the de-humanisation process began, how Jews
were taken from their houses, how they were herded, how they were put onto
cattle-trucks, and deported to Auschwitz. Cavaglion's two main currents have
blurred boundaries and common themes unite them. In this sense, the four texts
analysed in this book can be included in the wider field of Italian Holocaust writing
and examined in relation to Holocaust culture in Italy.

Debenedetti's *16 ottobre 1943*, published first in 1944 in a journal and then in 1945
as a book, was the earliest attempt at re-elaborating and capturing in narrative form
the Roman round-up. It started a process of integrating the persecution of the Jews
in Italy into the national narrative and national literature, as Robert Gordon points
out.[13] It became a point of reference for all the literary works which followed. It is
quoted, incorporated, alluded to, and re-phrased in *La Storia*, *La parola ebreo*, and
Portico d'Ottavia 13. These four representations of Rome during the round-up turn
16 October into the representative event of discrimination and persecution in the
Italian territories under German occupation. In the Italian context, these are the
most influential Italian literary texts dedicated to the Roman round-up, but there
are others which prompt, albeit sometimes only indirectly, reflections on the event
and give us a sense of the spread of the re-elaboration of the Roman round-up in
the last eighty years. There are fourteen other examples.

In *Scorciatoie e raccontini*, first published in 1945, Umberto Saba referred
sporadically to the Jewish massacre.[14] He mentioned the Roman round-up only
twice. In *scorciatoia* number 75, he referred to Debenedetti's works: *16 ottobre 1943*,
Otto ebrei (a short account of a post-war trial in Rome), and 'Campo di ebrei' (a
review of *Le Camp de la mort lente*, a book published by Jean Jacques Bernard in

1944).[15] In *scorciatoia* number 131, Saba mentioned the Roman Jewish collaborator Celeste di Porto, also remembered as 'Pantera Nera'. This is his last reference to the deportation of the Roman Jews.

In the late 1960s, Giacoma Limentani wrote *In contumacia* (1967), and in the early 1990s, Lia Levi published *Una bambina e basta* (1994).[16] Both these books are literary re-elaborations of the childhood of the authors, who included the Roman round-up among the events that had affected their development, and they give us a sense of how the round-up was perceived by young people of their generation.[17] In Limentani's work, it is indirectly recalled by the narrator, who comments on the absence of some families in the Tempio Maggiore in Rome. In Levi's work, the round-up is remembered by the narrating voice through the worries and tears of her mother who had been a witness to it. In 1995 and 1996 two other people published a re-elaboration of their experiences of the Roman round-up: Gianni Campus, who avoided deportation during the German occupation and wrote a memoir entitled *Il treno di piazza Giudia* (1995); and Settimia Spizzichino, who published *Gli anni rubati* (1996), a work where she reported her arrest on 16 October and deportation to Auschwitz on 18 October.[18] Spizzichino was the only woman among the sixteen people who survived and returned to Rome after the end of the war.

The Italian journalist Enzo Forcella gave a brief description of 16 October in *La resistenza in convento* (1999), a posthumously-published work in the form of a diary.[19] In it, he included reflections on the role played by the Church during the deportation from Rome. He combined his own experiences with historical data. He reported the story of Enza Pignatelli Aragona Cortes and, her connections with Pius XII, and her attempt on 16 October to inform the Pope of the round-up. He included long extracts from the work by Robert A. Graham, an American Jesuit priest and Second World War historian, *Il Vaticano e il nazismo* to corroborate his argument that the Pope tried to intervene in favour of the captured Jews.[20] Forcella's account of events is to be read in relation to a period, the late 1990s, in which historians began again to examine the role of the Vatican and Pius XII during the Holocaust. This controversy has continued up to the present day and has entered a new period of intensity with the opening, in 2020, of the Vatican archives dedicated to Pius XII. Within this context, Forcella's text has been repeatedly cited as a source by the historian Gabriele Rigano.[21]

In 2005, Renzo Modiano published *Di razza ebraica*, a memoir reporting life in hiding in Rome from the German occupation onwards.[22] Two of the fifteen chapters of the book are devoted to the Roman round-up. These two chapters narrate the arrest of one of Renzo's friends, Rachel. There is a shift from the first-person narrator of the memoir to an extra-diegetic, intrusive third-person narrator which portrays the inner feelings of Rachel in order to describe the arrest on 16 October and the deportation to Auschwitz.

Between 2010 and 2020, seven books, including variously explicit references to 16 October 1943, were published in Italy. In 2010, Gianni Clementi published a play entitled *Ladro di razza*, where he discusses the appropriation of the property and of the goods of Italian Jews from 1938.[23] The round-up is described through the vicissitudes of the three main characters: Tito, a thief released from Regina Coeli prison, Oreste, an indigent workman, and Rachele, a wealthy Jewish spinster who lives in the ghetto. Tito and Oreste decide to rob Rachele's apartment on a Saturday morning, the morning of 16 October 1943. All three are arrested by SS officers. In 2014 and 2016, Francesca Romana De'Angelis and Federica Pannocchia published two fictional novels which include a representation of the round-up: *Per infiniti giorni* and *Quando dal cielo cadevano le stelle*, respectively.[24] Romana De'Angelis set her love story between two young musicians, Davide, who is Jewish, and Regina, who is Catholic. They live in Rome during the years of discrimination and then persecution and the round-up is reported through a choral description of attempts to save Jews from deportation: Davide, for example, hid on the eve of the round-up and disappeared with the help of a friend. In *Quando dal cielo cadevano le stelle*, Pannocchia told of a young Jewish girl, Lia, who is captured during the round-up and deported to Auschwitz. The description of the round-up and the events that followed 16 October are described from her perspective, through her fear and despair. Also, in 2016, Alberto Ciarafoni published a collection of seventy sonnets written in Roman and Roman Jewish dialects that describe the round-up from the collective perspective of the Jews of the ghetto: *Quer 16 ottobbre*.[25] In 2017, Amedeo Osti Guerrazzi and Maurizio Molinari published *Duello nel ghetto*, a popular historical narrative which reports the Roman round-up, in which the authors re-elaborated diaries and memories of Pacifico di Consiglio, a young Jewish man who had fought against the Nazi occupiers of Rome.[26] The representation of the ghetto, however, is multi-voiced: the authors give space to the stories of those who were captured and of those who managed to escape. In the same year Corrado Plastino published a play, *La valigia*, in which the protagonist is an old lady who has a suitcase; through this object, she recounts to her grandchildren the discrimination and persecution in Italy, her story culminating in the description of the round-up.[27] Finally, in 2020 Lia Tagliacozzo published *La generazione del deserto*, the most recent work to include the Roman round-up.[28] Tagliacozzo re-wrote her family history, including a description of the round-up, as the daughter of one of the Jews who avoided deportation by hiding in an ecclesiastical institution until the liberation of Rome in June 1944.

From within this fluid field of texts which evoke and elaborate a literary-historical account of the events of 16 October 1943, this book concentrates on four texts by Debenedetti, Morante, Loy, and Foa. These authors will be considered in terms of their generation and other factors such as their Jewish or non-Jewish background, both in its own right and in relation to the persecution and the risk of deportation during the war, and the extent of their first- or second-hand experience of persecution.

In Holocaust studies, Marianne Hirsch's generational approach fruitfully links the fields of Holocaust and cultural memory studies. Hirsch believes that writers can either bear testimony to their own past and transmit it to their own generation, all the while seeking to reach the next, or else represent a past that they did not experience for their own generation and the next to reflect on. The first group belongs to a generation which transmits memories of first-hand experiences; the second group is what she defines as the generation of 'postmemory'. Hirsch says that:

> Postmemory describes the relationship that the generation after those who witnessed cultural or collective trauma bears to the experiences of those who came before, experiences that they 'remember' only by means of the stories, images, and behaviors among which they grew up.[29]

Postmemory is different from memories of life. It is not always assumed to be re-worked in and through media, as in the case of Landsberg's prosthetic memory, but instead is a result of an inter- and trans-generational dialogue and connection, and of a re-embodiment in the present of distant individual and family memories. In literary terms, writers mediate experiences which they did not live through and make them compelling, appropriable, and understandable to their own generation and the next.

Hirsch's generational approach prompts fruitful reflections on *16 ottobre 1943*, *La Storia*, *La parola ebreo*, and *Portico d'Ottavia 13*. Debenedetti and Morante can be included in the generation of first-hand experiences, even though neither of them is a Holocaust witness strictly speaking. Born in 1901 and 1912 respectively, they experienced the war in their adulthood and lived under the Fascist regime. Their texts contain explicit or implicit references to their own adult experiences of the war. Loy and Foa can be said to belong to the generation of postmemory. Loy was born in 1931 into an upper middle-class family, and her childhood memories of the war are blurred and only indirectly related to the persecution of the Jews; Foa was born in 1944 into an anti-Fascist family and experienced the war and Fascist anti-Semitism only through what her parents told her. Hirsch tailored the notion of postmemory to second-generation Jews who experienced discrimination and persecution through their parents' experiences and stories. I will therefore stretch the notion of postmemory to include Loy, a Roman Catholic child during the war. Loy's autodiegetic narrator in *La parola ebreo*, as will be explained later in Chapter 5, can be, I think, effectively analysed through Hirsch's theory of postmemory.

Being conscious of the fragmentary nature of the image of Roman round-up, I believe that *16 ottobre 1943*, *La Storia*, *La parola ebreo*, and *Portico d'Ottavia 13* add tiles to the mosaic of 16 October and can be defined together as inter- and trans-generational transmissions of that traumatic experience. So, they are examined and re-read in themselves, in dialogue with each other, and in light of the theoretical framework explained in Chapter 1 that is based on cultural memory studies and theories of emotions. *16 ottobre 1943* and *La parola ebreo* are written by merging what Erll defines as the 'experiential' and the 'reflexive' modes.[30] Historical facts and personal stories are re-elaborated in narrative forms which transmit the past in and through lived experience. Also, they more explicitly observe how the Roman round-up is remembered and offer new ways for its recollection. *La Storia* is written in the 'experiential' mode; *Portico d'Ottavia 13* in the 'reflexive'. Despite these differences, there is common ground between these four texts. They all fulfil a multitude of mnemonic functions because they create vicarious memories and vicarious perceptions of the Roman round-up in their readers, negotiate compelling memories of the event, and mediate the recollection of it. They employ a variety of literary techniques, including first-person narratives and in-depth, intimate portrayals of daily life. To direct attention to key passages of their story, they engage readers in an intimate way, with direct, spontaneous communication. By involving readers in the story, these techniques forge ties within and across generations and favour a critical reading of the representation of that past. My attention is not driven by reader-response criticism, but through the notions of cultural memory explored in Chapter 1, I will discuss further literary strategies and techniques which facilitate the understanding and recollection of the narrated past from the personal perspective of the reader.

From the wider perspective of collective memory, the four books have enacted some of the five ways in which, according to Rigney, literature interacts with cultural memory, and have transmitted historical knowledge. We can illustrate this by collating a table of Rigney's categories and how they pertain to *16 ottobre 1943*, *La Storia*, *La parola ebreo*, and *Portico d'Ottavia 13*:

	Relay station	Stabilizer	Catalyst	Object of recollection	Calibrator
16 ottobre 1943	✕	✕	✕	✕	—
La Storia	✕	✕	✕	✕	—
La parola ebreo	✕	✕	✕	—	✕
Portico d'Ottavia 13	✕	✕	—	✕	✕

TABLE 1. Categories from Ann Rigney, 'The Dynamics of Remembrance: Texts Between Monumentality and Morphing', in *A Companion to Cultural Memory Studies*, ed. by Astrid Erll, Ansgar Nünning, and Sara Young (New York: De Gruyter, 2010), pp. 345-56.

All four texts can be said to work as 'relay stations' and 'stabilizers'. They convey earlier forms of recollection of the round-up and succeed in representing it in memorable ways, thus becoming a stabilising factor in the cultural memory of 16 October. The first three works are also 'catalysts' because they focus on details of the round-up which had been previously neglected. The first two and the last one are 'objects of recollection' in the sense that a documentary in 1961 and two theatre plays and a graphic novel in 2018 were made of *16 ottobre 1943*, and a film and a television series were made of *La Storia* in 1986. A picture book intended for children was made of *Portico d'Ottavia 13* in 2015. The last two are 'calibrators' because they are benchmarks for critical reflection on the Roman round-up. They contribute to the larger discussion of the ways in which Italian society has recollected the round-up and the Holocaust more broadly because they implicitly portray the complexity and the heterogeneity of the process of remembering and show how it changes through time.

Before turning to the individual works in Part II, in this final section of the chapter I contextualise the Roman round-up in historical terms, recapitulating the key phases of it, and reflecting on the historiography of it from the Liberation to the present day. However, since my methodological assumption is that history and literature run in parallel and intersect at blurred boundaries, I don't describe just a sequence of events but examine which elements and phases have been emphasised and investigated more closely in its historiography alongside literature.

Beyond History

On 25 July 1943, the Fascist Grand Council removed Mussolini from power. On 8 September, Marshal Badoglio, Mussolini's successor, proclaimed the armistice between Italy and the Allies. The following day he left Rome with King Vittorio Emanuele III. On 10 September, the Germans occupied the capital. With several divisions already in Italy, they swept through the peninsula to occupy most of the country in just a few days. From allies, they turned into occupiers. On 12 September, an SS parachute unit rescued Mussolini, who had been confined in a mountaintop resort in the Apennines. On 15 September in Berlin, Mussolini announced the reconstruction of the Fascist Party, and, a week later, the formation of the collaborationist Italian Social Republic (RSI), headed by himself.

From September 1943 to June 1944, the Germans occupied Rome and surrounded the Vatican. The Gestapo took over a former apartment building in via Tasso 145 and used it as their headquarters. The German diplomat Eitel Friedrich Moellhausen became the German ambassador in Italy; Karl Wolff, the Chief of Personal Staff Reichsführer-SS, was transferred to Italy as Supreme SS and Police Leader; the German officer Reiner Stahel was appointed Military Commander of the City of Rome; and the German SS functionary Herbert Kappler was appointed head of the German police and security service.[31] In these nine months of occupation, Roman citizens lived through a time of deprivation, hunger, and oppression, and of resistance, torture, imprisonment, and death. The Fosse Ardeatine massacre can be seen as the epitome of this period: on 23 March, a group of Roman partisans from the Gruppi di azione patriottica (GAP) bombed a central Roman street, via Rasella. Thirty-three German-speaking soldiers were killed. A communication from Berlin ordered a ten-for-one reprisal within twenty-four hours. On 24 March, 335 people were arrested or taken from Regina Coeli prison, brought to the Fosse Ardeatine quarry and catacombs, and shot in the head in groups of five.[32]

During the occupation, the Jewish community took no official precautions to protect themselves from the German occupiers, they did not want to attract attention to themselves. Israele Zolli, the Rabbi of Rome, was one of the very few public figures who, from September 1943, informally advised the closure of the synagogue, destruction of the files on the members of the community, and provision of subsidies to the poorest. He left his apartment and went into hiding and advised Jews to leave their homes and hide, but most of them remained in their homes.[33]

The first history book to include the Roman round-up, though it was described in only a few pages, was published in 1961: *Storia degli ebrei italiani sotto il fascismo* by Renzo De Felice, commissioned by the Jewish community in Rome and published by Einaudi, its focus on the discrimination against and the persecution of the

Italian Jews before and after the promulgation of the Racial Laws introduced in 1938. In 1961, the Comunità Israelitica di Roma itself published *Ottobre 1943: cronaca di un'infamia*.[34] This concise volume was the first to be dedicated entirely to the Roman round-up, containing the testimony of Ugo Foà, President of the Comunità Israelitica di Roma, after the ransom of fifty kilos of gold which occurred on 26 September, and extracts of the diary of Rosina Sorani, who in October 1943 was the synagogue secretary. From 1961 to 1963, Paolo Foa and Guido Valabrega edited three volumes entitled *Gli ebrei in Italia durante il fascismo*, published by the Centro Documentazione Ebraica Contemporanea (CDEC), which included a detailed chapter on the Roman round-up, written by Michael Tagliacozzo, who became one of the most renowned witnesses of that period.[35] In 1969 the American writer and journalist Robert Katz published *Black Sabbath*, the first reconstruction of the Roman round-up written outside Italy. The volume was translated and published by Rizzoli in 1973 with the title *Sabato nero*.[36] It was not particularly appreciated by the Roman Jewish community, who saw limits in Katz's historical representation, especially in his assumption that the round-up had affected only the poorest families in the ghetto.[37] Finally, in 1994 the essayist and journalist Fausto Coen wrote *16 ottobre 1943: la grande razzia degli ebrei di Roma*, in which he discussed and castigated the Rabbi of Rome and reported testimonies of the days before the round-up and the defence mechanism of Italian Jews in relation to the German occupiers.[38] He included a couple of poignant pages on Celeste di Porto, too.

There were few further scholarly publications in the field of historiography until the 2000s when scholars began to examine and reconstruct the phases of this event from new perspectives. *Roma, 16 ottobre 1943: anatomia di una deportazione* (2006), edited by Silvia Haia Antonucci, Claudio Procaccia, Gabriele Rigano, and Giancarlo Spizzichino, is the first historiographical volume entirely dedicated to the Roman round-up and the events that preceded it, gathering testimonies, interviews, press reviews, and archival and unpublished documents.[39] For the seventieth anniversary of the Roman round-up in 2013, an exhibition was held at the Complesso Vittoriano in Rome. It was curated by Marcello Pezzetti, who, in the same year, edited a book of documents, pictures, and drawings from the exhibition, *16 ottobre 1943: la razzia degli ebrei di Roma*.[40] The book includes official messages to and from Germany, personal letters, family photographs, and the first illustrations of the round-up by Aldo Gay, a Jew who made some sketches while SS officers were in the ghetto. In 2016, Martin Baumeister, Amedeo Osti Guerrazzi, and Claudio Procaccia edited and published *16 ottobre 1943: la deportazione degli ebrei romani tra storia e memoria*.[41] The book sets the Roman round-up within the framework of the Holocaust in Europe and includes chapters on the recollection and commemoration of the event in Rome, and in Italy more broadly. Finally, focusing on a group of Office of Strategic Services documents held at the US National Archives and Records Administration, in 2020 Liliana Picciotto published an article which traces the process of decision and preparation for the round-up of 16 October and reconsiders the relations between the Church and the German occupiers of Rome.[42]

The historians Rigano and Pezzetti suggest that the dynamics of the Roman round-up are better understood in relation to some events that preceded 16 October, specifically on 26, 29, and 30 September and 11 October.[43] Narrative writings on the Roman round-up refer repeatedly to these and indeed other contiguous episodes and re-elaborate them to contextualise their accounts of the deportation. On 26 September, there was a first meeting between the occupying authorities and representatives of the Jewish community: Kappler brought together Ugo Foà and Dante Almansi, President of the Unione delle comunità ebraiche italiane. Kappler threatened that two hundred heads of household would be deported if the Jewish community did not collect fifty kilos of gold within the following thirty-six hours. The gold was gathered over the next day from within the Jewish community. Many Catholics also donated money and jewellery. The Vatican gave a pledge to loan fifteen kilos of gold, to be repaid in four years' time, but the Jewish community did not take up the pledge. On 28 September, by 4 pm, an hour before the deadline, a sealed box with fifty kilograms of gold arrived in Kappler's office in the Gestapo headquarters in via Tasso. That evening, the box was put on a train to Berlin, addressed to Ernst Kaltenbrunner, the head of the Reich Security Main Office (RSHA). After the end of the war the box was found unopened in Kaltenbrunner's office and in 1948 it was sent to Israel.[44]

Historians' interpretation of this event vary: it is still not clear who decided to demand that the Jews collect fifty kilos of gold nor why. Rigano thinks that the request might have been Kappler's initiative to avoid the deportation of the Roman Jews, that Kappler wanted to demonstrate how the Jews could still be useful in raising a large amount of money to sustain the German war effort, and, at the same time, to avoid antagonising the Catholic Church with the deportation of Jews from Rome.[45] Michele Sarfatti suggests that the demand for gold was intended as recuperation from the victims the costs of their own imminent deportation by rail.[46] In literary terms, Debenedetti, Morante, Loy, and Foa all describe and prompt reflections on this episode. Debenedetti's text, indeed, became the most authoritative source for cinema as well, in particular for two films which came out in 1961: a short documentary, *16 ottobre 1943* by Ansano Giannarelli, and a feature-film, *L'oro di Roma* by Carlo Lizzani.[47]

On 29 and 30 September, the SS officers broke into the Jewish community buildings, where they stole two million lire, which had been collected in addition to the gold, and took archival documents, including the lists that recorded the addresses of Roman Jews. Most of the Jews remained in their homes over September and October. Scholars suggest that there were two main factors behind this choice. Firstly, not all families, especially those living in the ghetto, could afford to leave their homes or find refuge elsewhere as their resources had been greatly diminished after the Racial Laws of 1938 had restricted their ability to work and earn money. Without help or collaboration, it was difficult to hide children and the old. Secondly, the majority of them believed that the Germans, having obtained the gold, would spare their lives, they did not believe that there would be deportations from Italy, and above all they did not believe that there would be deportations from Rome.

They felt that the proximity of the Pope gave them protection.[48] Gabriele Rigano agrees, saying that this was 'il meccanismo psicologico che trasse in inganno gli ebrei' [the psychological mechanism that misled the Jews].[49]

On 30 September, representatives from the Einsatzstab Reichsleiter Rosenberg (ERR), a special commando unit established in 1940 by Alfred Rosenberg for the refashioning of German and European culture after the war, appeared at the synagogue in the ghetto.[50] Approximately twenty officials took a register of what was held in both the Biblioteca Comunale and the Biblioteca del Collegio Rabbinico. Rosina Sorani's diary, which is now held in New York at the YIVO Institute for Jewish Research, reports what happened in buildings close to the synagogue on 30 September and the following day. It reports that on 11 October an officer of the Einsatzstab Reichsleiter Rosenberg made a phone call to an international shipping company and arranged the transportation out of Rome of the books of both libraries.[51] Sorani noted that the books were under sequestration. Almansi and Foà addressed a letter of protest to the competent Italian authorities in which they stressed the value of the library collections and the loss to Italy as well as to the Jewish community from the confiscation; they did not receive a reply.[52] On 14 October at 8.30 am, officials of the ERR and workers from the transport company started collecting the contents of the two libraries and loading them onto the railway trucks which would take them to Germany.[53] Debenedetti's *16 ottobre 1943* is the only literary text in our corpus which fully and vividly describes the episode of the books. It has become a source of information on this episode for many historiographical volumes and articles, among them Katz's *Black Sabbath*, Stanislao Pugliese's article 'Bloodless Torture', and Rigano's chapter '16 ottobre 1943'.[54]

Preparation for the deportations of 16-18 October probably began early in that month. The organisation was supervised by Theodor Dannecker, an SS-captain (*Hauptsturmführer*) who had previously carried out deportations from Bulgaria, Greece, Poland, Belgium, and Holland, and had co-directed the Vel d'Hiv round-up in Paris on 16 and 17 July 1942.[55] He arrived in Rome on 3, 4, or 5 October with a letter ordering the deportation of the Roman Jews and signed by Heinrich Müller, at that time chief of the Gestapo.[56] Dannecker did not stay in the Gestapo headquarters in via Tasso, but more than three kilometres away in Albergo Bernini in via Po. A few days later, 365 SS troops arrived in Rome. They were divided into groups and Rome itself into twenty-six areas. During the round-up on 16 October, each group was in charge of one area and Italian police officers were excluded.[57] According to the deposition Kappler made under interrogation between 20 and 28 August 1947, Dannecker informed him in the late evening of 15 October that the round-up would take place the next day. He told him that the Italian police officers could not be trusted and would not be used.[58]

On 15 October, in the evening, a Jewish woman ran up and down the streets of the ghetto screaming that two hundred families would be deported the next day — no one paid any attention to her. During the night, there were gunshots near the ghetto; they were not linked to the round-up, but there are testimonies that people were scared and remained at home longer than usual the next morning.[59] At around 4 am, a few people left their homes and queued for the weekly cigarette ration outside a tobacconist, which was not yet open, between the two bridges of the Isola Tiburtina.[60] They were unaware of the round-up when it started. Debenedetti vividly describes the woman running up and down the streets of the ghetto. She was Elena di Porto, he called her 'Celeste'. Morante too created a powerful portrait of Elena di Porto on the basis of Debenedetti's report, and Katz and Rigano mention it as a source for the night before 16 October.[61] In 2022, Gaetano Pertraglia published *La matta di piazza Giudia*, a book of popular history entirely dedicated to Elena di Porto, and mentions both Debenedetti and Morante.[62]

On Saturday 16, at 5.30 am, the SS started to arrest Jews around Rome.[63] They broke into apartments, cut telephone wires, and handed residents written instructions in Italian and in German. The residents had twenty minutes to pack food, blankets, money, and jewellery, and to lock the door:

> 1) Insieme con la Vostra famiglia e con gli altri ebrei appartenenti alla vostra casa sarete trasferiti / 2) Bisogna portare con se / a) viveri per almeno 8 giorni / b) tessere annonarie / c) carta d'identità / d) bicchieri / 3) si può portar via / a) valigetta con effetti e biancheria personali / b) denaro e gioielli / 4) chiudere a chiave l'appartamento / prendere con sé la chiave / 5) Ammalati anche casi gravissimi non possono per alcun motivo rimaner indietro. Infermeria si trova nel campo / 6) Venti Minuti dopo presentazione di questo biglietto la familia deve essere pronta per la partenza.[64]

> [1) You, your family, and other Jews in your household are being moved / 2) You must take with you / a) food for at least eight days / b) ration cards / c) identification cards / d) drinking glasses / 3) You may take with you / a) a small suitcase with personal effects and belongings, linen, blankets / b) money and jewellery / 4) Lock your apartment up / take along the key / 5) The sick, even those gravely ill cannot under any circumstances remain behind / There are hospitals in the camp / 6) Your family must be ready to leave twenty minutes after receipt of this card.]

According to Kappler's deposition, the round-up ended at 2 o'clock in the afternoon.

The role of Pius XII on and after 16 October is particularly intensely debated.[65] Some historians believe that the Pope intervened to attempt to stop the deportation from Rome.[66] Others do not: among them, Rigano widely studied the correspondence between Monsignor Alois Hudal, the Austrian bishop in Rome during the occupation, and Stahel, and concluded that Hudal asked for the end of the deportation in the hope of avoiding intervention by Pius XII.[67] Similarly, Sara Berger has studied the testimonies left by some of the SS officers who conducted the round-up, which state that the round-up lasted only a few hours and they were supposed to go back to the Gestapo headquarters as soon as they had traced the families on their list.[68] From the analysis of the investigations, Berger believes that the round-up stopped at 2 pm because the SS officers had completed their list and not due to Heinrich Himmler who, according to some supporters of Pius XII, was following an indirect request from the Pope which arrived via Stahel and Hudal.[69] This issue of the Church and its direct or indirect role in the round-up permeates several of the literary narratives under analysis: Loy and Foa both dedicate several passages to Pius XII and the Church; Debenedetti and Morante only mention it in passing.

By the evening of 16 October, 1259 people had been gathered in a temporary detention centre: the Collegio Militare Italiano, in the Palazzo Salviati in via Lungara, close to both the Vatican and Regina Coeli prison. From among the Jews, the SS officers enlisted Arminio Wachsberger, a German-speaker from Fiume, as an interpreter.[70] His first assignment was to calm people as they arrived at the Collegio Militare and to explain that they were all to be sent to a labour camp in the North. The old and the children would be assigned light jobs to earn their keep, the young would be given hard labour. Wachsberger helped to divide the Jews from those whom the Germans defined as non-Jews.[71]

On 17 October, before dawn, 252 people were set free: they were from mixed marriages; children one of whose parents was an Italian Catholic; Catholics arrested by mistake; and Jewish citizens of countries where deportations were not occurring. Among them, some Jews pretended to be Catholic evacuees from the Allied bombing of San Lorenzo on 19 July 1943. They survived.[72] Later in the morning, Don Igino Quadraroli, an officer of the Vatican Secretariat of State, went into the Collegio Militare to provide assistance. According to Susan Zuccotti, there is no evidence that he or anyone from the Vatican intervened in the screening process.[73] The rest of the people captured on 16 October stayed in the Collegio one more night; they were obliged to give any money and jewellery they possessed to pay for the upkeep of children and the elderly in the camp. Much of this money and jewellery ended up in SS pockets.[74] In the evening, an obstetrician went into the Collegio to help Marcella Perugia, who gave birth to a premature child. The child was deported to Auschwitz with two older siblings, their mother, and all the others.[75] Only *16 ottobre 1943* and *Portico d'Ottavia 13* mention Marcella Perugia and her new-born.

On 18 October, in the morning, 1015 people were taken by truck to Stazione Tiburtina where they were put into twenty-eight cattle-trucks.[76] In each cattle-truck, there were roughly forty people. A Jewish woman, Costanza Calò Sermoneta, came to the railway station and persuaded some of the SS officers to let her on to the cattle-truck which held her husband and children. This episode has been widely cited in historiography as well as in both Debenedetti's and Morante's works, and is briefly mentioned in Loy's text.[77] There were thus 1016 people on the train, which left at 2 pm; the driver was Quirino Zazza.[78] On 19 October, documents of the Roman police station reported that on Monday 18 October at 2 pm, a train consisting of twenty-eight wagons with about one thousand Jews, including men, women, and children, left Stazione Tiburtina heading for the Brenner Pass.[79]

On Tuesday 19 October, at noon, the train made an unscheduled stop in Padua. Women of the Red Cross were permitted to distribute water and soup, after some Italian Fascists persuaded the SS officers to open the cattle-trucks and let the Jews out.[80] On Friday 22 October, in the night, the train arrived at Auschwitz after a journey of five days during which seven people died. On Saturday 23 October, in the morning, Arminio Wachsberger was again chosen to be the interpreter, this time for Josef Mengele, one of the most notorious German SS officers and a physician in Auschwitz, mainly remembered for his deadly experiments on prisoners. At the end of the line, Mengele ordered the people off the train.[81] He divided the weak, the sick, the elderly, and the children from those who were suitable for work; he explained that families would be reunited each evening; he chose about 450 people for hard labour. Then, he told them they could either walk, and that it would be a walk of ten kilometres, or ride with the other group. In total 149 men and 47 women chose to walk. The walk was in fact less than half a kilometre. The rest were sent directly to the gas chambers. Sixteen people returned to Rome after the end of the Second World War.[82] Among the four texts analysed here, only *La Storia* reports this phase of the deportation. The numbers of the deportees and of the survivors are inaccurate, but the figures were still unverified when Morante published *La Storia*:

> La marcia del treno piombato fu lentissima: i prigionieri stavano là dentro da cinque giorni quando, nell'alba del sabato, sbarcarono al campo di concentramento di Auschwitz-Birkenau, dove erano destinati. Non tutti però arrivarono vivi: e questa fu una prima selezione [...]. Dei vivi, soltanto una minoranza fu valutata idonea per servire nel campo. Tutti gli altri, in numero di 850, subito all'arrivo furono mandati a morte inconsapevoli nelle camere a gas. Oltre ai malati, ai minorati, e ai meno robusti, in questo numero si comprendevano tutti, in totale, i vecchi, i ragazzetti, i bambini e gli infanti [...]. Per i rimanenti 200, serbati alla vita del campo in quel sabato dell'arrivo, il viaggio, incominciato il 16 ottobre '43, ebbe durate diverse a seconda della resistenza. Alla fine, dei 1056 partiti in folla dalla Stazione Tiburtina, in totale 15 ne tornarono indietro vivi.
>
> E di tutti quei morti, i più fortunati di certo i primi 850. La camera a gas è l'unico punto di carità, nel campo di concentramento.[83]

> [The progress of the sealed train was very slow: the prisoners had been inside it for five days when, at dawn on Saturday, they reached the concentration camp of Auschwitz-Birkenau, to which they were assigned. Not all, however, reached there alive: and this was a first selection [...]. Of the living, only a minority of about two hundred individuals was judged able to work in the camp. All the others, numbering about eight hundred and fifty, promptly on arrival were sent to death, unaware, in the gas chambers. In addition to the ill, the handicapped, and the less strong, this number included almost all the old people, the children, and babies [...]. For the remaining two hundred, destined to the life of the camp on that Saturday of their arrival, the journey begun on October 16th, 1943, was of varying duration according to their strength. In the end, of the one thousand fifty-six who had left, in a body, from the Tiburtina station, a total of fifteen came back alive.
>
> And of all those dead, the luckiest were surely the first eight hundred and fifty. The gas chamber is the only seat of charity, in a concentration camp.][84]

The Nazis considered the round-up of 16 October a failure: they had managed to deport only one eighth of the Jews who lived in Rome.[85] The capture was neither efficient nor carried out in full; the 365 SS troops did not know Rome and lost their way in the maze of streets. Rigano also argues that Kappler's deposition suggests that the Italian police sabotaged the operation: they were supposed to draw up a list of addresses of all the Jews, but they arranged them in a way that deliberately confused the SS. The confusion was even greater because not all the apartments in a building had been assigned to the same group of SS men.[86] This gave some Jews time to warn each other, escape, and hide. Many families survived. Some, as witnesses testified, were intentionally set free by individual SS soldiers;[87] some were saved by Catholics, as Kappler's deposition reports;[88] some Catholics managed to hide Jews in their apartments, others tried to intervene in the arrests.[89] Debenedetti, Morante, Loy, and Foa devote passages of their texts to the description of those who decided to help, protect, and save Jews.

Between the round-up and the Liberation of Rome on 4 June 1944, at least 835 more Roman Jews were arrested by Italian police officers or individual citizens motivated by anti-Semitism and/or pro-Nazism. Among them was Celeste di Porto, also known as 'Stella' [Star] or 'Pantera Nera' [Black Panther]. She was Jewish and lived in the ghetto but betrayed fifty Jews by informing on them, and was directly responsible for their arrest.[90] There is no monograph dedicated to Celeste, but her life was fictionalised in a historical novel, *Stella di Piazza Giudìa*, by Giuseppe Pederiali and in a book of popular history co-authored by Anna Foa and Lucetta Scaraffia, *Anime nere*.[91] Of the four texts, only *Portico d'Ottavia 13* dedicates a chapter to Celeste; a play about Celeste, entitled *Celeste* and written by Fabio Pisano, was staged in 2018.

Notes to Chapter 2

1. My research has been greatly facilitated by the following works: Robert S. C. Gordon, 'Which Holocaust? Primo Levi and the Field of Holocaust Memory in Post-war Italy', *Italian Studies*, 61.1 (2006), 85-113; Paola Bertilotti, 'Contrasti e trasformazioni della memoria dello sterminio in Italia', in *Storia della Shoah in Italia: vicende, memorie, rappresentazioni*, ed. by Marcello Flores and Simon Levis Sullam, 2 vols (Turin: Utet, 2010), II, 58-114; Gordon, *The Holocaust in Italian Culture*.

2. During this period of lack of interest, there are a few exceptions, even if the readership was scant: the small-scale publication of memoirs, among which Primo Levi, *Se questo è un uomo* (Turin: De Silva, 1947), and Liana Millu, *Il fumo di Birkenau* (Milan: La Prora, 1947), as well as literary works such as the novella by Giorgio Bassani, 'Una lapide in via Mazzini' [1952], in *Cinque storie ferraresi* (Turin: Einaudi, 1956), and the first public exhibition on the deportation and the extermination camps in 1955 in Carpi, which possibly marked the first breach of the earlier neglect.

3. See Manuela Consonni, 'The Impact of the "Eichmann Event" in Italy, 1961', *Journal of Israeli History*, 23.1 (2004), 91-99.

4. See: Giorgio Bassani, *Il giardino dei Finzi-Contini* (Turin: Einaudi, 1962); Primo Levi, *La tregua* (Turin: Einaudi, 1963); Natalia Ginzburg, *Lessico famigliare* (Turin: Einaudi, 1963).

5. These myths find their roots in a particular diplomatic strategy of the 1940s of the new Italian government to get Italy accepted as an ally of the Western democracies and to be included in the United Nations and other international bodies. See: Filippo Focardi, 'La memoria della guerra e il mito del "bravo italiano": origine e affermazione di un autoritratto collettivo', *Italia contemporanea*, 220.21 (2000), 93-99, and *Il cattivo tedesco e il bravo italiano: la rimozione delle colpe della Seconda guerra mondiale* (Rome: Laterza, 2013); Angelo Del Boca, *Italiani, brava gente? Un mito duro a morire* (Vicenza: Neri Pozza, 2005); John Foot, *Italy's Divided Memory* (New York: Palgrave, 2009); Gordon, *The Holocaust in Italian Culture*, pp. 148-56.

6. See: Nicola Caracciolo, *Gli ebrei e l'Italia durante la Guerra 1940–45* (Rome: Bonacci, 1986); Susan Zuccotti, *The Italians and the Holocaust: Persecution, Rescue, and Survival* (London: Halban, 1987); Alexander Stiller, *Benevolence and Betrayal: Five Italian Jewish Families under Fascism* (New York: Summit Books, 1991).

7. See: Michele Sarfatti, *Gli ebrei nell'Italia fascista: vicende, identità, persecuzione* (Turin: Einaudi, 2000); *Gli ebrei in Italia tra persecuzione fascista e reintegrazione postbellica*, ed. by Ilaria Pavan and Guri Schwarz (Florence: Giuntina, 2001); *Jews in Italy under Fascist and Nazi Rule, 1922–1945*, ed. by Joshua D. Zimmerman (Cambridge: Cambridge University Press, 2005); Rebecca Clifford, *Commemorating the Holocaust: The Dilemmas of Remembrance in France and Italy* (Oxford: Oxford University Press, 2013); Simon Levis Sullam, *I carnefici italiani: scene dal genocidio degli ebrei, 1943–1945* (Milan: Feltrinelli, 2015); Filippo Focardi, *Nel cantiere della memoria: fascismo, resistenza, Shoah, foibe* (Rome: Viella, 2020). Also, on International Holocaust Remembrance Day see for example, Gordon, 'The Holocaust in Italian Collective Memory'.

8. Numerous articles in the most prominent newspapers in Italy, *La Repubblica*, *Corriere della sera*, and *La Stampa*, refer to this growing anti-Semitism. See for example: Liliana Segre, 'Siate farfalle che volano sopra i fili spinati', *La Repubblica*, 29 January 2020 <https://www.repubblica. it/politica/2020/01/29/news/siate_farfalle_che_volano_sopra_i_fili_spinati-247109535/> [accessed 29 January 2020]; Carlo Verdelli, 'Indagine Eurispes: il 15,6% crede che la Shoah non sia mai esistita, erano 2,7% nel 2004', *La Repubblica*, 30 January 2020 <https://www.repubblica. it/cronaca/2020/01/30/news/indagine_eurispes_il_15_6_crede_che_la_shoah_non_e_ mai_esistita_erano_il_2_7_nel_2004-247140837/> [accessed 8 February 2020]; Gad Lerner, 'Quel normale antisemitismo', *La Repubblica*, 12 February 2020 <https://www.repubblica.it/ commenti/2020/02/12/news/quel_normale_antisemitismo-300805182/> [accessed 12 February 2020].

9. On Liliana Segre see Silvana Greco, 'Liliana Segre, or the Courageous Struggle against "Indifference" and for Social Recognition', *Academicus*, 19 (2019), 9-31.

10. See Francesca Koch and Simona Lunadei, 'Il 16 ottobre nella memoria cittadina', in *La memoria della legislazione e della persecuzione antiebraica nella storia dell'Italia Repubblichina*, ed. by the Istituto romano per la storia dell'Italia republicana (Milan: Franco Angeli, 1999), pp. 55-70; Mario Toscano, '16 ottobre 1943. La costituzione della memoria: i difficili inizi', in *16 ottobre 1943*, ed. by Baumeister, Osti Guerrazzi, and Procaccia, pp. 109-33 (p. 111).

11. See for example Guri Schwarz and Arturo Marzano, *Attentato alla sinagoga: Roma, 9 ottobre 1982, il conflitto israelo-palestinese e l'Italia* (Rome: Viella, 2013), pp. 183-225.

12. Koch and Lunadei, 'Il 16 ottobre nella memoria cittadina', p. 69.

13. Robert S. C. Gordon, *An Introduction to Twentieth-century Italian Literature: A Difficult Modernity* (London: Duckworth, 2005), p. 93.

14. Umberto Saba, *Scorciatoie e raccontini*, in *Tutte le prose* (Milan: Mondadori, 2001), pp. 3-106.

15. Details of the earliest editions of these works can be found in Chapter 3. Giacomo Debenedetti, *Otto ebrei*, in *Saggi* (Milan: Mondadori, 1999), pp. 65-91, and 'Campo di ebrei', in *Saggi*, pp. 858-65 (this 1999 Mondadori edition hereafter referenced simply as *Saggi*); Jacques Bernard, *Le Camp de la mort lente* (Paris: Arc-en-ciel, 1945).

16. Giacoma Limentani, *In contumacia* (Milan: Adelphi, 1967); Lia Levi, *Una bambina e basta* (Rome: E/O, 1994).

17. On Limentani and Levi, among others, see for example Lucamante, *Forging Shoah Memories*, pp. 113-49.

18. Gianni Campus, *Il treno di piazza Giudia* (Cuneo: L'arciere, 1995); Settimia Spizzichino and Isa Di Nepri Olper, *Gli anni rubati: le memorie di Settimia Spizzichino, reduce dai Lager di Auschwitz e Bergen-Belsen* (Cava de' Tirreni: Comune di Cava de' Tirreni, 1996).

19. Enzo Forcella, *La resistenza in convento* (Turin: Einaudi, 1999).

20. Robert A. Graham, *Il Vaticano e il nazismo* (Rome: Cinque Lune, 1975).

21. Rigano, '16 ottobre 1943', p. 51 n., and 'Il Vaticano e la razzia del 16 ottobre 1943', in *16 ottobre 1943*, ed. by Baumeister, Osti Guerrazzi, and Procaccia, pp. 63-85 (pp. 76 n., 77 n., 80 n.).

22. Renzo Modiano, *Di razza ebraica* (Milan: Scheiwiller, 2005).

23. Gianni Clementi, *Ladro di razza*, in *L'ebreo; Ladro di razza* (Riano: Editoria & Spettacolo, 2010).

In 2013, a stage play adaptation of the book was performed, as will be later discussed in the Conclusion.

24. Francesca Romana De'Angelis, *Per infiniti giorni* (Bagno a Ripoli: Passigli, 2014); Federica Pannocchia, *Quando dal cielo cadevano le stelle* (Trento: Eden, 2016).

25. Alberto Ciarafoni, *Quer 16 de ottobre* (Padua: Il Torchio, 2016).

26. Maurizio Molinari and Amedeo Osti Guerrazzi, *Duello nel ghetto: la sfida di un ebreo contro le bande nazifasciste nella Roma occupata* (Milan: Rizzoli, 2017).

27. Corrado Plastino, *La valigia* (Milan: StreetLib, 2017). In 2017, *La valigia* was produced and performed at secondary school level, as will be later discussed in the conclusion of this book.

28. Lia Tagliacozzo, *La generazione del deserto: storie di famiglia, di giusti e di infami durante le persecuzioni razziali in Italia* (Lecce: Manni, 2020).

29. Hirsch, 'The Generation of Postmemory', p. 106.

30. Erll, *Memory in Culture*, pp. 158-59.

31. Standard historiography on this period of Italian history includes: Lutz Klinkhammer, *L'occupazione tedesca in Italia 1943–1945* (Turin: Bollati Boringhieri, 1993), and *Stragi naziste in Italia: la guerra contro i civili 1943–1944* (Rome: Donzelli, 2006); Gabriele Ranzato, *La liberazione di Roma: alleati e resistenza (8 Settembre 1943–4 Giugno 1944)* (Bari: Laterza, 2019). On occupied Rome see: Cesare De Simone, *Roma città prigioniera: i 271 giorni dell'occupazione nazista (8 settembre '43–4 giugno '44)* (Milan: Mursia, 1994); Liliana Picciotto Fargion, *Il libro della memoria: gli ebrei deportati dall'Italia (1943–1945)* (Milan: Mursia, 2002), pp. 858-66.

32. On the Fosse Ardeatine massacre, see for example: Robert Katz, *Death in Rome* (London: Cape, 1967); Alessandro Portelli, *L'ordine è già stato eseguito: Roma, le Fosse Ardeatine, la memoria* (Roma: Donzelli, 1999); John Foot, 'Via Rasella, 1944: Memory, Truth, and History', *Historical Journal*, 43.4 (2000), 1173-80.

33. On Israele Zolli see: Eugenio Zolli, *Prima dell'alba: autobiografia autorizzata* (Cinisello Balsamo: San Paolo, 2004); Gabriele Rigano, *Il caso Zolli: l'itinerario di un intellettuale in bilico tra fedi, culture e nazioni* (Milan: Guerini e Associati, 2006).

34. *Ottobre 1943: cronaca di un'infamia*, ed. by Comunità Israelitica di Roma (Rome: Dapco, 1961).

35. Michael Tagliacozzo, 'La comunità di Roma sotto l'incubo della svastica: la grande razzia del 16 ottobre 1943', in *Gli ebrei in Italia durante il fascismo*, ed. by Foa and Valabrega, III, 8-38.

36. Robert Katz, *Sabato Nero*, trans. by Enrica Labò (Bologna: Rizzoli, 1973).

37. On this debate see, for example, Koch and Lunadei, 'Il 16 ottobre nella memoria cittadina', p. 68.

38. Fausto Coen, *16 ottobre 1943: la grande razzia degli ebrei di Roma* (Florence: Giuntina, 1994).

39. *Roma, 16 ottobre 1943*, ed. by Antonucci and others.

40. Pezzetti, *16 ottobre 1943*.

41. *16 ottobre 1943*, ed. by Baumeister, Osti Guerrazzi and Procaccia.

42. Picciotto, 'The Decision-making Process of the Roundup of the Jews of Rome'. Other significant historiographical works on 16 October include: Liliana Picciotto Fargion, *L'occupazione tedesca e gli ebrei di Roma: documenti e fatti* (Rome: Carocci, 1979); Sarfatti, *Gli ebrei nell'Italia fascista*; Amedeo Osti Guerrazzi, *Caino a Roma* (Rome: Cooper, 2005); Gordon, *The Holocaust in Italian Culture*, pp. 86-107; Luca Pietrafesa, *16 ottobre 1943. Viaggio nella memoria: voci, testimonianze e immagini del rastrellamento e della deportazione degli ebrei di Roma* (Rome: Reality Book, 2014).

43. See for example: Rigano, '16 ottobre 1943', pp. 19-74; Pezzetti, *16 ottobre 1943*, pp. 65-187.

44. See: Katz, *Black Sabbath*, p. 102; Susan Zuccotti, *Under His Very Windows: The Vatican and the Holocaust in Italy* (New Haven, CT: Yale University Press, 2000), p. 154; Gordon Thomas, *The Pope's Jews: The Vatican's Secret Plan to Save the Jews from the Nazis* (New York: Thomas Dunne Books, 2012), p. 157.

45. Rigano, '16 ottobre 1943', pp. 19-74.

46. Sarfatti, *Gli ebrei nell'Italia fascista*, p. 243.

47. *L'oro di Roma*, dir. by Carlo Lizzani (Ager Film, Sancro Film, C.I.R.A.C., Contact Organisation, Lux Film, 1961); *16 ottobre 1943*, dir. by Ansano Giannarelli (REIAC film, 1961). Cinematographic representations of 16 October will be explored in the Conclusion.

48. In *Il libro della Shoah italiana*, Marcello Pezzetti collects testimonies of Jews who lived through

those days. Marcello Pezzetti, *Il libro della Shoah italiana: i racconti di chi è sopravvissuto* (Turin: Einuadi, 2009), pp. 53–63.

49. Rigano, '16 ottobre 1943', p. 63. All translations are mine unless otherwise stated.

50. The Einsatzstab Reichsleiter Rosenberg was composed of two formal divisions: work groups made up of regional organisations and special staff whose responsibility included the fields of art and historical artefacts. See Stanislao G. Pugliese, 'Bloodless Torture: The Books of the Roman Ghetto under the Nazi Occupation', *Libraries and Culture*, 34.3 (1999), 241–53 (p. 243).

51. The diary of Rosina Sorani is partially reproduced in *Ottobre 1943: cronaca di un'infamia*, ed. by Comunità Israelitica di Roma, pp. 35–43.

52. Rigano, '16 ottobre 1943', p. 33.

53. On this episode see Pugliese, 'Bloodless Torture', p. 248.

54. Katz, *Black Sabbath*, pp. 123, 145, 166, 167 n.; 224, 302 n.; Pugliese, 'Bloodless Torture', pp. 252–53 n.; Rigano, '16 ottobre 1943', pp. 28, 33, 34, 37 n., 40, 41 n., 42 n., 44, 56, 71 n., 73.

55. On Theodor Dannecker see for example: Helmut Krausnick and others, *Anatomy of the SS State*, trans. by Richard Barry and others (London: Collins, 1968); Robert S. Wistrich, *Who's Who in Nazi Germany* (London: Weidenfeld & Nicolson, 1982); Claudia Steur, *Theodor Dannecker: ein Funktionär der Endlösung* (Essen: Klartext, 1997); Sara Berger, 'I persecutori del 16 ottobre 1943', in *16 ottobre 1943*, ed. by Baumeister, Osti Guerrazzi, Procaccia, pp. 21–39.

56. There are controversies surrounding the arrival of Dannecker. On 6 October, Kappler sent a telegram to Wolff, the Supreme SS and Police Leader, saying that Dannecker was in Rome. See Rigano, '16 ottobre 1943', pp. 34–35.

57. On the division of Rome see: Claudio Procaccia and Giancarlo Spizzichino, 'I sommersi e la città', in *Roma, 16 ottobre 1943*, ed. by Antonucci and others, pp. 75–88; Sabrina Gremoli and Keti Lelo, 'La localizzazione della popolazione ebraica romana arrestata e deportata nell'ottobre del 1943', in *Roma, 16 ottobre 1943*, ed. by Antonucci, and others, pp. 89–94.

58. The interrogation of Herbert Kappler in the preliminary phase of the trial against him between 20 and 28 August 1947 is kept at the Tribunale Militare Territoriale of Rome. See Gabriele Rigano, 'Appendice', in *Roma, 16 ottobre 1943*, ed. by Antonucci, and others, pp. 147–200 (pp. 151–71).

59. See Berger, 'I persecutori del 16 ottobre 1943', p. 30.

60. Katz, *Black Sabbath*, p. 173.

61. Ibid., pp. 160–61; Rigano, '16 ottobre 1943', p. 40.

62. Gaetano Petraglia, *La matta di piazza Giudia: storia e memoria dell'ebrea romana Elena di Porto* (Florence: Giuntina, 2022), pp. 34, 142–44, 146, 167–70, 175, 200–02.

63. See for example: Rigano, '16 ottobre 1943', p. 41; Klinkhammer, *L'occupazione tedesca in Italia 1943–1945*, pp. 403 and 606 n.

64. A picture of one of these instructions is in Pezzetti, *16 ottobre 1943*, p. 65.

65. On Pius XII and the Roman round-up see for example: Andrea Riccardi, *L'inverno più lungo: 1943–44. Pio XII, gli ebrei e i nazisti a Roma* (Rome: Laterza, 2008); Rigano, 'Il Vaticano e la razzia del 16 ottobre 1943', pp. 63–85; Frank Coppa, 'Between Morality and Diplomacy: The Vatican's "Silence" During the Holocaust', *Journal of Church and State*, 50.3 (2008), 541–68; Gabriele Rigano, 'Pio XII e il 16 ottobre: note sul dibattito storiografico', *Rivista di Storia della Chiesa in Italia*, 68.1 (2014), 165–86. On the Vatican and the Second World War see for example: Giovanni Miccoli, *I dilemmi e i silenzi di Pio XII* (Bologna: Rizzoli, 2000); Zuccotti, *Under His Very Windows*; *Pope Pius XII and the Holocaust*, ed. by Carol Rittner and John K. Roth (London: Bloomsbury, 2016).

66. Jacques Nobécourt, 'Il silenzio di Pio XII', in *Dizionario storico del papato*, ed. by Philippe Levillain (Milan: Bompiani, 1996), pp. 1883–89 (p. 1886); Pierre Belt, *Pio XII e la seconda guerra mondiale negli archivi vaticani* (Cinisello Balsamo: San Paolo, 1999), p. 283; Andrea Tornielli, *Pio XII: Eugenio Pacelli, un uomo sul trono di Pietro* (Milan: Mondadori, 2007), pp. 407–08; Gary L. Krupp, *Pope Pius XII and World War II: The Documents of Truth* (London: Xlibris, 2012), pp. 100–01.

67. Rigano, 'Il Vaticano e la razzia del 16 ottobre 1943', pp. 76–77.

68. See Berger, 'I persecutori del 16 ottobre 1943', pp. 21–40.

69. Ibid., p. 36.

70. See: Arminio Wachsberger, 'Testimonianza di un deportato da Roma', in *L'occupazione tedesca e gli ebrei di Roma*, ed. by Picciotto Fargion, pp. 173-207; Gabriele Rigano, *L'interprete di Auschwitz: Arminio Wachsberger, un testimone d'eccezione della deportazione degli ebrei di Roma* (Milan: Guerini, 2015).

71. Wachsberger, 'Testimonianza di un deportato da Roma', p. 176.

72. See: Tagliacozzo, 'La comunità di Roma sotto l'incubo della svastica', p. 26; Klinkhammer, *L'occupazione tedesca in Italia 1943–1945*, p. 606; Rigano, '16 ottobre 1943', p. 51.

73. Zuccotti, *Under His Very Window*, p. 155 n.

74. Rigano, *L'interprete di Auschwitz*, p. 92.

75. See for example: Pezzetti, *16 ottobre 1943*, p. 145; Wachsberger, 'Testimonianza di un deportato da Roma', pp. 177-78.

76. For further information on the registered number of people who left the Collegio Militare see for example Rigano, '16 ottobre 1943', pp. 45 and 83 n.

77. See: Katz, *Black Sabbath*, p. 234; Rigano, '16 ottobre 1943', p. 56.

78. On Quirino Zazza see Katz, *Black Sabbath*, p. 235.

79. Rigano, '16 ottobre 1943', p. 56.

80. The police station of Rome recorded the train's departure in its daily reports to the Ministry of the Interior, and Kappler sent a telegram to Berlin. A picture of these documents can be found in Pezzetti, *16 ottobre 1943*, p. 161.

81. Rigano, *L'interprete di Auschwitz*, pp. 95-96.

82. Wachsberger, 'Testimonianza di un deportato da Roma', pp. 177-78; Tagliacozzo, 'La comunità di Roma sotto l'incubo della svastica', pp. 34-37; Katz, *Black Sabbath*, pp. 269-72; Zuccotti, *The Italians and the Holocaust*, pp. 121-25.

83. Elsa Morante, *La Storia*, in *Opere*, 2 vols (Milan: Mondadori, 1990), II, 255-1036 (p. 621); hereafter referenced in the main text as *S*.

84. Elsa Morante, *History: A Novel*, trans. by William Weaver (New York: Aventura, 1984), pp. 266-67; hereafter referenced in the main text as *H*.

85. Rigano, '16 ottobre 1943', pp. 48-50.

86. Ibid., p. 44. See also Berger, 'I persecutori del 16 ottobre 1943', p. 27.

87. Picciotto Fargion, *Il libro della memoria*, pp. 858-66; Berger, 'I persecutori del 16 ottobre 1943', pp. 31-34.

88. See Kappler's deposition in De Felice, *Storia degli ebrei italiani sotto il fascismo*, pp. 469-70; Katz, *Black Sabbath*, p. 223.

89. De Felice, *Storia degli ebrei italiani sotto il fascismo*, pp. 469-70; Katz, *Black Sabbath*, p. 223; Rigano, '16 ottobre 1943', p. 45.

90. Katz, *Black Sabbath*, pp. 179, 296; Zuccotti, *The Italians and the Holocaust*, p. 192; Silvia Haia Antonucci, 'Le interviste', in *Roma, 16 ottobre 1943*, ed. by Antonucci and others, pp. 96-131.

91. Giuseppe Pederiali, *Stella di Piazza Giudìa* (Florence: Giunti, 1995); Anna Foa and Lucetta Scaraffia, *Anime nere: due donne e due destini nella Roma nazista* (Venice, Marsilio, 2021).

PART II

CHAPTER 3

❖

❖

Giacomo Debenedetti,
16 ottobre 1943

An Introduction

16 ottobre 1943 was the first detailed account to be published about the Roman round-up, from dawn on 16 October to the deportation to Auschwitz on 18 October. It was written in Rome in November 1944 by the literary critic and writer Giacomo Debenedetti, who was in the capital on 16 October.[1] During the round-up, he hid in his neighbour's house in via Sant'Anselmo 32. The following is the only indication of this in the text: 'Chi scrive questo racconto passò la mattinata del 16 ottobre in casa di una sua vicina' [The writer of this account spent the morning of October 16 in the house of a neighbor].[2] Debenedetti's daughter confirmed this fact, adding that her father was in Rome for practical reasons.[3]

16 ottobre 1943 appeared for the first time in December 1944 in the Roman monthly journal *Mercurio*, taking up just over twenty pages. The director, Alba de Céspedes, had asked Debenedetti to publish it in her journal, as stated in a 1962 letter in which she asked for a signed copy of the new edition of *16 ottobre 1943*: 'Caro Giacomino, [...] mi piacerebbe tanto avere il suo "16 ottobre 1943": non l'ho avuto e mi sarebbe caro riceverLo da Lei, con la Sua firma, poiché *ho il merito di averglielo chiesto io, con tanta insistenza, per "Mercurio"'* [Dear Giacomino, [...] I would very much like to have your '16 ottobre 1943': I haven't got it and I would love to receive it from you, with your signature, since *I have the merit of having asked you for it, with so much insistence, for 'Mercurio'*].[4] The issue of *Mercurio* in which '16 ottobre 1943' appeared was highly significant: published while Italy was still at war, albeit Rome had been liberated, it was entirely dedicated to the Resistance. In around three hundred pages, it contained almost seventy contributions with first-hand accounts of the experience of the war. Eugenio Montale, Natalia Ginzburg, Alberto Moravia, and Guido Piovene, along with key figures in the Roman Resistance, were among the contributors.[5] According to Debenedetti, this issue was a channel of transmission to the north of Italy which was still under German occupation:

> Per noi questo fascicolo di 'Mercurio' sarà forse il primo ambasciatore, il primo latore che si incaricherà di portare una nostra parola oltre il cordone sanitario che ancora ci separa dal Nord. Perciò queste note noi non riusciamo a stenderle se non come una lettera indirizzata a persone, per le quali abbiamo trepidato

fino al giorno in cui non riusciremo ad avere notizia. Lassù abbiamo un fratello con tutta la sua famiglia né potevamo incaricare coloro che passavano le linee di collegarci con lui, data la situazione razziale che avrebbe reso impudente violarne il nascondiglio — abbiamo parenti, abbiamo amici. Che se poi queste note, per l'economia della rivista, prendon forma di un resoconto letterario, esse saran continuamente tentate di sconfinare dal soggetto e di toccare toni i più immediati tanto per noi quanto per loro, che speriamo riusciranno a leggerci.[6]

[For us this volume of 'Mercurio' will perhaps be the first ambassador, the first bearer who will take a word from us beyond the cordon sanitaire that still separates us from the North. Therefore, we cannot write these notes if not as a letter addressed to the people, for whom we will be anxious until the day when we will be able to get news. Up there we have a brother with his whole family; we could ask those who crossed the lines to connect us with him, but given the racial situation it would be imprudent to violate his hiding place — we have relatives, we have friends. And if these notes, for the economy of the magazine, take the form of a literary account, they will be continually tempted to trespass on the subject and touch the most immediate tones for us as well as for them, who, we hope, will be able to read us.]

In this sense, *16 ottobre 1943* is also to be re-read as a means by which Debenedetti was able to pass personal information about his situation to his loved ones in the north. In the text, he includes private messages which are disguised in the polyphonic descriptions of the round-up. As previously indicated, he mentions that he was in Rome when the round-up occurred and back again in July 1944 (*SO*, p. 58; *OS*, p. 56). By publishing the text, he demonstrates that he was back in Rome, this time out of danger.

In November 1945, after Einaudi refused it, a small Roman publisher, OET, published *16 ottobre 1943* as a short book.[7] A second edition appeared in 1959 with Il Saggiatore, in Milan, as the volume had long become unobtainable. Since then, several editions have appeared, a second edition with Il Saggiatore and others with a number of different publishers such as Riuniti, Sellerio, and Einaudi, variously including prefaces and notes by some of the most renowned writers and critics of the time: Alberto Moravia, Ottavio Cecchi, and Natalia Ginzburg.[8] Since 1973, *16 ottobre 1943* has been published with another short piece by Debenedetti written in late 1944, *Otto ebrei*, dedicated to the trial of the police commissioners Pietro Caruso and Raffaele Alianello.[9] To date, it has been published thirteen times and translated into five languages. This publishing history already suggests that *16 ottobre 1943* has played an evolving role in the historical and literary transmission of memory of the persecution of the Roman Jews.

In *16 ottobre 1943* Debenedetti writes a sober but vivid account of the unfolding of the crime, building upon his own impressions and memories, albeit very limited, and the direct testimonies he collected, which are the historical elements he had access to at the time and which he used to corroborate his work.[10] He narrows the focus of history down to the individual and transforms personal memories into a powerful and incisive means of recalling the round-up. He conveys the immediate sense of reality of 16 October and illustrates the round-up in its heterogeneity and complexity by way of the combination of individuals' stories. He relates each of these testimonies to each other, makes them interact, compares them, and by placing them within the social framework of occupied Rome, he verifies them. The work merges the genres of historical chronicle, essay, testimony, memoir, and short story and in this sense is a clear example of the triangular relationship between history, memory, and literature.

The two following sections offer some details of Debenedetti's life during the war and help to contextualise the genesis of *16 ottobre 1943* in a period which Debenedetti mainly devoted to journalism. The essays and the articles analysed identify Debenedetti's commitment to the study of the discrimination against, persecution of, and deportation of Jews in Italy, and establish how this highly influential text came to take its unique form.

Personal Experiences

Debenedetti was born into a Jewish family in the northern town of Biella in 1901.[11] In 1913 he moved to Turin with his family, and in 1922, after graduating in law, he enrolled in the Facoltà di Lettere e Filosofia at the University of Turin. In the same year, he set up the short-lived magazine *Primo Tempo*, and started a collaboration with *Il Baretti*, the fortnightly journal directed by Piero Gobetti. In 1923, after the cessation of *Primo Tempo*, he wrote for several literary magazines including *Solaria*, *Quindicinale*, and *Pegaso*, and in 1926 published his first volume of short stories, *Amedeo ed altri racconti*.[12] In 1929, the first of the three volumes of *Saggi critici*, a significant body of critical essays which show the evolution of his critical methodology, appeared.[13] Debenedetti began his career as an exponent of Crocean aesthetics, but he soon developed his own critical methodology, which included elements of Freudian and Jungian psychoanalysis and cultural and anthropological approaches.[14]

In 1936, Debenedetti and his family moved from Turin to Rome where they lived in via Sant'Anselmo 32. In 1938, after the promulgation of the Racial Laws, he was forced to abandon or hide his newspaper and literary activities because he was Jewish. In December 1938, he was unable to publish his second volume of *Saggi critici*, intended for publication by Vallecchi in Florence. In 1941, using the name of his wife Renata Orengo, he signed an essay dedicated to D'Annunzio published in *Argomenti*.[15] Between 1938 and 1943, he worked in the Italian cinema as a scriptwriter and artistic supervisor: he anonymously collaborated on at least thirteen screenplays.[16] Among the works he did not publish, published anonymously, or published under the name of Renata Orengo in this period, there are two exceptions: a 1940 translation of George Eliot's *The Mill on the Floss* for Mondadori, and an article in a 1942 volume dedicated to Benedetto Croce published by Laterza.[17]

When Marshal Badoglio signed the armistice with the Allies and the Germans occupied the Italian peninsula in early September 1943, Debenedetti was in Rome. Between 8 and 13 September, he wrote a diary (now held at the archive of the Gabinetto Vieusseux, Florence) in which he meticulously recorded the vicissitudes he lived through hour by hour and the measures he took to take his family to safety. On 9 September, a day after the proclamation of the armistice between Italy and the Allies, Debenedetti and his family left their apartment and hid in a hotel in the city centre. The filmmaker Oreste Biancoli booked a room for Debenedetti at the Boston Hotel close to the Villa Borghese to ensure that he and his family were safe. Debenedetti wrote in the diary: '9 sett. Ore 15 [...] Biancoli per parte sua mi telefona di avermi fissato delle camere in centro; per telefono non può dirmi particolari, ma ha buone ragioni per sconsigliarmi di rimanere a casa mia' [9 Sept 3 pm [...] Biancoli telephones me he says he has booked some rooms in the city centre for me; he cannot give me details over the phone, but he has good reason to suggest that I should not stay at home].[18]

A few days later, the literary critic Pietro Pancrazi, a close friend of Debenedetti, persuaded him to leave Rome and so, on 13 September, Debenedetti and his family left the capital for Cortona, where they stayed for more than ten months from September 1943 to August 1944, during which time he made two short trips to Rome, as previously mentioned: the first was on or around 16 October 1943, the other in July 1944. In Cortona, at first, they stayed at Pancrazi's home, then they rented Villa Baldelli, in Cegliolo, a hamlet a few kilometres from the town.[19] In *La piccola patria* by Pietro Pancrazi, Debendetti included his reflections on Cortona, described as place of refuge, and on the sense of guilt and powerlessness he felt because of the persecution of his Jewish community:

> Caro Pancrazi, nessuno meglio di te è in grado di sapere che cosa abbia rappresentato Cortona, il tuo caro e bellissimo paese, per gente a cui l'8 settembre e i mesi successivi potevano creare difficoltà di vita quasi insormontabili [...]. Io viaggiavo con mia moglie e coi bambini [...]. E io avevo come vergogna di me stesso, come se fossi stato io personalmente, per un colpo di testa, per un errore di calcolo, a trascinare i miei bambini in un'avventura di cui non potevo assicurare l'esito.[20]

> [Dear Pancrazi, no one is more able than you to understand what Cortona, your dear and beautiful village, represented for people for whom 8 September and the following months could create almost insurmountable difficulties in life [...]. I was travelling with my wife and children [...]. And I was ashamed of myself, as if it had been me personally, through a blow to the head, through a miscalculation, to drag my children into an adventure whose outcome I could not guarantee.]

In June 1944, the Fascists arrived in Cortona looking for Jews. Debenedetti's wife recounted those days in her diary, *Diario del Cegliolo*: 'Arriva in bicicletta Gaetano, l'uomo Guercio, il finto tonto ad avvertirci: Giacomo è cercato, bisogna che se ne vada subito [...]. Poco dopo lo vediamo arrampicarsi e sparire per l'erto sentiero che porta a Cantalena da Don Rodolfo' [Gaetano arrives by bicycle, the Guercio man, the fake idiot, he warns us: Giacomo is being sought, he must leave immediately [...]. Shortly after, we see him climb and disappear on the steep path that leads to Cantalena to Don Rodolfo].[21] Debenedetti left Villa Baldelli from 9 to 16 June, taking refuge with the partisan forces in the rectory of Cantalena on Monte Sant'Egidio.[22] On 13 June, the Fascists left Cortona and Debenedetti could return home, as his wife reported: 'i fascisti di Cortona sono fuggiti col camion della Misericordia. Le liste sono bruciate. Giacomo potrà, se vuole, tornare' [In Cortona, the fascists fled with the Misericordia truck. The lists are burned. Giacomo will be able, if he wants, to come back].[23]

During the ten months in Cortona, after he had witnessed and hidden from the October round-up, he wrote two pieces of literary criticism which, although apparently detached from contemporary events, nonetheless relate to the war: *Vocazione di Vittorio Alfieri* and 'Camilla'. Giuliano Manacorda suggests that in these two works, Debenedetti developed a form of political commitment through literary commentary, in particular through his exploration of an idea of freedom and of revolutionary struggle.[24] In these two texts, Debenedetti disclosed, albeit in a veiled way, the thoughts that gripped him during the war. The two works had different destinies: *Vocazione di Vittorio Alfieri* was published as a book only posthumously in 1977, although the main themes of the essay appeared in two articles published between 1945 and 1946 in two literary magazines, *Poesia* and *La fiera letteraria*;[25] 'Camilla' appeared in 1945, in a later issue of *Mercurio*.[26]

Vocazione di Vittorio Alfieri is a long essay dedicated to the eighteenth-century poet, playwright, and writer Vittorio Alfieri (1749-1803). In it, Debenedetti proposes an analysis of Alfieri's *Vita scritta da esso* in which some reflections on the concepts of freedom and tyranny are read in light of the Fascist regime: 'Potrebbe darsi che per gente come noi, così malcapitata sul pianeta, in un'era così soffocante, il primo invito dell'Alfieri, e il più decisivo, emani da quella parola "libertà" che romba, tuona e vola nelle sue pagine' [It could be that for people like us, so unfortunate on the planet, in such a suffocating era, Alfieri's first invitation, and the most decisive, comes from the word 'freedom' that roars, thunders and flies through its pages].[27] A passage in which Debenedetti imagines being admonished by a commissioner to read and comment on Alfieri's words confirms this reading: 'Commissario, che andate cercando? Questo è Vittorio Alfieri, poeta d'altro secolo, e ce l'aveva col re, coi preti e coi francesi' [Commissioner, what are you looking for? This is Vittorio Alfieri, a poet from another century, and he was angry with the king, with the priests and with the French].[28] Debenedetti defends himself and sarcastically notes that Alfieri's words refer only to 'altro secolo', but by re-contextualising those words in the present in which he is writing he reinforces their effectiveness.

'Camilla' is a short essay dedicated to the armed virgin described by Virgil in the eleventh book of the *Aeneid*. It was written immediately after Debenedetti had returned from Rome following 16 October 1943, as stated in the footnote for the later edition of *Saggi critici*: 'queste note sul personaggio di Camilla furono scritte nell'ottobre 1943, pochi giorni dopo la razzia dei nazisti nel Ghetto di Roma' [these notes on the character of Camilla were written in October 1943, a few days after the round-up the Nazi carried out in the Roman ghetto].[29] It includes, like *Vocazione di Vittorio Alfieri*, several references that implicitly relate to the political and social situation in Italy. The description of the mythological character of Camilla and the battle Latinus undertook alongside Turnus, echoes the war Mussolini had undertaken alongside Hitler. In the aforementioned footnote, Debenedetti explicitly traces a parallel between the historical and mythological figures, Latinus as Mussolini, Turnus as Hitler: 'queste note [...] contengono anche troppi accenni che avrebbero dovuto aprire gli occhi dei lettori sull'intenzione dello scritto' [these notes [...] also contain too many hints that should have opened the readers' eyes to the intention of the writing].[30] He comments, 'sia malaugurata questa battaglia che Latino è costretto nolente a intraprendere per imposizione di Turno, il duro alleato a cui si è stretto in un momento di aberrazione politica e militare' [May this battle go badly, the battle Turnus forced on an unwilling Latinus, Turnus, the hard ally Latinus joined in a moment of political and military aberration].[31] Considering the Pact of Steel, which was signed on 22 May 1939 and which marked the beginning of the formal alliance between Fascist Italy and Nazi Germany, Debenedetti indirectly describes Mussolini as passive towards Hitler and having waged a war he did not believe in from June 1940.

Vocazione di Vittorio Alfieri and 'Camilla' are the first works to hint at the beginning of Debenedetti's considerations of the war he was living through, considerations which reached their acme with the publication of *Otto ebrei* and *16 ottobre 1943*.

Engaging with History

In August and September 1944, Debenedetti spent a short period in Gragnano at the house of his brother-in-law, Nicola Gaudioso. In late September, he returned to Rome and joined the Communist Party. Between September and December 1945, he devoted himself to journalism. He wrote articles about the war, including several about the persecution of the Jews, revealing in him a new political commitment. These articles are cited here as part of Debenedetti's attempt to spread awareness of the discrimination against and persecution of the Jews by paying attention to both persecutors and persecuted, and are read in relation to *16 ottobre 1943* specifically.

The first of these articles was 'Otto ebrei'. Written in September 1944, it appeared across three issues of *Il Tempo* from 11 to 15 October 1944 and by the end of the same year it had been published as a book by Atlantica.[32] Its subject is the trial on 20 September 1944 of the police commissioner of Rome, Pietro Caruso, who was accused of collaboration with the Nazi occupiers, as he had drawn up the list of victims to be shot on 24 March 1944 at the Fosse Ardeatine. The trial began with the courtroom testimony of policeman Raffaele Antonio Alianello, who had deleted ten names from the list because the number of hostages was higher than expected — eight of whom he had chosen from among the Jews on the list — and had released these ten people. In court he claimed mitigation for this act.

In *Otto ebrei*, Debenedetti investigates the reasons behind Alianello's behaviour and draws attention to a new subtle and dangerous form of discrimination, hidden behind mercy: 'Perché gli ebrei ebbero il privilegio, la precedenza? Perché su dieci posti se ne portarono via otto?' [Why did the Jews merit privilege, take precedence? Why of ten exemptions did they get eight?]. According to Debenedetti, 'nel salvare preferenzialmente gli ebrei in vista dei propri meriti futuri, l'Alianello [...] sottolineò un partito preso [...] una "campagna" di riparazione che rovescia una "campagna" di distruzione' [In preferentially saving Jews with an eye to possible future credit to himself, Alianello was following an advertising campaign [...] he emphasized his deliberate choice [...] a reparative 'campaign' to reverse a destructive 'campaign'] (*OE*, p. 76; *OS*, p. 72). Debenedetti was concerned that Jews could again be treated as different from others: 'se prima negli ebrei si puniva l'ebreo, oggi [...] può nascere il dubbio che *negli ebrei si perdoni l'ebreo. E il perdono richiama l'idea di una colpa, di un trascorso*' [if, formerly, Jews were punished for their Jewishness, on viewing the current situation [...] it gives rise to the suspicion that *Jews are being forgiven for their Jewishness. Forgiveness recalls the concept of guilt, of transgression] (*OE*, p. 83; *OS*, p. 79, my emphasis). In the manuscript of *Otto ebrei*, held in the archive of the Gabinetto Vieusseux, Debenedetti wrote a sentence, then crossed it out in the final version of the text, which confirms a link and a continuity between forgiveness, condemnation, and otherness: 'il perdono immediato, conferma l'idea di una condanna immediata' [immediate forgiveness confirms the idea of immediate condemnation].[33] He states directly what Jews should aim for: 'la pretesa [...] è unicamente di non accampare, né vedersi riconosciute, speciali pretese. Il diritto di non avere speciali diritti. Speciali cioè razziali' [the claim [...] is not to assert title to, nor to see ourselves accorded, any special rights. The right to not have special rights. Special, meaning racial] (*OE*, p. 83; *OS*, p. 84). In *Otto ebrei*, Debenedetti considers the experiences the Jews of Rome during the German occupation mostly by looking at the Fosse Ardeatine massacre; but he also includes, for the first time, a brief comment on the round-up of 16 October:

> A Roma, [...] non c'è famiglia ebraica nella quale, tornando dopo questi mesi, non si abbia paura di chiedere notizie dei congiunti più stretti. Già troppe volte ci siamo visti opporre dei visi chiusi [...]: — 'Presi deportati quella mattina del 16 ottobre. Non se ne è saputo più niente'. (*OE*, p. 72)

> [In Rome, where one can say there isn't a Jewish family which, on returning after all these months, one wouldn't be afraid to inquire about closest kin. Too many times already, we've come across closed, severe faces [...]. Taken, deported, that morning of October 16. Never another word about them.] (*OS*, p. 67)

Less than two months later, Debenedetti published the chronicle–narrative–essay '16 ottobre 1943' in form of an article, thus continuing and broadening his consideration of the round-up. His journalistic career intensified still further after the publication of '16 ottobre 1943'.

Between February and December 1945, Debenedetti was chief editor of *L'Epoca*, a daily journal founded by Leonida Répaci.[34] Describing his editorial staff, Répaci said a few words about Debenedetti and mentioned the article 'Otto ebrei', thus showing the relevance it had at the time: 'una redazione di primordine che nessun altro quotidiano a Roma può vantare [...]. Come redattore l'amico Giacomo Debenedetti, critico illustre, che già invitai a pubblicare sul *Tempo* uno straordinario servizio sulla *via crucis* degli ebrei di Roma' [a first-rate editorial staff that no other newspaper in Rome can boast [...]. As an editor, my friend Giacomo

Debenedetti, an illustrious critic, whom I had already invited to publish in *Tempo* an extraordinary report on the *Via Crucis* of the Jews of Rome].[35] While he was chief editor of *L'Epoca*, Debenedetti wrote twenty articles, ten signed in full and ten with the initials 'g. d.'.[36] Among these twenty works, he wrote four about the conflict and persecution of the Jews: 'Lupi in plenilunio', 'Febbre a 40', 'Libertà dalla paura', and 'Trincea degli ebrei'.[37] These four articles are not the only ones that Debenedetti dedicated to the persecution of the Jews: there is one further important essay, published in *La Nuova Europa* in April 1945, entitled 'Campo di ebrei'.[38]

In 1945 Debenedetti contributed to other magazines and journals, among which *La Nuova Europa*, a weekly magazine directed by Luigi Salvatorelli.[39] As noted by Salvatorelli himself, the magazine was divided into three parts:

> Una prima parte di politica attuale; una seconda dedicata alla letteratura e alle arti; una, che potrei chiamare 'storico-morale' o anche, con termine più largo, sociale, in cui si intrecciano discussioni di idee, ed esposizioni di fatti non attinenti propriamente né alla politica né alla letteratura [...]. I limiti fra le tre parti [...] sono fluttuanti.[40]

> [A first part of current politics; a second dedicated to literature and the arts; one, which I could call 'historical-moral' or even, with a broader term, social, in which discussions of ideas and expositions of facts not strictly related to politics or literature are interwoven [...]. The boundaries between the three parts [...] fluctuate.]

Debenedetti wrote five articles for *La Nuova Europa* between December 1944 and July 1945, among them 'Campo di ebrei', which is briefly analysed in relation to his willingness to discuss the persecution of the Jews in Italy and the Jewish massacre in Europe.[41] 'Campo di ebrei', published on 1 April 1945, is in part a literary review of the French book *Le Camp de la mort lente* by Jacques Bernard, but more than that, it is also a text full of reflections on the war, on the Jewish deportations in Italy, on the lack of information about them, and on the denigration and violence that the Jews suffered.

Le Camp de la mort lente, published in December 1944, is about Bernard's experience of the German occupation of Paris, of his arrest in December 1941, and of his deportation to Royallieu, a concentration camp close to Compiègne, where he was imprisoned until March 1942. From the beginning of the article, Debenedetti draws parallels between Bernard's experience and that of the Roman Jews on 16 October:

> È quasi sicuro infatti che il racconto del Bernard, almeno fino a un certo punto, può far testo anche per i *nostri* deportati. Intanto, fin dove sappiamo, il procedimento seguito nella razzia di Roma collima con quello descrittoci dal Bernard, al punto da far supporre che l'analogia continui anche dove dei *nostri* non sappiamo più nulla. A Parigi come a Roma i tedeschi si presentarono nelle case degli ebrei verso l'alba, col solito foglio di istruzioni [...]. Unica differenza fondamentale: invece che le intere famiglie, nella razzia parigina furono presi soltanto gli uomini, anzi soltanto gli iscritti su certi elenchi. Differenza accessoria: non furono subito gli autocarri a portarli via, ma comode macchine chiuse, che li condussero fino alla mairie dell'arrondissement [...]. Da questo punto le due storie tornano a coincidere: a pugni e pedate, soprattutto contro

chi si attardi perché vecchio o malato o stanco o impaurito, gli ebrei vengono ammassati sui tetri autocarri [...]. Finalmente si fermano alla Scuola Militare. Collegio Militare a Roma, Scuola Militare a Parigi: senza dubbio la coincidenza è fortuita, ma accresce la suggestione dell'analogia. (*CE*, p. 859, my emphasis)

[Indeed, almost certainly Bernard's account, at least up to a certain point, can also be used for *our* deportees. Meanwhile, as far as we know, the procedure followed in the round-up in Rome coincides with that described to us by Bernard, to the point of suggesting that the analogy continues even where we no longer know anything *about ours*. In Paris as in Rome, the Germans showed up in the apartments of the Jews towards dawn, with the usual instruction sheet [...]. The only fundamental difference: instead of entire families, only men were taken in the Parisian round-up, in fact only those registered on certain lists. Accessory difference: it was not the trucks that took them away immediately, but comfortable closed vehicles, which led them to the town hall of the arrondissement [...]. From this point the two stories coincide again: punching and kicking, especially of those who linger because they are old or sick or tired or afraid, the Jews are piled onto the bare trucks [...]. Finally they stop at the Military School. Military College in Rome, Military School in Paris: undoubtedly the coincidence is fortuitous, but it augments the suggestion of the analogy.]

There are three points to stress. In the first two sentences, Debenedetti uses 'nostro' twice. By doing so, he shows a sense of belonging and a sense of community with the Jews deported from Rome. Then, he briefly describes two differences between the two round-ups ('differenza fondamentale', 'differenza accessoria'). He comments that the Roman round-up was far more dramatic. Women and children, as mentioned in Chapter 2, were the majority of the people arrested on 16 October, and they were taken away in 'autocarri' and not in 'comode macchine chiuse'. After that, he goes back to drawing comparisons, stating that 'le due storie tornano a coincidere'. He was convinced that *Le Camp* could offer an idea of what happened to the Roman Jews after their departure from Stazione Tiburtina and their arrival at the railway station in Florence:

Esistono qui in Roma centinaia di famiglie ebraiche, le quali da circa venti mesi vivono nella più angosciosa ignoranza di ciò che sia successo ai loro congiunti, prelevati nella famosa razzia del 16 ottobre 1943 [...]. Della razzia romana si è giunti a ricostruire il decorso fino al momento in cui le vittime, sul treno piombato in rotta verso il nord, giunsero alla stazione di Firenze. Ma da Firenze comincia la notte inesorabile. Il Bernard è penetrato nel cuore di quella notte, ne ha vissute alcune ore, scontandone attimo per attimo la sostanza per noi così crudelmente enigmatica, poi ne è riemerso a dirci com'era. Lo si interroga [...]. *Le risposte che il Bernard ci dà noi le riassumiamo soprattutto a intenzione dei nostri amici dell'ex-ghetto di Roma, che non potranno leggere il libro.* (*CE*, p. 859, my emphasis)

[There are hundreds of Jewish families here in Rome, who for about twenty months have been living in the most anguished ignorance of what happened to their relatives, taken in the famous round-up of 16 October 1943 [...]. The course of the Roman round-up has been reconstructed until the moment in which the victims, on the sealed train en route to the north, arrived at the train station in Florence. But the inexorable night begins in Florence. Bernard penetrated the heart of that night, for a few hours he lived moment by moment the reality so cruelly unknown to us, then he emerged to tell us what it was like. He questions it [...]. *We summarise the answers that Bernard gives us above all for the sake of our friends from the former ghetto of Rome, who will not be able to read the book.*]

In 1945, it was still unclear what had happened to the Roman Jews.[42] Debenedetti describes this lack of information as 'la notte inesorabile'. His glosses on Bernard's descriptions of deportation suggest his commitment to remembering the Roman round-up and to making his readers reflect on what the Jews experienced:

> Quello che il Bernard ci ha detto non è forse moltissimo. Per fortuna sua, egli fece un'esperienza solo parziale e forse attenuata. Inoltre, nel riferirla, per certe ragioni personali che bisognerà discutere, ci defrauda di quella che dovette essere l'intima, la specifica psicologia, la condizione umana degli ebrei deportati. Comunque, in confronto col nulla che fin qui sapevamo, anche il poco sembra già qualche cosa. (*CE*, p. 865)

> [What Bernard told us is perhaps not very much. Fortunately for him, he had only a partial and perhaps attenuated experience. Furthermore, in reporting it, for certain personal reasons that we must discuss, he deprives us of what must have been the intimate, the specific psychology, the human condition of the deported Jews. However, in comparison with the nothing we knew up to now, even the little seems something.]

Although Bernard had not been deported to an extermination camp and thus his memoir could not provide a complete picture of deportation, Debenedetti prompts embryonic reflections on the process of dehumanisation that it produced. He pays attention to the descriptions of the abuses Bernard lived through and comments that the Nazis began to vilify the Jews by turning their physiological needs into something to be ashamed of: 'solo a distanza ci si rende conto che la prima di quelle torture, sugli inizi quasi imprecisabile, [...] consiste nel trasformare i bisogni naturali in una ossessione' [only from a distance do we realise that the first of those tortures, almost imprecise at the beginning, [...] consists of transforming natural needs into an obsession] (*CE*, p. 861). In 1945, before the first survivors could share what they had lived through, Debenedetti understood the process of progressive dehumanisation that the Nazis operated on the Jews.

Examined together, 'Campo di ebrei' and the articles mentioned above provide a crucial foundation for understanding the value Debenedetti that attributed to journalism and his choice to publish '16 ottobre 1943' as an article in *Mercurio*. As Marcello Ciocchetti notes, journalism was a means by which Debenedetti was able to write and to be published again after a period in which the Fascist regime had prevented him from doing so.[43] And, in general, towards the end of 1944 journalism had become the most powerful, immediate, and widely-read medium in Italy. Through it, Debenedetti, perhaps for the first time, committed himself to a moment of collective rethinking, using it as a powerful conduit for his thoughts and opinions. In his articles for *L'Epoca* and *La Nuova Europa*, he adopted a more direct and impactful style than he had used in his literary criticism in the *Saggi critici*.

When at the end of 1945 he resigned from *L'Epoca*, he wrote a letter, published as an article entitled 'Piantatori di datteri' on 1 January 1946, in which he offered reflections on journalism.[44] He saw it as a meeting point between intellectuals and the public: 'questo giornalismo quotidiano, rimane ancora la forma incomparabile per conciliare l'intervento nella vita associata con la riflessione solitaria, la piazza con il tavolino' [this daily journalism still remains the incomparable form for reconciling the intervention in life associated with solitary reflection, the piazza with the table].[45] From 1946, Debenedetti radically limited his journalistic career: 'in questi giorni di bilanci, una domanda si pone: se andiamo avanti così, se tutti serviamo la politica militante, chi rimarrà per quell'altra politica?' [in these days of record, a question arises: if we go on like this, if we all serve militant politics, who will remain for the other policy?].[46] According to Ciocchetti, by 'altra politica' Debenedetti meant 'lavoro educativo' [educational work], and from 1946 he only sporadically published articles, most of them in the Communist newspaper *L'Unità*.[47] In the same year, he joined the jury of the literary prize Premio Viareggio and started a collaboration with the publishing house Arnoldo Mondadori. In 1950, he obtained a teaching post at the University of Messina and his role and career to a degree left behind this brief but intense period of public commitment closely linked to the Nazi persecution of the Jews.

The articles considered here represent Debenedetti's willingness to provide the first testimony to various aspects of the war, and the deportations of 16 October in particular, at a time when the tendency to cover up or forget Italian guilt and complicity in this history was already beginning to emerge. His articles are crucial elements through which to understand the sociocultural background against which *16 ottobre 1943* was written, and the following section looks more closely at *16 ottobre 1943* itself in this light. It proposes a textual analysis of Debenedetti's narrative techniques and broader considerations on the modalities that this key text, and by extension literature in general, uses to influence its readership and to shape cultural memory.

Voices From the Ghetto

In *16 ottobre 1943*, Debenedetti wrote a chronicle-narrative-essay of the round-up and of the ex-ghetto on the days that preceded and followed 16 October. He begins his text by reporting the night of 15 October. Through flashbacks, he recounts the ransom of the 50 kilos of gold on 26 September and the plunder of the Jewish Community Library on 11 October. He then goes back to describe the round-up from the dawn of 16 October through the combination of the testimonies he had collected.

Astrid Erll is convinced that 'what the past appears to be in a given culture of memory [...] arises not so much from the remembered events themselves, but from the specific mode of re-presenting these events'.[48] This analysis of how Debenedetti represented the Roman round-up in *16 ottobre 1943* does not read the text sequentially from its start but instead examines it from three standpoints.

Firstly, it looks at Debenedetti's representation of the events through two notions of time: one historical or linear, the other biblical or cyclical. It then focuses on the re-elaboration of the testimonies he gathered in writing it and descriptions of the habits, personal perceptions, impressions, and gestures of the Jews of Rome which he recounted and imaginatively elaborated. Lastly, it considers and analyses Debenedetti's opinions about the events concerning the round-up that he expresses in his text.

Debenedetti situates the round-up within the historical timeline of occupied Rome, and at the same time represents it alongside and in light of the history of the Jews as narrated in the Bible. He provides an immediate contextualisation of 16 October by describing the events which took place between 26 September and 11 October, making readers directly aware of his process of historical reconstruction by using the first person plural: '*chiediamo* scusa di questa digressione, ed eventualmente delle altre in cui *incorreremo*; ma per intendere l'intera atrocità del dramma che *cercheremo* di ricostruire, è opportuno conoscere un po' meglio i personaggi' [*We beg* forgiveness for this digression, and for any others in which *we might indulge*, but in order to understand the full horror of the drama which *we seek* to reconstruct, it is necessary to know the people involved a little better] (SO, p. 33; OS, p. 26, my emphasis).[49] The first of the events narrated is the ransom of the 50 kilos of gold:

> La sera del 26 Settembre 1943, il presidente della Comunità Israelitica di Roma e quello dell'Unione delle Comunità Italiane [...] erano stati convocati per le ore 18 all'Ambasciata Germanica [...]. Il governo dei Reich imponeva loro una taglia di 50 chilogrammi d'oro, da versarsi entro le ore 11 del successivo martedì 28. In caso di inadempienza, razzia e deportazione in Germania di 200 ebrei. (SO, pp. 33-34)

> [In fact, on the evening of the 26th of September, 1943, the presidents of the Roman Jewish community and of the Union of the Italian Communities had been summoned [...] to a 6 pm meeting at the German Embassy [...]. The government of the Reich was levying a tribute of 50 kilograms of gold, to be produced before 11 am of the following Tuesday, the 28th. Nonfulfillment would result in the roundup and deportation to Germany of two hundred Jews.] (OS, p. 26)

The second is the plunder of the rabbinical college and Jewish community libraries:

> Una strana figura [...] appare l'11 ottobre nei locali della Comunità. Anche lui accompagnato da una scorta di SS, a vederlo si direbbe un ufficiale tedesco [...]. Mentre i suoi uomini cominciano a buttare all'aria la biblioteca del collegio rabbinico e quella della Comunità, l'ufficiale con mani caute e meticolose, da ricamatrice di fino, palpa, sfiora, carezza papiri e incunaboli, sfoglia manoscritti e rare edizioni, scartabella codici membranacei e palinsesti [...]. Poco dopo sulla linea tranviaria della Circolare Nera, giungono tre carrozzoni merci. Le SS vi caricano le due biblioteche. I carrozzoni ripartono. Libri, manoscritti, codici e pergamene hanno preso la strada di Monaco di Baviera. (SO, pp. 38-40)

> [A strange figure [...] appears at the offices of the Jewish community on October 11. He too is escorted by SS troops and appears to be just another German officer [...]. While his men commence ransacking the libraries of

the rabbinical college and the Jewish community, the officer, with hands as cautious and sensitive as those of the finest needlewoman, skims, touches, caresses papyri and incunabula, leafs through manuscripts and rare editions, peruses parchments and palimpsests [...]. Shortly thereafter, three large freight cars arrive on the tracks of the Black Tram line. The SS load the two libraries onto them. The cars leave. Books, manuscripts, codices, parchments are on their way to Munich.] (*OS*, p. 33)

Debenedetti ends his text by providing what little information he could gather about Monday 18 October and the deportation, mentioning the stops the train made between Stazione Tiburtina and Bologna:

> Verso l'alba del lunedì, i razziati furono messi su autofurgoni e condotti alla Stazione di Roma-Tiburtina, dove li stivarono su carri bestiame [...]. Alle 13.30 il treno fu dato in consegna al macchinista Quirino Zazza [...]. Il treno si mosse alle 14 [...]. Nei pressi di Orte, il treno trovò un semaforo chiuso e dovette fermarsi per una decina di minuti [...]. A Chiusi, altra breve fermata, per scaricare il cadavere di una vecchia, deceduta durante il viaggio. A Firenze il signor Zazza smonta [...]. Cambiato il personale di servizio, il treno proseguì per Bologna. (*SO*, pp. 62-63)

> [Toward dawn on Monday, the prisoners were boarded onto motor vans and taken to the Rome Tiburtino station [...]. At 1:30 pm the train was assigned to motorman Quirino Zazza [...]. The train began moving at 2 pm [...]. Near Orte the train encountered a closed semaphore signal and had to stop for about ten minutes [...]. At Chiusi, another short stop, to drop off the body of an old woman who had died during the trip. At Florence, Signor Zazzi left [...]. With a change of service personnel, the train continued on to Bologna.] (*OS*, p. 61)

As these passages show, in giving his readers a context and chronological order to the events narrated, his style is concise and paratactic, his language clear and simple. The descriptions of the day of the round-up itself, however, are quite different: the language is more complex and lyrical, employing analogies and metaphors, and giving, for example, descriptions of Jewish religious and ancestral rituals within the context of the Bible. A good example of this is the passage in which he describes the evening of Friday 15 October, where he writes about the religious ritual of the Sabbath. As narrated in Exodus, God commanded that it should be a holy day of rest:

> Fino a poche settimane prima, ogni venerdì sera, all'accendersi della prima stella, si spalancavano le grandi porte della Sinagoga, quelle verso la piazza del tempio [...]. Ogni venerdì, si celebrava il ritorno del Sabato [...]. Dall'alto della cantoria, nella romba osannante dell'organo, il coro di fanciulli gloriava un cantico di sacra tenerezza, l'inno dell'antico cabbalista, 'Lehà Dodì Lichrà Calà': Vieni, o amico, vieni incontro al Sabato... Era il mistico invito ad accogliere il Sabato che giunge, che giunge come una sposa. (*SO*, p. 29)

> [Until a few weeks ago, on Friday evenings, at the appearance of the first star, the great doors of the synagogue, those facing the Temple Square, would be opened wide [...]. Every Friday evening [...] the return of the Sabbath was celebrated. Not the thin psalmody of the cantor, lost at the distant altar, but from the choir stall above, amid the resounding praises of the organ, the chorus

of young voices raised high in a song of holy love; the old kabbalists' hymn, *Lekhah dodi, likrat Kallah*, 'Come, my beloved, come to meet the Sabbath'. It was the mystical invitation to greet the approaching Sabbath, the Sabbath that arrives like a bride.] (*OS*, p. 21)

The Roman Jews were used to coming together and celebrating it in the synagogue 'ogni venerdì sera', but on the night of Friday 15 they were at home, as they had been since the German occupation:

> Quella sera le famiglie erano già tutte raccolte nelle case. Qualche madre accendeva la lampada sabbatica [...] mentre i vecchi con la *teffilà* sui ginocchi recitavano le benedizioni, e passavano dal borbottio della preghiera all'invettiva iraconda e chioccia contro i nipotini disturbatori. (*SO*, p. 30)

> [On that evening as well, families were already gathered in their homes. Mothers were lighting candles in Sabbath candlesticks [...] while old men with *tephilal* prayer books in their laps were reciting the blessings and alternating between mumbling prayers and hoarse and angry tirades against their noisy grandchildren.] (*OS*, p. 23)

Debenedetti continues the comparison with the lost communal rituals of the Sabbath when he describes Portico d'Ottavia on late Saturday morning:

> Verso le 11 [...] un poco di sole brillò sulle selci del Portico di Ottavia [...]. Nei Sabbati ormai lontani, quel raggio di sole attraversava le vetrate della Sinagoga, andava ad accendere le canne dell'organo, che gli rispondeva nel registro più d'oro. E lo riversava, quel raggio, sui fedeli in concenti di giubilazione, in uno sfolgorare di santa allegrezza. I fanciulli cantavano: *Santo, Santo, Santo, il Dio degli Eserciti, della Sua gloria tutta la terra è colma*. Ora, dal fondo della fossa in cui stanno spettando di essere deportati, quei fanciulli non levano altro che pianto, un pianto che non fa coro, che non si innalza al cielo come il fumo dei sacrifizi; che il cielo tornato basso sembra respingere, fa ricadere sulle loro spalle. (*SO*, pp. 58-59)

> [The weather [...] cleared briefly at about 11 am a little sunshine glowed on the paving stones of the Portico di Ottavia [...]. On by now distant Sabbaths, that ray of sunlight would pierce the windows of the synagogue and gild the organ pipes, which would reply to it in their most golden register. And that ray of light would pour down on the faithful in a harmony of jubilation, in a glow of holy joy. The children would sing, *Holy, holy, holy, the Lord of hosts. All the earth is filled with His glory*. Now, from the depths of the pit in which they stand awaiting deportation, these children raise only laments, laments not joined in chorus, which do not rise toward heaven like the smoke of sacrifice; and which heaven, dark and low once again, seems to reject and send falling back upon their shoulders.] (*OS*, p. 57)

He contrasts the image of the children herded together in Portico d'Ottavia with the image of joyful children singing 'nei Sabbati ormai lontani', lit up by the sun through the coloured glass windows of the synagogue. He then makes references to the Bible, portraying the ghetto after the round-up as the Jerusalem told of in The Lamentations of Jeremiah I. 1: 'la razzia si protrasse fino verso le 13. Quando fu la fine, per le vie del Ghetto non si vedeva più anima, vi regnava la desolazione della

Gerusallemme di Geremia: *quomodo sedet sola civitas'* [the roundup lasted until about
1 pm when it was over, there wasn't a soul to be seen on the streets of the Ghetto,
the desolation of Jeremiah's Jerusalem was upon it, *quomodo sedet sola civitas*] (*SO*, p.
59; *OS*, p. 57). He ends his reportage of Saturday 16 October with metaphors from
Exodus 2. 22 while describing the birth of two infants in the Collegio Militare
Italiano, and comparing their hopeless destiny to that of Gershom, the first of the
two children of Moses and Zipporah:

> Due neonati aprirono gli occhi sulle tenebre di quel malaugurato cortile.
> Quali nomi saranno stati dati a questi primogeniti di una nuova schiavitù di
> Babilonia? (Gheresciòm aveva chiamato Mosè il figlio della servitù, 'pellegrino
> in terra straniera', natogli da Sipporà, ma i due nati di quella notte senza Mosè
> erano pellegrini verso le camere dei gas.) (*SO*, p. 61)

> [Two newborns opened their eyes in the shadows of the ill-omened courtyard.
> What names were given to these two first-borns into a new Babylonian slavery?
> (Moses named the son born to him of Zipporah, while in servitude, Gershom,
> [wayfarer in a strange land], but the two born that night without a Moses were
> on their way to gas chambers.] (*OS*, pp. 60–61)

Of our four authors, Debenedetti is the only one who pays such attention to Jewish
ritual and tradition in narrating 16 October. His description of the event is intimate,
familiar to his fellow Jews, and unexpected, unconventional to non-Jewish
readers. His reconstructions of events guarantee easily memorable association of
images which partly explains why *16 ottobre 1943* has so widely influenced both
individual and cultural memory, becoming an intertextual reference in both the
historiography and subsequent literary texts of the Roman round-up. Two other
factors also explain the influence of Debenedetti's work: first, the collage that he
creates from the testimonies collected, which provides multifocal perspectives on
the episode; second, his sharing, as a participant narrator, of his own opinions and
bitter commentary.

Debenedetti describes Saturday morning through a combination of testimonies,
personal impressions, and sensory perceptions. After a few pages dedicated to the
events that preceded the arrests on 16 October, he brings his readers to the middle
of the ghetto through the description of the shouts of an unknown Jewish woman,
Letizia:

> Pare che il primo allarme l'abbia dato una donna di nome Letizia [...]. Verso
> le 5, costei fu udita gridare: 'Oh Dio, i *mamonni*!' 'Mamonni' in gergo giudìo-
> romanesco significa gli sbirri, le guardie, la forza pubblica. Erano infatti i
> tedeschi che col loro passo pesante e cadenzato (conosciamo persone per cui
> questo passo è rimasto il simbolo, lo spaventoso equivalente uditivo del terrore
> tedesco), cominciavano a bloccare strade e case del Ghetto. Il proprietario di un
> piccolo caffè del Portico di Ottavia [...] dice che i passi cadenzati, lui cominciò
> a sentirli verso le 5 e mezzo (sulle ore non è stato possibile mettere d'accordo
> i testimoni; quel tempo di sciagura deve essere stato terribilmente elastico,
> soggetto a valutazioni soltanto psicologiche). (*SO*, p. 44)

> [It appears that a woman named Letizia sounded the first alarm [...]. Toward 5
> am she was heard shouting, 'Oh God, i *mammoni*.' Mammoni in Roman Jewish

slang means cops, guards, police. In fact, it was the Germans, who, with the heavy, cadenced steps (we know people for whom that step has remained the symbol, the terrifying audio equivalent, of the German horrors) had begun to barricade streets and houses of the Ghetto. The owner of a small cafe near the Portico di Ottavia [...] says that he himself first heard the rhythmic steps toward 5:30 (it hasn't been possible to get the witnesses to agree on the exact time: that disastrous moment must have been dreadfully elastic, subject only to psychological measure).] (*OS*, pp. 39-40)

Debenedetti appears to walk around the ghetto and enter the houses of the ordinary characters he follows:

> Entriamo ora in una casa di via Sant'Ambrogio, nel Ghetto. Potremo seguire la razzia in tutte le sue fasi. Verso le 5 (ora psicologica, ripetiamo), la signora Laurina S. viene chiamata dalla strada. È una nipote che le grida: 'Zia, zia, scendi! I tedeschi portano via tutti!' Questa ragazza, qualche momento prima, uscendo di casa in via della Reginella aveva veduto portar via una intera famiglia con sei bambini [...]. Qui si domanderà come abbia potuto la nipote gridare così dalla via, e parole tanto esplicite, alla presenza di due tedeschi [...]. Ripetiamo che i tedeschi, in massima, non rastrellarono la gente per via: fuor di casa furono presi soltanto quelli che, infelici, vollero farsi prendere. Né bisogna credere che la tragedia si sia svolta in un'atmosfera di muta e trasecolata solennità: le persone seguitavano a parlare tra di loro, a gridarsi degli avvisi, delle raccomandazioni. (*SO*, p. 46)

> [Now we enter a house on via S. Ambrogio in the Ghetto. We'll be able to watch the entire raid from here. Toward 5 am (a psychologically meaningful time, we repeat) Signora Laurina S. hears herself called from the street. It's her niece shouting, 'Auntie, auntie, come down! The Germans are taking everyone away'. A few minutes before, on leaving her house on via della Reginella, this girl had seen an entire family with six children be taken away [...]. Here, one wonders how the niece could have shouted such explicit words in the presence of the Germans [...]. And we must explain again that for the most part the Germans did not round up people on the street. Out of doors they took only those poor souls who took no precautions to keep from being taken. Nor is it necessary to think that the tragedy was enacted in an atmosphere of muted and astonished solemnity. People went on talking among themselves, shouting out news, suggestions.] (*OS*, pp. 41-42)]

Debenedetti draws his readers into the ghetto both temporally and geographically: with the exhortative 'Entriamo' he invites his readers into a Jewish house; events take place in 'un piccolo caffè in Portico d'Ottavia', in 'una casa di via Sant'Ambrogio', in 'via Reginella'; the arrests happen 'verso le 5'. Parenthetically he again makes his readers aware of his attempt to corroborate each testimony with reference to others, and of the difficulty of establishing a precise timeline, given that individual perception of time is subjective. Having taken the reader into the ghetto, he focuses on the experiences of the witnesses and vividly evokes the soundtrack of the events of the morning of 16 October by reproducing their conversations, ways of speaking, warnings ('Zia, zia, scendi! I tedeschi portano via tutti!'), and cries ('Oh Dio! I *Mamonni*'). Such sounds, and use of Roman-Jewish dialect in particular (as in *mammoni* here) throughout the book, bring the events graphically to life for the readers, allowing them to participate in what the Jews of the ghetto lived through.[50] As both the passages cited above show, Debenedetti is both a link and a mediator between the Jewish victims and his readers: he anticipates the questions that his readership might plausibly raise ('Qui si domanderà come'); and uses first person plural narratorial forms repeatedly — 'conosciamo', 'entriamo', 'potremo', 'ripetiamo' — thus showing him to be among both the Jewish residents of the ghetto and his readers.

As if in a cinematic long shot, Debenedetti moves around the arrests:

> Nel mezzo della via passano, in fila indiana un po' sconnessa, le famiglie rastrellate: una SS in testa e una in coda sorvegliano i piccoli manipoli, li tengono su per giù incolonnati, li spingono avanti con i calci dei mitragliatori, quantunque nessuno opponga altra resistenza che il pianto, i gemiti, le richieste di pietà, le smarrite interrogazioni. (*SO*, p. 47)

> [The captured families are straggling single-file down the middle of the street. SS troopers at the head and the tail of each little band are guarding them, keeping them more or less in line, prodding them on with the butts of their machine guns although no one is resisting with anything more than tears, moans, cries for mercy, confused questions.] (*OS*, p. 44)

He then zooms in on this aural scene and reveals that it is made up of a collage of individual feelings and perceptions. He briefly depicts the physical and emotional traits of some of the Jews waiting to be loaded into the cattle-trucks and brought to the Collegio Militare with a series of highly suggestive vignettes of hopelessness and fear. He depicts frightened children and powerless fathers, the old and the sick, a young mother with an infant in her arms:

> I ragazzi cercano negli occhi dei genitori una rassicurazione, un conforto che questi non possono più dare [...]. Taluno bacia le proprie creature [...] certi padri tengono la mano sul capo dei figlioli, col medesimo gesto con cui nei giorni solenni hanno impartito la *Birchàd Choanìm*: 'Ti benedica il Signore e ti protegga...'. (*SO*, p. 48)

> [The children search their parents' eyes for reassurance, comfort the latter can no longer give [...]. Some of them kiss their children [...]. And there are fathers who keep their hands on their child's head in the very same manner with which, on holy days, they had bestowed the *Birchad Choanim*: 'May the Lord bless you and keep you...'.] (*OS*, pp. 44-45)

> Una vecchia di ottant'anni mezza andata di mente: si trascinava tra gli altri, come un po' saltellando, senza capire che cosa le facessero fare, e rispondeva con saluti e sorrisi ebeti e perfino un po' fatui agli sguardi della gente; ma poi trasaliva d'improvviso e si spaventava, biascicando frammenti di preghiere, quando i tedeschi si rimettevano a urlare [...]. Passa un'altra vecchia di ottantacinque anni, sorda e malata. Passa un paralitico, portato a braccia sulla sedia. (*SO*, p. 48)

> [An old woman about eighty-years old and half out of her mind, in the line. She was swept along among the others, almost skipping a little, without understanding what was happening her, and was responding to the stares of people around her with greetings and inane, even fatuous smiles. But, she

jumped with fright and begun murmuring fragments of prayers when the Germans started shouting again [...]. Another old woman, eighty-five years old, deaf and sick goes by. A paralytic carried aloft in his chair goes by.] (*OS*, p. 45)

Una donna con un lattante in collo si slaccia la camicetta, estrae la mammella e la spreme per mostrare al soldato che non ha più latte per la creatura: ma quello le punta il mitragliatore contro il fianco perché cammini. (*SO*, p. 48)

[A woman with a nursing child in her arms opens her blouse and takes out a breast and presses it to demonstrate to a soldier that there is no longer any milk for her child. But he pokes his machine gun into her side to get her to walk.] (*OS*, p. 45)

He ends the overview by zooming out to portray the crowd once again, allowing his readers to see the ghetto from a loftier perspective, so that they can imagine the exact place in which the Jews were rounded up:

Le file vengono spinte verso la goffa palazzina delle Antichità e delle Arti, che sorge al gomito del Portico di Ottavia di fronte alla via Catalana, tra la Chiesa di Sant'Angelo e il Teatro di Marcello. Ai piedi della palazzina si estende una breve area di scavi, ingombra di ruderi, qualche metro più bassa della strada. Entro questa fossa venivano raccolti gli ebrei, e messi in riga ad aspettare il ritorno dei tre o quattro camion, che facevano la spola tra il Ghetto e il luogo dove era stabilita la prima tappa. (*SO*, p. 49)

[The lines were being directed toward the ugly little Museum of Antiquity and Fine Arts, which rises at the summit of Portico di Ottavia in front of via Catalana, between the church of Sant' Angelo and the Teatro di Marcello. At the foot of the museum building, there's a small excavated area, several meters below street level, that's cluttered with ruins. The Jews were gathered together in this pit and arranged in lines to await the return of three or four trucks, which were shuttling back and forth between the Ghetto and the site that had been set up as the first staging area.] (*OS*, p. 46)

These intimate depictions, as a contrast to the bare facts of the historical event of the round-up, encourage the readers to become involved in what they read, to recognise and identify with the characters, and so memorise the facts of the event in a more personal and deeply felt way. The emotional repertoire shared by the readers and characters bridges the spatial and temporal gaps between them; the readers read the fear, the anguish, and the hopelessness of Debenedetti's characters, immerse themselves in these emotions, and momentarily blur the distinction between self and other.

The power of Debenedetti's account of 16 October, and thus also possibly its influence, is strengthened by his sharing of his personal opinions as a narrator close to the events. The first time Debenedetti explicitly comments in his own critical narratorial voice is when he describes the meeting between Kappler and the Jewish community leaders, Foà and Almansi, on 26 September:

Herbert Kappler [...] li fece accomodare e per qualche momento parlò del più e del meno, in tono di ordinaria conversazione. Poi entrò nel merito: gli ebrei di Roma erano doppiamente colpevoli, come italiani (ma meno di due mesi dopo, un decreto germano-fascista, auspici Rahn, Mussolini e Pavolini, doveva disconoscere agli ebrei d'Italia la cittadinanza italiana; e allora Maggiore Kappler?), come italiani per il tradimento contro la Germania, e come ebrei perché appartenenti alla razza degli eterni nemici della Germania. (*SO*, p. 33)

[They were received [...] by SS Major Herbert Kappler, who made them comfortable and spoke to them for a few minutes about this and that in conversational tones. Then he went to the heart of the matter. Roman Jews were doubly guilty, as Italians (but less than two months later a German-Fascist decree, sponsored by Rahn, Mussolini, and Pavolini, will no longer recognize Italian Jews as citizens of Italy, and what then Major Kappler?), for their betrayal of Germany, and as Jews because they belong to a race eternally inimical to Germany.] (*OS*, pp. 26-27)

Debenedetti's account of Kappler's conversation with the Jewish community leaders was probably based on a reading of the testimony that Foà left in November 1943.[51] By interrupting the reconstruction of the conversation by pointing out a contradiction in Kappler's argument to Kappler himself, Debenedetti leads his readers to ask the same questions.

Two further examples worth mentioning come from Debenedetti's description of the SS soldiers who conducted the round-up. First, he reflects on how they diligently followed orders yet did not bother to seek out those Jews they had not found in their houses:

Tutto sommato, rimane l'impressione che le SS, in un genere di operazioni a cui avevano ormai fatto il callo, abbiano agito quella mattina con una sorta di rigore professionale, di coscienza del mestiere, piuttosto che stimolati da un preciso accanimento. La brutalità che mostravano faceva parte della tecnica e non divenne, salvo eccezioni, sadismo individuale [...]. Così quella mattina la razzia non si mutò, generalmente parlando, in una caccia all'ebreo [...]. In sostanza, le SS agirono soprattutto *come se* il loro incarico fosse di fornire ai mandanti un certo — e senza dubbio assai cospicuo — numero di ebrei. E, visto che stavano facilmente raggiungendolo, non si siano dati la briga di andare per il sottile, di fare lo zelo supplementare. (*SO*, pp. 55-56)

[All things considered, the impression remains that the SS, already inured to this type of operation, had acted that morning with a kind of professional rigor, with a consciousness of their trade, rather than from the stimulus of specific fury. The brutality that they demonstrated, one could say, was part of their technique and only exceptionally became an act of individual sadism [...]. For that reason, the roundup that morning did not, generally speaking, turn into a hunt for Jews [...]. In essence, the SS acted primarily *as if* their responsibility was to furnish their superiors a certain — and without doubt — a very considerable number of Jews. And seeing that goal was easy to reach, they didn't trouble themselves to put too fine a point on it, or to get overzealous in the attempt.] (*OS*, pp. 53-54)

Debenedetti gives his readers a view of the round-up from the unusual perspective of the SS troops and catches their attention through the use of informal and colloquial language: popular sayings such as 'fatto il callo', 'dati la briga', and 'andare per il sottile' to describe the behaviour of the Germans; and syntagmatic phrases such as 'tutto sommato', 'salvo eccezioni', 'generalmente parlando', 'in sostanza', 'senza dubbio', and 'facilmente' to give a sense of a critical perspective and reflection upon the significance of the events.

Debenedetti continued his analysis of the attitude of the SS when he described them driving trucks full of Jews on sightseeing tours of the capital:

> Le SS che compirono questa razzia appartenevano a un reparto specializzato, giunto dal Nord la sera prima, all'insaputa di tutte le altre truppe tedesche di stanza a Roma [...]. A taluni di quei giovanotti non sembrò vero di poter disporre di un automezzo, sia pure carico di ebrei razziati, per fare un po' di giro turistico della città. Sicché prima di raggiungere il luogo di concentramento, i disgraziati che stavano all'interno dovettero subire le più capricciose peregrinazioni, sempre più incerti sul loro destino e, ad ogni nuova svolta, ad ogni nuova via che infilassero, assaliti da diverse e tutte inquietanti congetture. Naturalmente, la meta più ambita di quei turisti era Piazza S. Pietro, dove parecchi dei camion stazionarono a lungo. Mentre i tedeschi secernevano i *wunderbar* da costellarne il racconto che si riservavano di fare, in patria, a qualche Lilì Marlén, dal di dentro dei veicoli si alzavano grida e invocazioni al Papa, che intercedesse, che venisse in loro aiuto. Poi i camion ripartivano, e anche quest'ultima speranza era svanita. (*SO*, pp. 59-60)

> [The SS who performed this roundup belonged to a special unit which, unknown to all the other German troops stationed in Rome, had arrived from the North the previous evening [...]. It was irresistible to some of the young soldiers finding themselves with a motor vehicle at their disposal, even if it was full of rounded-up Jews, to take a tour of the city. So that before reaching the detention center, the poor souls standing inside the trucks had to suffer the most capricious peregrinations — always more uncertain of their destination, and at every new turn, at every new street that they traveled, assailed by various and always alarming conjectures. Naturally, the most popular goal of these tourists was St. Peter's Square, where several trucks stopped for long periods of time. While the Germans uttered the *Wunderbars* with which they would sprinkle the tales they intended to tell their Lili Marleens back home, from within the truck came shouts and invocations to the Pope, asking that he intercede, that he come to their aid. Then the trucks were on their way again, and even that last hope was gone.] (*OS*, pp. 58-59)

To engage with his readers, he refers to a well-known cultural figure of the time, Lili Marleen, the protagonist of the 1939 German song by Norbet Schultze, which became widely known in Italy when it was re-written by Nino Rastelli in 1942 and sung by Lina Termini. By picturing the Jews invoking the help of the Pope in St Peter's Square, Debenedetti covertly questions the silence of Pope Pius XII on the deportation of the Jews of Rome while alluding to the common belief of the Roman Jews that nothing would happen to them in Rome because the Pope would protect them. His comment that 'anche quest'ultima speranza era svanita' strongly but quietly implies that the Pope did nothing. Even though in Rome, and despite the Pope, Jews were deported to Auschwitz.[52]

By melding historiographical and biblical contexts with his own narratorial voice and perspectives, and by inviting the reader to reflect on particular aspects of the event, Debenedetti creates incisive images of the round-up which lead to a vivid evocation, recollection, and remembering of the events of 16 October, amongst a variety of communities of readers: readers of *Mercurio* and readers in the Jewish community, for example. *16 ottobre 1943* is a bearer of historical knowledge and a medium of memory; it engages in a fruitful dialogue with writers from his own and later generations as well as with historians on the interpretation of that past.

Constructing and Observing Cultural Memory

With *16 ottobre 1943*, Debenedetti created a work capable of providing a transmission of the macro-history of 16 October through a combination of micro-histories in a compelling narrative form that reveals the complex bond between historical facts, personal memory, the form of narrative, and the process of remembering. In this way, his work was one of the earliest and most crucial active ingredients in the ongoing cultural process of making the Roman round-up knowable. This move from the individual to the collective can be explained in terms of Astrid Erll's two modes of the 'experiental' and the 'reflexive' and of four of Ann Rigney's five types of narrative as cultural memory: 'relay station', 'catalyst', 'object of recollection', and 'stabilizer'.

Erll's 'experiential' mode is seen in Debenedetti's detailed, intimate descriptions of the morning of the round-up, his vivid glimpses into the life of the Jews of the ghetto, conveyed in the present tense, that embody the immediate experience of arrests, gatherings, trucks, sounds, and gestures; and her 'reflexive' mode in his narrative voice, as he merges personal testimonies with his own acerbic commentary.

16 ottobre 1943 functions as Rigney's 'relay station' because it is the first channel of transmission of personal memories of the Roman round-up, providing details and teasing out the complexities of it, making the event knowable even when Italy was still at war and before a general conception of the Holocaust had been formed. It fosters prosthetic memories of the event and favours the recollection of 16 and 18 October through the particular forms of writing we have analysed, thus linking together the processes of writing, reading, and remembering.

16 ottobre 1943 can be thought of as a 'catalyst' because it is instrumental in establishing the topic of the Roman round-up as socially and culturally relevant. When it was published in *Mercurio* in 1944 and re-printed as a book by OET in 1945, it became a tool with which to circulate knowledge of the round-up outside the Jewish community, potentially nationally. When it appeared in Lugano in the daily newspaper *Libera Stampa* in 1945 and in France in the journal *Les Temps modernes* in 1947, it gained an international readership, and the Roman round-up began to be read about in relation to events in the rest of Europe.[53] To date, as mentioned, it has been published in thirteen editions and translated into five languages: Dutch, English, French, German, and Hebrew.

16 ottobre 1943 is an 'object of recollection'. In 1961, Ansano Giannarelli directed and produced in collaboration with Marina Piperno the homonymous short documentary film on the Roman round-up which was based entirely on Debenedetti's work. The narrative voiceover, by Vittorio Foà, reads extracts of *16 ottobre 1943* as a commentary on images of the ex-ghetto.[54] In 2010, Simonetta

De Nichilo and Francesca Gatto based their play dedicated to the round-up on Debenedetti's text. It was entitled *Roma, 16 ottobre 1943*. In 2018, theatre director Giancarlo Monticelli turned *16 ottobre 1943* into a homonymous play which was performed by the amateur theatre company Bovisateatro in Milan for the first time on 16 October 2018, at the seventy-fifth commemoration of the Roman round-up.[55] Also in 2018, Sarah Laing, an Australian graphic novelist and designer, published *Rome 16 October 1943*, a visual adaptation of Debenedetti's *16 ottobre 1943* accompanied by her own translation of his words.[56]

Finally, *16 ottobre 1943* works as a 'stabilizer' because it has become a point of comparison for subsequent representations of the Roman round-up and has provided a cultural frame for later recollections. As mentioned in Chapter 2, it has been used as a source for later historiographical studies, including work by Renzo De Felice, Robert Katz, Anna Foa, Stanislao Pugliese, Gabriele Rigano, and Gaetano Petraglia.[57] In the literary sphere, Gordon points out that *16 ottobre 1943* works as something like an urtext for several lines of both Holocaust literature and testimony in Italy. It was the start of a long process of integrating the persecution of Italian Jews into a national narrative and national literature: '[it] was crucial as a model for the early post-war decades, in its reportage and chronicle, linked like several deportation testimonies to the neorealist movement, in its engagement with justice, national identity and collective responsibility'.[58] Similarly, Cavaglion finds in *16 ottobre 1943* the origin of one of the two groups into which he divides Italian writing on the Holocaust and suggests that every literary representation of 16 October is indebted to Debenedetti's text.[59] As the following chapters will demonstrate, *16 ottobre 1943* was the dominant and most authoritative literary source for all the other texts examined here, whose authors all cite it, as we shall see.

Rigney's categorisations should not be taken as inflexible and do not establish rigid boundaries. Instead, they help to weigh *16 ottobre 1943* in relation to its various publications, as well as its influence in the sphere of historiography and cultural and literary expression, and to demonstrate therefore that it is in many respects the point of genesis of the process of cultural memory of the Roman round-up. Since 1944, Debenedetti has come to be the keeper of the memory of the ghetto at the time when the SS erupted into the spaces of its daily life with terrible destructive force.

Notes to Chapter 3

1. On Debenedetti see: *Giacomo Debenedetti 1901–1967*, ed. by Cesare Garboli (Milan: Il Saggiatore, 1968); Angela Borghesi, *La lotta con l'angelo: Giacomo Debenedetti critico letterario* (Venice: Marsilio, 1989); *Il Novecento di Debenedetti*, ed. by Rosita Tordi (Milan: Mondadori, 1991); Antonio Debenedetti, *Giacomino* (Milan: Rizzoli, 1994); Paola Frandini, *Il teatro della memoria: Giacomo Debenedetti dalle opere ai documenti* (Lecce: Manni, 2001); Walter Pedullà, *Il Novecento segreto di Giacomo Debenedetti* (Milan: Rizzoli, 2004); Marcello Ciocchetti, *Prima di piantare datteri: Giacomo Debenedetti a Roma (1944–1945)* (Pesaro: Metauro, 2006).

2. Giacomo Debenedetti, *16 ottobre 1943*, in *Saggi*, pp. 25–63 (p. 58); all further quotations are taken from this edition (hereafter referenced in the main text as *SO*). Giacomo Debenedetti, *October 16, 1943; Eight Jews*, trans. by Estelle Gilson (Notre Dame, IN: University of Notre Dame Press, 2001), pp. 21–62 (p. 56); all further English translations are taken from this edition (hereafter referenced in the main text as *OS*).

3. Elisa Debenedetti, '16 ottobre 1943 nel ghetto di Roma rivissuto da Giacomo Debenedetti', *Strenna dei Romanisti*, 21 (2017), 159-68.

4. De Céspedes is referring to the 1962 Saggiatore edition: Giacomo Debenedetti, *16 ottobre 1943* (Milan: Il Saggiatore, 1962). Exchange of letters with Alba de Céspedes held at the Archivio contemporaneo 'Alessandro Bonsanti' -Gabinetto Vieusseux. The letter of 13 August 1962 is now reproduced in Ciocchetti, *Prima di pianteare datteri*, p. 33 (my emphasis).

5. On *Mercurio*, see: Franco Contorbia, 'Appunti per un saggio su "Mercurio"', *La Rassegna della Letteratura Italiana*, 1 (2004), 29-43; Laura Di Nicola, 'Il progetto "Mercurio" negli anni del dopoguerra', *Rivista di Letteratura Italiana*, 1-2 (2005), 407-12, and *Mercurio: storia di una rivista 1944-1948* (Milan: Il Saggiatore, 2012).

6. Unpublished documents quoted as 'da un manoscritto inedito in Archivio Debenedetti Roma', in Marco Edoardo Debenedetti, 'Cronologia', in *Saggi*, pp. lxix-lvxx (p. lxxvi).

7. Ciocchetti examined the exchange of letters between Debenedetti and OET and confirmed that the first edition of *16 ottobre* appeared in November 1945: *Prima di piantare datteri*, pp. 34-35. Marco Edoardo Debenedetti notes that the collaboration with OET started 'dopo il fallimento dei contatti intrapresi con la Einaudi' [after the failure of contacts with Einaudi]: 'Cronologia', p. lxxvii. Paola Frandini comments that *16 ottobre* had been 'rifiutato dalla Einaudi': *Il teatro della memoria*, p. 309.

8. Giacomo Debenedetti, *16 ottobre 1943; Otto ebrei*, ed. by Cesare Garboli, preface by Alberto Moravia (Milan: Il Saggiatore, 1973); *16 ottobre 1943*, ed. by Ottavio Cecchi (Rome: Riuniti, 1978); *16 ottobre 1943*, preface by Natalia Ginzberg (Palermo: Sellerio, 1993).

9. The practice of offering these two texts by Debenedetti together in book format has been largely respected in publications in translation outside Italy as well.

10. As far as the testimonies are concerned, Marco Edoardo Debenedetti ('Cronologia', p. lxxvi) claims that the author listened to several witnesses among whom Mario Spizzichino, Luciano Camerino, and Aldo Sorani. According to the CDEC (Fondazione Centro di Documentazione Ebraica Contemporanea) Mario Spizzichino was arrested on 10 February 1944, deported to Auschwitz on 5 April 1944 and repatriated on 8 May 1945. Aldo Sorani was arrested in Florence in December 1943, and he returned to Rome after the liberation of Auschwitz in 1945. If the information Marco Edoardo Debenedetti gives is correct, then Debenedetti would have met Spizzichino and Sorani before he left Rome for Cortona, straight after the round-up occurred, or sometime before July 1944. However, it is not documented whether Debenedetti returned to Rome before July 1944. By contrast, Luciano Camerino was arrested on 16 October and deported two days later, thus it is unlikely Debenedetti could have heard his testimony. Several times throughout the text Debenedetti refers to the testimonies of Ugo Foà and Rosina Sorani that he might have listened to or read. As we saw in Chapter 2, they were respectively President of the Comunità Israelitica di Roma and the synagogue secretary who was working when the ERR ordered the SS to plunder the Jewish community library. Foà filed his report on 15 November 1943; later it appeared in Ugo Foà, 'Relazione del Presidente della Comunità Israelitica di Roma Ugo Foà circa le misure razziali adottate in Roma dopo l'8 settembre (data dell'armistizio Badoglio) a diretta opera delle Autorità Tedesche di occupazione', in *Ottobre 1943*, ed. by Comunità Israelitica di Roma, pp. 9-29. It is possible that Debenedetti read Sorani's diary, which later appeared in 'Dal diario di Rosina Sorani impiegata della Comunità di Roma nel periodo dell'occupazione tedesca', in *Ottobre 1943*, ed. by Comunità Israelitica di Roma, pp. 35-43.

11. On Debenedetti's life see: Renata Orengo, *Diario del Cegliolo: cronaca della guerra in un comune toscano, giugno-luglio 1944* (Milan: Scheiwiller, 1965); A. Debenedetti, *Giacomino*; M. E. Debenedetti, 'Cronologia'; Frandini, *Il teatro della memoria*.

12. Giacomo Debenedetti, *Amedeo e altri racconti* (Turin: Baretti, 1926).

13. Giacomo Debenedetti, *Saggi critici* (Florence: Solaria, 1929).

14. On Debenedetti as a literary critic see: Borghesi, *La lotta con l'angelo*; Francesco Mattesini, *La critica letteraria di Giacomo Debenedetti* (Milan: Garzanti, 1994); Frandini, *Il teatro della memoria*; Emilio Jona and Vanni Scheiwiller, *Giacomo Debenedetti: l'arte del leggere* (Milan: Libri Scheiwiller, 2001); *Il Novecento di Debenedetti*, ed. by Tordi.

15. Renata Orengo [i.e. Giacomo Benedetti], 'Nascita del D'Annunzio. Ritratto di Gabriele D'Annunzio come poeta: "Intermezzo"', *Argomenti*, 1.7-8 (September-October 1941), 55-62.

16. M. E. Debenedetti, 'Cronologia', p. lxxii.

17. George Eliot, *Il mulino sulla Floss*, trans. by Giacomo Debenedetti (Milan: Mondadori, 1940); Giacomo Debenedetti, 'Lo stile del Croce', in *L'opera filosofica storica e letteraria di Benedetto Croce: saggi di scrittori italiani e stranieri e bibliografia dal 1922 al 1941*, ed. by Edmondo Cione (Rome: Laterza, 1942), pp. 264-74.

18. Florence, Archivio contemporaneo 'Alessandro Bonsanti' - Gabinetto Vieusseux, Fondo Debenedetti, II. 149.

19. Frandini, *Il teatro della memoria*, p. 166.

20. Giacomo Debenedetti, 'Testimonianza di gratitudine', in *La piccola patria: cronache della guerra in un comune toscano giugno-luglio 1944*, ed. by Pietro Pancrazi (Florence: Le Monnier, 1946), pp. 135-40 (p. 135).

21. Orengo, *Diario del Cegliolo*, pp. 39-40.

22. M. E. Debenedetti, 'Cronologia', p. lxxv.

23. Orengo, *Diario del Cegliolo*, p. 49.

24. Giuliano Manacorda, 'Giacomo Debenedetti: *16 ottobre 1943* e *Otto ebrei*', in *Il Novecento di Debenedetti*, ed. by Tordi, pp. 303-11 (p. 303).

25. Giacomo Debenedetti, 'L'Alfieri: "Ingegnoso nemico di se stesso"', *Poesia*, 1 (1945), 44-45, and 'Discorso sull'Alfieri', *La fiera letteraria*, 1.38 (1946), 11. The works were later included in *Saggi critici: terza serie* (Milan: Il Saggiatore, 1959); then as *Vocazione di Vittorio Alfieri* (Rome: Riuniti, 1977); then included in *Saggi*, pp. 765-824 (hereafter I will cite this last edition of 'Alfieri').

26. Giacomo Debenedetti, 'Camilla', *Mercurio*, 2.15 (November 1945), 109-16; then in *Saggi critici: terza serie* and in *Saggi*, pp. 827-36 (hereafter I will cite this last edition of 'Camilla'). 'Camilla' was also included in the *Dizionario letterario Bompiani delle opere e dei personaggi di tutti i tempi e di tutte le letterature*, 9 vols (Milan: Bompiani, 1947-50), VIII, 144-45.

27. Debenedetti, 'L'Alfieri', p. 765.

28. Ibid.

29. Debenedetti, 'Camilla', p. 832 n.

30. Ibid.

31. Ibid., p. 834.

32. Originally published as Giacomo Debenedetti, 'Otto ebrei. 1) Ori e Settebello', *Il Tempo*, 11 October 1944, pp. 1-2; 'Otto ebrei. 2) Il Ghetto e l'Arca di Noè', *Il Tempo*, 13 October 1944, pp. 1-2; 'Otto ebrei. 3) Gli aratori del vulcano', *Il Tempo*, 15 October 1944, pp. 1-2.; in *Saggi*, pp. 65-91 (hereafter I will cite this last edition and reference it as *OE*). Giacomo Debenedetti, *Otto ebrei* (Rome: Atlantica, 1944) (hereafter this work will referenced as *OS*).

33. Florence, Archivio contemporaneo 'Alessandro Bonsanti' - Gabinetto Vieusseux, Fondo Debenedetti, II. 154.

34. On this see: Marcello Ciocchetti, *Moravia e Piovene tra giornali e riviste del dopoguerra* (Pesaro: Metauro, 2010), pp. 100-03; Ciocchetti, *Prima di piantare datteri*, pp. 45-62 and 64 n.

35. Leonida Répaci, *Taccuino segreto: prima serie (1938-1950)* (Lucca: Fazi, 1967), pp. 351-52. Répaci here refers to 'Otto ebrei' published, as mentioned, in three issues of *Il Tempo* between 11 and 15 October 1944. At the time, Répaci was still co-director of *Il Tempo* with Renato Angiolillo.

36. According to Ciocchetti, the articles signed 'g. d' are by Debenedetti: *Prima di piantare datteri*, p. x.

37. Giacomo Debenedetti, 'Lupi in plenilunio', *L'Epoca*, 15 March 1945, p. 3, and 'Trincea degli ebrei', *L'Epoca*, 8 May 1945, pp. 1-2; 'g. d.' [i.e. Giacomo Debenedetti], 'Febbre a 40', *L'Epoca*, 12 February 1945, p. 1, and 'Libertà dalla paura', *L'Epoca*, 13 April 1945, p. 1. For further information see Ciocchetti, *Prima di piantare datteri*.

38. Giacomo Debenedetti, 'Campo di ebrei', *La Nuova Europa*, 1 April 1945, p. 8. Then included in *Saggi critici: terza serie* and in *Saggi*, pp. 858-65 (hereafter I cite this last edition of 'Campo de ebrei' and reference it as *CE*).

39. Ciochetti, *Prima di piantare datteri*, pp. 89-91.

40. Luigi Salvatorelli, 'Come faccio il mio giornale', *Cosmopolita*, 17 May 1945, p. 4.

41. Giacomo Debendetti, 'Gide ritrovato', *La Nuova Europa*, 24 December 1944, p. 8, 'Il silenzio del mare', *La Nuova Europa*, 28 January 1945, p. 6, 'Campo di ebrei', and, 'Paul Valéry', *La Nuova Europa*, 29 July 1945, p. 5; 'g. d.' [i.e. Giacomo Debenedetti], 'Contrabbandi alla storia', *La Nuova Europa*, 31 December 1944, p. 8.

42. Further information on this is given in Chapter 2, in the section titled 'Beyond History'.

43. Ciocchetti, *Prima di piantare datteri*, p. 17.

44. Giacomo Debenedetti, 'Piantatori di datteri', *L'Epoca*, 1 January 1946, p. 1.

45. Ibid.

46. Ibid.

47. Ciocchetti, *Prima di piantare datteri*, p. 176.

48. Astrid Erll, 'Re-writing as Re-visioning: Modes of Representing the "Indian Mutiny" in British Novels, 1857 to 2000', *European Journal of English Studies*, 10.2 (2006), 163-85 (p. 179).

49. 'Personaggi' here refers to the characters in the narration, but in this case of course the characters coincide with real people.

50. In the preface to the 1959 edition published by Il Saggiatore, Debenedetti explained that the mixture of the two dialects, *romanesco* and *giudio*, is recognisable in both direct and indirect speech. Terms used include *resciud* [run away], *manhòd* [money], and *nharèl* [Catholic]: Giacomo Debenedetti, *16 ottobre 1943* (Milan: Il Saggiatore, 1959), pp. 8-9.

51. See n. 10 above.

52. This emphasis on the Pope's involvement is explored further in Chapter 5.

53. Giacomo Debenedetti, '16 ottobre 1943', *Libera stampa*, 27 April 1945, and '16 ottobre 1943', *Les Temps modernes*, 2 (August–September 1947), 305-26.

54. On Giannarelli's document see Damiano Garofalo, ' "Non dimenticarlo il nostro ottobre": la retata del 16 ottobre 1943 sullo schermo', in *16 ottobre 1943*, ed. by Baumeister, Osti Guerrazzi, and Procaccia, pp. 151-68.

55. On this see for example <https://www.bovisateatro.com/> [accessed 12 February 2023].

56. Giacomo Debenedetti, *Rome 16 October 1943*, illus. and trans. by Sarah Laing (Wellington: Holocaust Centre of New Zealand, 2018).

57. De Felice, *Storia degli ebrei italiani sotto il fascismo*, p. 526; Katz, *Black Sabbath*, p. 382; Anna Foa, *Diaspora: storia degli ebrei nel Novecento* (Rome: Laterza, 2009), p. 157; Pugliese, 'Bloodless Torture', p. 247; Rigano, '16 ottobre 1943', p. 33; Petraglia, *La matta di piazza Giudia*, pp. 34, 142-44, 146, 167-70, 175, 200-02.

58. Gordon, *The Holocaust in Italian Culture*, p. 47.

59. Cavaglion, 'Il grembo della Shoah'.

CHAPTER 4

❖

Elsa Morante,
La Storia

An Introduction

Published by Einaudi in 1974, *La Storia* by Elsa Morante is an account of the life of a woman and her children during the periods which immediately preceded and followed the Second World War. Set in Rome, it unfolds between 1941 and 1947 and includes the story of the parents of the protagonist, which dates to the beginning of the twentieth century, her own marriage in 1921, and a brief account of her death in 1956. The protagonist is a middle-aged teacher of Jewish origin, Ida Ramundo, whose husband dies in 1936 leaving her alone to raise their teenage son, Nino. In 1941, a young German soldier, Gunther, due to leave for North Africa, rapes her. She becomes pregnant and gives birth to a boy, Giuseppe, afterwards called 'Useppe' whom she always leaves at home, afraid people will ask about her illegitimate son. In 1943, Nino runs away from home to join the army, a battalion of Camicie Nere destined for the north of Italy; a few months later he is in the Resistance. He only occasionally returns to visit his mother, who struggles to nurse, help, and protect Useppe. In summer 1943, after the bombing of their small apartment in San Lorenzo, Ida and Useppe go to live in a shelter at Pietralata, where they stay for more than a year. At the end of 1944, Ida manages to rent a bedroom in another small apartment, in Testaccio, and starts teaching again. At the end of the war, Nino becomes a smuggler and then dies in 1946 in a police chase. In the same year, Useppe is diagnosed with epilepsy, which he has inherited from his mother and maternal grandmother. The plot ends when he has his last, fatal, attack in 1947. Ida is traumatised, declines into apathy, and dies nine years later.

In *La Storia*, Morante painted a vast canvas of ordinary life in and around the Second World War in Rome. As part of this project, she narrated in part the history of the Italian Jews following the introduction of the Racial Laws in 1938 and during the Second World War. Two of the characters of Jewish origin that she created who are described in some depth are Nora and Davide. Some touching passages are dedicated to Nora, Ida's mother, who is depicted as a shy and fearful woman who foresees that she will be persecuted for her Jewish identity:

> Nei riguardi del suo segreto ebraico, essa [Nora] aveva spiegato alla figlia, fino da piccolina, che gli ebrei sono un popolo predestinato dall'eternità all'odio

vendicativo di tutti gli altri popoli; e che la persecuzione si accanirà sempre
su di loro, pure attraverso tregue apparenti, riproducendosi sempre in eterno,
secondo il loro destino prescritto. Per tali motivi, era stata lei stessa a volere
Iduzza battezzata cattolica, come il padre. (*S*, p. 281)

[As for her Jewish secret, she had explained to her daughter, from early childhood, that the Jews are a people destined, since time began, to suffer the
vindictive hatred of all other peoples; and that even during apparent periods of
truce, persecution will always dog them, eternally recurring, as their prescribed
destiny. For these reasons, she herself had insisted on having Iduzza baptized a
Catholic, like her father.] (*H*, p. 20)

Nora drowns in a poorly-planned attempt to reach Palestine after the promulgation
of the Racial Laws in 1938. Davide in contrast is a young man, an anarchist and
a poet. He is the only member of his family to avoid deportation. He meets Ida
and Useppe in Pietralata and joins Nino in the Resistance. After the end of the
war he suffers from a form of post-traumatic stress disorder and a sense of guilt
and dies of a morphine overdose in 1947. Other Jewish characters briefly but
poignantly portrayed include some Jews of the ghetto: Celeste Di Segni and Vilma
in particular, as will be seen later. Through Ida's experiences and her relationships
with these characters, there is a powerful focus on the Roman round-up and the
deportation of the Jews to Auschwitz between 16 and 18 October, which also
become a synecdoche in some way for the round-ups which occurred in Italy
from the start of the German occupation, and indeed for the wider history of the
Holocaust. As Stefania Lucamante suggests, 'Morante collects the memory of events
deposited on the bottom and narrates to Italians the Story of the Shoah as situated
in the geographical space of the Roman Ghetto'.[1]

La Storia is a striking example of the triangular relationship between history,
memory, and literature as analysed in Chapters 1 and 2. Historical data, personal
memories, and fiction are deeply intertwined as the title, *La Storia: romanzo*, and
the photo-montage of the cover of the first edition reveal. The title establishes
key interpretative coordinates for the text. The Italian word *storia* is semantically
ambiguous because it means both 'history' and 'story'. Its use in the title implicitly
argues that official history, *La Storia* (the novel was published using the capital 'S'),
with its silences and biases, is a construct, a fiction. Similarly, the fiction, *romanzo*, is
a bearer of history because it gives an account of voices and stories put into historical
frames.[2] Morante is in line here with the contemporary considerations that Hayden
White expressed in *Metahistory*.[3] Morante and White both believe that history is
culturally, socially, and politically relativist. They suggest that all views of history
are shaped by politics, and that images of the past are artificial and subjective.
With her novel, Morante sets out to reveal historical erasures and then juxtaposes
with them a narrative space which compensates the historical discourse and shows
ordinary experiences of ordinary people.

The photo-montage on the cover of the first edition of *La Storia* also indirectly
suggests how provocatively Morante deals with the link between reality and
imagination, history and fiction. The image of the photo-montage has been
mistakenly attributed to Robert Capa, an error that probably originated from the

tagline relating to the image on the back cover of the first edition: 'un particolare di una foto di Robert Capa (Agenzia Magnum)' [a detail of a photograph by Robert Capa (Magnum Agency)].[4] At first, Morante chose a photograph by Capa, 'The Falling Soldier', which represents a partisan shot to death and falling backwards. Then she must have changed her mind and chosen another one representing a lifeless body sprawled on a pile of rubble. At the time, the picture was attributed to Capa but had actually been shot in Spain in 1937 by Gerda Taro, who was one of the first female war photographers.[5] Taro was in Spain with Capa during the Civil War and died on the frontline in 1937.[6] Morante had her photograph edited in a garish red tint and so, already, her work appears not to be a precise historical reconstruction, but a back-and-forth between historical sources and fictional stories of fictional characters.

La Storia is built on historical sources, testimonies, and memories of the war, so framing the narrative within socio-historical evidence, as Morante herself reveals in a note at the end of the book:

> Riguardo alla bibliografia — ovviamente, interminabile — sulla Seconda Guerra Mondiale, io non posso che rinviare i lettori a qualcuno dei tanti cataloghi disponibili ovunque in proposito. Qui devo limitarmi a citare — anche a titolo di ringraziamento — i seguenti autori, che con le loro documentazioni e testimonianze mi hanno fornito degli spunti (reali) per alcuni singoli episodi (inventati) del romanzo. (S, p. 1036)

> [As far as the bibliography of the Second World War is concerned, since it is obviously vast, I can only refer readers to some of the many accounts everywhere available on the subject. Here I must limit myself to mentioning — also by way of thanks — the following authors who, with their documentation and testimony, have given me some (real) suggestions for some (invented) individual episodes in the novel.] (H, p. 561)

Crucially for our purposes, among the few texts she cites are Debenedetti's *16 ottobre 1943* — we will see below that this is a foundational source for Morante — as well as *Black Sabbath* by Robert Katz, *Guerriglia nei castelli romani* by Pino Levi Cavaglione, *Perchè gli altri dimenticano* by Bruno Piazza, and *La strada del Davai* and *L'ultimo fronte* by Nuto Revelli.[7] The manuscripts of *La Storia* show the scrupulous historical notes Morante compiled to build the plot: on the verso of every leaf of the original text there are historical references which corroborate the images of the past she was depicting. Both the manuscripts and the majority of Morante's books are stored in the Biblioteca Nazionale Centrale in Rome. Among her volumes there are roughly thirty concerning the Second World War. They are national and international publications which provide a macro-historical picture of the war against which the Italian conflict can be contextualised. All of them have Morante's signature at the beginning or at the end, or signs of having been read. Monica Zanardo, who has conducted research on the historiographical sources Morante used to write *La Storia*, suggests that the novel is based on historical details and facts which were not discussed in depth in historical records and volumes. In the novel, these are examined extensively as elements in the narrative of personal experiences.[8] There is in other words a process of mediation and remediation. Morante rewrites historical facts in her novel and turns archival and experiential traces into shareable and shared representations. As we will see, this process is central to Morante's re-elaboration of the round-up and deportation of 1943.

The relationship Morante established with historical sources, personal memories, and literary strategies and techniques can also be read through feminist theories. While it would be inconsistent with Morante's image and aesthetic to read *La Storia* as a pamphlet for feminist change, her novel is a passionate indictment against reductive representations of the past.[9] In this sense, therefore, Morante can be seen as a precursor of those Italian female scholars who between the late 1980s and early 1990s began to problematise historical knowledge and representations of the past.[10] As Maria Ornella Marotti suggests, 'in their effort to include in historical rewriting the marginal and ex-centric, the new historicist and feminist perspectives offer a revaluation of both the method of historical research and the writing of official history'.[11] As Tiziana de Rogatis argues, in *La Storia*, Morante developed a 'female specificity in the face of war [one that] is a bio-cultural one and consists in the ability to inhabit the space of war and trauma through complementary, inclusive, multi-perspective and reversible approaches'.[12] Morante provided her readers with a new narration of the historical events of the war based on the reading of secondary sources and literary re-elaborations of personal experiences.[13]

La Storia has a binary structure. There is the reporting of historical events on the one hand, and the narrative of the characters' adventures, on the other. There are connections between the official and unofficial sources, as well as between reality and fiction. The novel moves between macro- and micro-temporal structures, namely history and personal stories, and combines them with literary imagination. Morante creates realities that do not contradict official historical records because the historical palimpsest on which the novel is built guarantees verisimilitude to the fiction; elements of the real world are re-elaborated to create poignant and dramatic fictional passages through which Morante offers alternative and ex-centric perspectives with which to observe and reflect upon the past.

The title of each chapter is the year in which the plot unfolds and each chapter is preceded by a chronicle of historical information, in which the major events of the year in question are presented.[14] These presentations form an integral paratext to the body of the novel. Although typographically limited to a few pages before each chapter, they are fluidly dialogic: historical events shape and direct the plot. Within these historical frames, as in historical records, human beings are an indistinct mass. In the fiction, by contrast, the focus is narrowed down to the individual and events are narrated through the mediation and perspective of ordinary characters, characters who are overwhelmed by the flow of history but at the same time constitute history itself. Each one is an infinitesimal part of the whole, a synecdoche for the hundreds and thousands of other individuals who have shared their experiences. Through them, Morante pays attention to the pluralised, unofficial, marginal, and unrecorded memories of ordinary people. She described their stories. By combining historical events, memories of the war, and imagined stories she gives voice to those who were side-lined by 'higher' politics and culture, and more broadly by what she saw as a dominant, hegemonic History. In her narrative, she shows socio-historical conditions through individual personal fortunes and prompts reflections on human experience during the war. She adds a personal vision of the events to the purely objective representations of the historical material collected. Through it, she establishes a relationship with her readers and, as we will see, facilitates their process of identification with her characters and the narrated story.

The persecution of Jews in Italy is a core feature of Chapter '1943'. In the chronicle, the text explains that in September and October 1943 the Germans started to arrest and deport Jews from Italy: 'come negli altri territori occupati, anche in Italia i Nazisti procedono alla "soluzione finale del problema ebraico"' [As in other occupied territories, also in Italy the Nazis proceed to the 'final solution of the Jewish problem'] (*S*, p. 421; *H*, p. 122). No specific round-up which occurred on the Italian peninsula is mentioned in the historical records of the time in Italy. And it seems that by doing so herself, Morante is referencing the fact that, in the early 1970s in Italy, the Holocaust was still broadly neglected in the historical discourse outside communal or survivor circles. It is through the following fictional pages that she gives space to memories of the persecution that up to that point had not been widely reflected in either literary or public discourse. The climax is reached in her description of 16 and 18 October.

Some episodes in Chapters '1942' and '1943' take the reader through aspects of the massacre of the Roman Jews: the transportation of a calf from Stazione Tiburtina and the death of Blitz, the beloved dog of Nino and Useppe, for example. In spring 1942, Useppe leaves his mother's apartment for the first time when Nino skips school and takes him on a tour of Rome. Together, they arrive by chance at Stazione Tiburtina, where they see a calf locked up in a cattle-truck and the description of the calf anticipates that of the transportation of the Jews to Auschwitz on 18 October.[15] Useppe is in Nino's arms when he sees the calf, just as he is in his mother's arms when he later witnesses the deportation of the Jews on 18 October:

> L'unico viaggiatore visibile, sui pochi carri là in sosta, era un vitello, affacciato dalla piattaforma scoperta di un vagone [...] dal collo, per una cordicella, gli pendeva una medagliuccia [...] sulla quale forse era segnata l'ultima tappa del suo viaggio. Di questa al viaggiatore non s'era data nessuna notizia; ma nei suoi occhi larghi e bagnati s'indovinava una prescienza oscura [...]. E forse fra gli occhi del bambino e della bestia si svolse un qualche sguardo inopinato, sotterraneo e impercettibile. D'un tratto, lo sguardo di Giuseppe subì un mutamento [...] una specie di tristezza o di sospetto lo attraversò. (*S*, p. 400)

> [The only visible traveler, on any of the few trains waiting there, was a calf, looking down from the open platform of a car [...] from its neck, hung a tiny medal, [...] on which the last stage of his journey perhaps was written. None of that information had been given the traveler; but in his broad, moist eyes you could sense a dark foreknowledge [...]. And perhaps between the child's eyes and the animal's there was some unforeseen exchange, subterranean and imperceptible. All of a sudden, Giuseppe's gaze underwent a curious change, [...] a kind of sadness or suspicion crossed his eyes.] (*H*, p. 108)

Blitz is a dog with a star-shaped marking on his belly: ' "Razza Bastarda" [...] Nino lo rimirava con orgoglio "La razza di Blitz [...] si chiama pure *razza stellata*. Blitz! fa' vedere il bel disegno di stella che ciài" ' [Nino watched him, with pride: "Blitz's breed," [...], "is also called the *starred breed*. Blitz! show them the nice star you have!"] (*S*, p. 376; *H*, p. 91).[16] Nino brings him home when Useppe is still an infant and Blitz loyally follows both of them as they grow up. On 19 July 1943, the dog dies in the bombing of the neighbourhood of San Lorenzo and Useppe faces death for the first time: 'il loro caseggiato era distrutto [...]. La vocina di Useppe continuava a chiamare: "Biii! Biiii! Biiiii!". Blitz era perduto [...]. Ma lui [...] ripeteva il suo grido: "Biii" con una pretesa sempre più urgente e perentoria' [Their building was destroyed [...]. Useppe's little voice continued calling: 'Biii! Biiii! Biiiii!'. Blitz was lost [...]. But [...] he repeated his cry: 'Biii!' with a more and more peremptory demand] (*S*, pp. 453–54; *H*, p. 146). And so, with Blitz's death Morante prepares her readers for the forthcoming massacre of the Roman Jews: the dog's star-shaped marking recalling the Star of David. Thus, the ground is laid for the account of 16 and 18 October in Chapter '1943' and for the intense experience of Ida and Useppe as witnesses.

Personal Experiences

Before turning to Morante's account of the Roman round-up and the deportation of Jews from Stazione Tiburtina as seen through the eyes of Ida and Useppe, we turn to further details of Morante's life during the war, her Jewish origins, and her marriage to Alberto Moravia in order to better understand her willingness to write about the discrimination against and persecution of the Jewish population. We then look at how Morante re-elaborated her experience of the war in a short story published in 1945, 'Il soldato siciliano', which undoubtedly fed into two crucial elements in *La Storia*: the representation of the war from multiple perspectives and the correlation between the author and her female narrator.

Morante was born in Rome in 1912 to a mother, Irma Poggibonsi, who was Jewish. Morante's consciousness of her own Jewish identity came when the rights of the Jews began to be severely limited following the promulgation of the Racial Laws in September 1938.[17] She even professed gratitude to Mussolini for making her aware of her heritage:

> I should be grateful to Mussolini. In 1938, by introducing the German racist laws he made me realize that I myself was a Jew; my mother was Jewish, but the thought had never crossed my mind that there was something peculiar about having a mother whose father and mother used to pray in a synagogue. At first, the Fascists were very loose in the enforcement of discrimination.[18]

Morante's family avoided direct Fascist discrimination as Elsa and her siblings had been baptised. In 1941 Morante married the writer Alberto Moravia, also of Jewish origin, in a Catholic wedding service conducted by Padre Tacchi Venturi, Mussolini's confessor, who knew both Elsa Morante and Irma Poggibonsi well. In the same year Morante published some of her work in journals, as well as her translation of *The Scrapbook* by Katherine Mansfield and her *Il gioco segreto*; in 1942, Einaudi published her fairy tale, *Le bellissime avventure di Caterì dalla trecciolina*.[19]

A few days after the dissolution of the Italian Army on 8 September 1943, Morante's life drastically changed. Moravia received threatening phone calls and was told his name was on the list of people to be deported. They both left their two-bedroom apartment in via Sgambati, and were hosted for two days by Carlo Lodovico Bragaglia: 'dopo due giorni Bragaglia ci consigliò, con molta gentilezza, di partire verso sud, per andare incontro agli americani' [two days later Bragaglia suggested, very kindly, that we left for the south, to meet the Americans].[20] They decided to leave Rome in the middle of September, taking a train to go south that was stopped at Fondi because the railway had been bombed in Ciociaria. Morante remembered that:

> When the Germans took over Rome in 1943, I learned a great lesson, I learned terror. I was afraid for myself but even more for Moravia... Jewishness to them was a race, a breed; they explained it through the barbaric, regressive imagery of 'blood' [...]. We escaped, Moravia and I, to the mountains of Ciociaria... We were finally given shelter by a peasant family.[21]

Moravia recalled that the shelter they found in Fondi: 'era una stanza che a dire sporca è poco: [...] ma non ci muovemmo di là per qualche tempo [...] poi i fascisti cominciarono la razzia di uomini. Allora pensammo di salire in montagna' [it was a room that to say dirty is not much: [...] but we did not move from there for some time [...] then the fascists began to round up the men. So we thought of going up to the mountains]. They found a hut up on a nearby mountain, in the little village of Sant'Agata, as Moravia described: 'stavamo in una capanna con un letto di tavole e sopra un pagliericcio di pannocchie. La coperta era un ferraiuolo da contadino' [we stayed in a hut with a bed made of planks and a pallet of corn on top. The blanket was a farmer's metal grid].[22] They remained there from the end of September 1943 until the end of June 1944. Between the end of October and the beginning of November, Morante went to Rome to get some warmer clothes, and immediately returned to Sant'Agata, as Moravia recalled:

> Quando arrivò il freddo, non avevamo panni per coprirci [...]. Elsa decise di partire per Roma; io restai per via dei rastrellamenti che tedeschi e fascisti seguitavano a fare [...]. Arrivata a casa riempì una valigia di roba di lana e tornò a Fondi: quel valigione glielo portarono per un tratto di strada persino dei soldati nazisti.[23]

> [When it got cold, we didn't have any clothes to warm us up [...]. Elsa decided to leave for Rome; I stayed because of the round-ups that Germans and Fascists continued to do [...]. When she got home, she filled a suitcase with wool clothes and she returned to Fondi: even Nazi soldiers carried that suitcase for her for part of the way.]

In August 1944 they moved to Naples and then returned to the capital in September.[24] On their arrival, they were told that their apartment had been searched five times by the SS during the German occupation.[25]

Morante, like Moravia who had started writing his war novel *La ciociara* in 1944,[26] re-elaborated facts of the Second World War and the insecurities and worries that gripped her during the period of persecution in writing 'Il soldato siciliano', a short story published in 1945 in the Milanese weekly magazine *L'Europeo*.[27] In 1963, she included it in *Lo scialle andaluso*, a collection of twelve short stories, of which only two, 'Il ladro dei lumi' and 'Donna Amalia', had not been published previously in *Il gioco segreto* or in journals.[28]

'Il soldato siciliano' narrates the journey of a woman from a village in the mountains of central Italy to Rome under German occupation. It is set in a hut where the woman sleeps for a night along the way. During the night, Gabriele, a Sicilian former soldier and now Resistance fighter, gets into the hut. Soaked by rain, covered in mud, exhausted, he sits next to the door on a suitcase. He starts talking to the woman and tells her why he joined the Italian army, then the partisans, and why he will join the English army at the end of the war. He says he cannot find peace after the death of his daughter, Assunta, whose story he then narrates. The text has three narrators: the woman, who tells of her journey to Rome, Gabriele, who explains why he cannot stop fighting and seeking peace, and Assunta. Gabriele becomes the mouthpiece for the third narrator, his daughter. Through his long speech, the story of Assunta is told: she was abandoned by her mother when she was an infant and raised by her father with whom she did not have a close relationship. Once grown, she left her home and started working in a village for an army officer, the Maresciallo. She was raped by the son of the Maresciallo and, then, because of this, committed suicide.

'Il soldato siciliano' is illuminating for the reading of *La Storia*. In it, Morante includes explicit autobiographical elements, and describes the war from three different view-points, in ways that feed into the narrative of *La Storia*. She re-elaborates her own experiences of the war in the nameless woman who is trying to reach Rome:

> Nel tempo che gli eserciti alleati, a causa dell'inverno, sostavano al di là del fiume Garigliano, io vivevo rifugiata in cima a una montagna, al di qua del fiume. Un giorno, per la salvezza di persone che amavo, fui costretta ad un breve viaggio a Roma. Era un amaro viaggio, poiché Roma, la città dove nacqui e dove ho sempre vissuto, era per me in quel tempo una città nemica. (*SS*, p. 1509)

> [During the time that the allied armies, because of the winter, stopped on the other side of the Garigliano river, I lived in a refuge on top of a mountain, on this side of the river. One day, for the safety of the people I loved, I was forced to take a short trip to Rome. It was a bitter journey, since Rome, the city where I was born and where I have always lived, was an enemy city for me at that time.]

As mentioned above, Morante was herself born in Rome and lived there throughout her life. From September 1943, she hid in the mountains in Ciociaria, and during the winter she went by herself to Rome to collect warmer clothes. Later in the text, the female narrator and character of 'Il soldato siciliano' makes another reference to a personal life event shared with Morante when she describes Sicily as the region her father was from: 'io pensavo quanto mi sarebbe piaciuto attraversare il fiume

Garigliano, e arrivare fino alla Sicilia [...]. Non sono mai stata laggiù, dov'è il paese di mio padre, e dove adesso avrei potuto vivere libera' [I thought how much I would have liked to cross the Garigliano river and reach Sicily [...]. I've never been there, which is where my father's town is, and where I could now live free] (SS, p. 1509).[29]

Through three personal stories, Morante conveys glimpses of the reality of the war, and by combining them creates a more layered and complex image to depict the multi-faceted nature of both reality and history. First, the woman narrator presents the war through the worries and insecurities of the journey she has to make to get to occupied Rome:

> Io mi disposi ad una notte di insonnia. Mi raffiguravo la folla dei miei compagni di treno, e le fermate in mezzo alle vuote campagne e alla strage; pensavo a ciò che avrei risposto se una voce improvvisa mi avesse ordinato di mostrare le mie carte, e il mio bagaglio. E poi mi domandavo, se avrei potuto mai giungere a Roma, giacché le ferrovie venivano bombardate ogni giorno. (SS, p. 1510)

> [I prepared myself for a night of insomnia. I pictured the crowd of my train companions, and the stops in the middle of the empty countryside and the massacre; I was thinking about what I would answer if a sudden voice ordered me to show my papers, and my luggage. And then I wondered if I would ever get to Rome, because the railways were being bombed every day.]

Then, the woman describes Gabriele before he starts talking about his daughter:

> Mi spiegò poi di aver guerreggiato nell'esercito, e di combattere adesso alla macchia, contro i tedeschi; e che più tardi si sarebbe unito agli inglesi per continuare la guerra. Così guerreggiando senza tregua, seguitò, sperava di raggiungere un certo suo scopo. (SS, p. 1511)

> [He then explained to me that he had fought in the army, and was now fighting with the resistance, against the Germans; and that he would later join the British to continue the war. Thus waging endless war, he continued, he hoped to achieve a sure end.]

Gabriele is not capable of committing suicide, so he joins the army in the hope of being killed. Once dead, he believes that his soul will return to Sicily, find Assunta, and stay with her. He presents the war as no more than a means of reaching his daughter, in his monologue there is no army, no battle, no gunfight. Lastly, Gabriele narrates the innermost thoughts of his daughter as if it were she who was telling the story:

> Assunta si liberava dibattendosi, gridava e piangeva; ma non osava dire niente al Maresciallo, né tanto meno a me. D'altra parte, non poteva lasciare quel posto [...] e come ritornare a casa, da un padre che odiava, e che non poteva neanche darle un pane? (SS, p. 1513)

> [Assunta struggled to be set free, screamed and wept; but she dared not say anything to the Marshal, much less to me. On the other hand, she could not leave there [...] and how to return home, to a father she hated, and who could not even give her bread?]

In Assunta's story, the perception of the war is partial: the only feature that connects her to the war is that the father of her rapist is an officer, a marshal, of the Italian army. However, read with the other two stories, that of Assunta provides further aspects of life during the war and another perspective on it. The rape is a narrative element that also recurs in *La Storia*. It is imbued with fear and shame and represents the double vulnerability of women, victims of the brutality of both men and war. In both texts, rape is a foundational element of the story. In 'Il soldato siciliano', after the rape of Assunta, Gabriele realises the failed relationship with his daughter and feels ashamed and guilty about it; he enlists in the army in a desperate attempt to be killed in order to be reunited with Assunta. In *La Storia*, the inextricable mother-son bond which is central to the novel — and more generally to Morante's aesthetic — is also rooted in the rape, Ida in fact becomes pregnant with Useppe after she is raped by the German soldier Gunther.[30]

The first-person narrator of *La Storia* is an experiencing 'I'. She is a female civilian victim of the war (in the Italian text, her gender is made evident by the past participles, but obviously this specificity is lost in the English translation). Critics are convinced that Morante herself is hidden in the figure of the narrator.[31] According to Cesare Garboli:

> *La Storia* è il solo romanzo della Morante a essere raccontato da Elsa Morante *ipse*, proprio da lei, con l'intonazione e il timbro della sua voce e non con una voce imprestata ad altri, in evidente armonia col proposito di abbassare il più possibile il tasso dell'immaginario e di dare al romanzo la forma di una cronaca.[32]

> [*La Storia* is the only novel by Morante to be told by Elsa Morante *ipse*, her true self, with the intonation and timbre of her voice and not with a voice lent to others, in evident harmony with the intention of lowering the expectation as far as possible that this will be a work of the imagination and to give the novel the form of a chronicle.]

Lucamante draws a comparison between Morante's experience of the war and the one that Ida lives throughout the book, and states that:

> Far from being an anachronistic novel, *La Storia* demonstrates how Morante sublimated the original subconscious perception of herself as the persecuted outsider [...] and made her most autobiographical narrating voice — Elsa, *ipse* — an indispensable one in which her own story collapses into one as enduring as her characters.[33]

In the manuscript of *La Storia* there is a passage, discarded in the final version, which strengthens the hypothesis of the correlation between Elsa Morante and the female narrator of the novel. The latter reveals herself when she greets Ida after Useppe's death. She re-introduces herself to Ida as Elsa:

> Portava delle calze grosse, legate sotto i ginocchi con piccoli nastri bianchi di cotone. I capelli bianchissimi erano ravviati, e meno ricci di un tempo. 'Ida...' la salutai. 'Mi riconosci? *Sono Elsa*. Ti ricordi? Ci conoscevamo quando tu insegnavi a Via Portuense...' Non capiva né la mia presenza né la mia voce; eppure ringraziava, col sorriso di un bambino che apre gli occhi dal sonno, in una barca, e intravede |in alto| la vela, su una immensa marina appena mossa.[34]

> [She wore thick stockings, tied below the knees with small white cotton

ribbons. Her very white hair was straightened, and less curly than it used to be. 'Ida...' I greeted her. 'You know me? *I'm Elsa.* Do you remember? We knew each other when you taught in Via Portuense...' She did not know it was me, she did not know my voice; yet she thanked me, with the smile of a child who opens her eyes from sleep, in a boat, and glimpses | aloft | the sail, on an immense sea that has just moved.]

This plausible correlation between the author and the female narrator of *La Storia* not only provides interesting insights into the literary recreation of Morante's personal memories of the war in a novel already based on a tight relationship between historical sources, personal memories, and fiction, but also provides a further understanding of her intention to discuss the second world war, an intention which, whether conscious or unconscious on Morante's part, can be read through feminist theories. Morante, and by extension her narrator, interpreted and narrated historical events through her female eye, looked at the past from the off-centre position of a female author of Jewish origin, and bore witness to the past by casting light upon what was marginalised, forgotten, or erased in the representation and interpretation of history. In her novel, Morante did not solely denounce the exclusion of women's experiences from history, she rather recounted the stories of the victims of history whose experiences were not included in the representations of the past and in this sense turned her novel into a counter-memory to what she considered as the official hegemonic history, as will be discussed later on in this chapter, and as de Rogatis suggests 'with its publication [*La Storia*] ha[s] been powerfully demolishing the "patriarchive"'.[35]

From the narrative point of view, the female narrator of *La Storia* has two voices, as Vittorio Spinazzola points out: the individual, feminine voice of a witness, and the tribal voice that is both maternal and sisterly.[36] As a chronicler and commentator on her own time and world, Morante rewrites historical facts and transcribes extra-literary, documentary sources within the narrative. In these passages her writing is systematic, precise, and objective:

> È stata diramata a tutti capi delle province, per l'immediata esecuzione, la seguente ordinanza di polizia: I — tutti gli ebrei, anche se discriminati a qualunque nazione appartengano, residenti nel territorio nazionale devono essere inviati in appositi campi di concentramento. Tutti i loro beni, mobili ed immobili devono essere sottoposti ad immediato sequestro in attesa di essere confiscati nell'interesse della Repubblica Sociale Italiana, la quale li destinerà a beneficio degli indigenti sinistrati dalle incursioni aeree nemiche. II — Tutti coloro che, nati da matrimonio misto, ebbero, in applicazione delle leggi razziali vigenti, il riconoscimento di appartenenza alla razza ariana, devono essere sottoposti alla speciale vigilanza degli organi di polizia. (*S*, p. 591)

> [To all provincial authorities, to be carried out immediately, the following police order has been sent: 1 — all Jews resident in Italian territory, even if granted special status, to whatever nation they may belong, must be sent to concentration camps set up for this purpose. All their property, real estate and other, must be immediately seized, until it can be confiscated by the Italian Social Republic, which will distribute it in the interest of indigent victims of enemy air raids. 2 — All those born of mixed marriages who, in application of

the existing racial laws, were recognized as members of the Aryan race, must be subjected to special surveillance by the police forces.] (*H*, p. 243)

However, when her narrator appraises and expresses opinions on historical events, Morante's language becomes evocative and figurative:

> Da parte sua, frattanto, il recente Fondatore dell'Impero, proprio con questo gran passo della carriera aveva, in realtà, messo il piede nella trappola che doveva consegnarlo all'ultimo scandalo del crollo e della morte. Proprio a questo passo lo aspettava, difatti, l'altro Fondatore del Grande Reich, suo complice presente e suo padrone predestinato. (*S*, p. 306)

> [For his part, meanwhile, the recent Founder of the Empire, taking this great step in his career, had actually put his foot in the trap that was to doom him to the final scandal, to his downfall and death. This step, in fact, led precisely to where he was being awaited by the other Founder of the Great Reich, his present accomplice and his preordained master.] (*H*, p. 38)

As Morante records the collective knowledge and personal memories of the people who lived in Rome with her while she was writing *La Storia*, so her female narrator reports the stories of the other characters. She, the female narrator, knows them: 'conosco Nora solo da una sua fotografia, del tempo che era fidanzata' [I know Nora only from a photograph taken in the days of her engagement]; she recognises them: 'mi sembra infatti di averla riconosciuta, non molto tempo fa [...]. Portava sempre il suo nastrino intorno alla testa, sebbene i suoi capelli fossero ridotti a pochi ciuffi lanosi' [in fact, I think I recognized her, not long ago [...]. She was still wearing her ribbon around her head, though her hair had been reduced to a few woolly clumps]; she tries to get information about them: 'Io, in quanto a me, le rare e frammentarie notizie che ho potuto raccoglierne, le ho avute in gran parte da Ninuzzo' [for myself, the scant and fragmentary information I have been able to gather came, to a large extent, from Ninnuzzu]; and she addresses them indirectly: 'Ida Ida dove vai hai sbagliato direzione' [Ida, Ida, where are you going?] (*S*, pp. 316, 820, 738, 803; *H*, pp. 45, 406-07, 350, 395). At the same time, however, Morante's female narrator goes beyond merely transcribing what she may have experienced herself by describing what she cannot remember and letting the narrative arise anew from her imagination. She envisages her characters' innermost feelings, 'provava solo una specie di commozione indulgente per lo sposo' [she was moved to a kind of tender indulgence towards her husband]; their dreams, 'le tornò il sogno solito che la visitava spesso, con qualche variazione, dall'ultima estate' [The usual dream returned to her, the one that had visited her often, with some variants, since the previous summer]; and their fears, 'segretamente essa temeva [...] che la gente [...] cominciasse a trattarlo da infermo e da minorato' [she was secretly afraid [...] that people [...] might begin treating him like an invalid or a backward child] (*S*, pp. 297, 536, 804; *H*, pp. 31, 204, 395). On the one hand, Morante's female narrator intimately feels part of the destiny of all the characters and presents the war through their sensory experiences, fears, worries, and hopes. On the other, Morante emphasises, as Sharon Wood suggests, the physicality, fragility, and vulnerability of human beings caught up in the violent maelstrom of history.[37] She describes war in physical, sensory, and emotional terms that are common to humankind, thus depicting the heterogeneity and complexity of historical events from engaging and intimate perspectives.

I now move on to focus on the purposes that Morante attributed to art, generally, and to *La Storia*, specifically, thus examining her socio-political commitment to writing about history in the 1970s in order to frame her treatment of the specific events of 16 and 18 October.

Engaging with History

The Second World War and Morante's imaginative re-elaboration of it became central to her work and her thinking about art and history. As an artist, she was convinced that 'il confronto con la Storia è un'altra delle prove necessarie che la presenza nel mondo richiede agli artisti [...] intesi all'azione' [the confrontation with history is another of the necessary tests that presence in the world requires of artists [...] intent on action].[38] Art creates the conditions for ethical thinking. In *La Storia*, Morante re-elaborates the events of the Second World War in literary terms and more broadly denounces all forms of Fascism, by sharing her idea of History, with a capital 'H', as 'uno scandalo che dura da diecimila anni' [a scandal that has lasted ten thousand years] (*S*, p. 259).[39]

Morante's intention to bear witness, make history accessible, and awaken the conscience of people influenced both the publication and marketing of *La Storia*.[40] The epigraph of the novel, quoting César Vallejo, reveals its intended inclusiveness: 'por analfabeto a quien escribo' [for illiterate to whom I write]. The book was published by Einaudi in its cheap paperback series 'Gli struzzi', at a cost of 2000 lire. The very low price, Einaudi's advertising campaign, and the debate around the book that erupted from July 1974 onwards pushed up book sales.[41] The timing of the novel's release was particularly favourable: it arrived in bookshops just before the Italian summer vacation, traditionally a period during which more books are sold, and currently popular titles are advertised and reviewed in the media. A few weeks before the novel's appearance, the publisher mounted an extensive advertising campaign in the mass media to announce it. Polemic about the book began on 18 July, when a letter, entitled 'Contro il romanzone della Morante', was sent to and published in *Il Manifesto*, a self-styled 'quotidiano comunista' [communist daily] founded in 1969 and one of the most prominent radical intellectual forums of the time.[42] The letter denounced Einaudi's publicity campaign, speculated about the profits made by Einaudi and Morante, and criticised the positive reviews written by Natalia Ginzburg, Carlo Bo, and Cesare Garboli which appeared in the *Corriere della Sera* on 30 June.[43] Even in outline, this debate illuminates the early popular and critical reception of the novel. Almost 20,000 copies were sold in the first few days, 465,000 in a year, and to date it has been reprinted thirteen times in Italy — a publishing history that suggests the novel has had a profond influence on Italian culture, certainly far beyond that of Debenedetti's *16 ottobre 1943*, for all the respectful reception that it received. Morante fulfilled her aim of bringing people into contact with a committed attempt at understanding the history of suffering.

From the 1960s, Morante had begun to avoid public life. She decided to give of herself only through her works and the meticulous control of their publication in which, according to Marco Bardini, the elaboration of a planned autobiography can be seen;[44] she made rare public appearances and wrote infrequent articles in journals and magazines.[45] However, in 1974 and in 1976, she talked publicly about *La Storia* and her willingness in writing it; and on 16 June 1974, nine days before the publication of *La Storia*, she published an article in *Il Messaggero* entitled 'Il 19 luglio 1943' which anticipated the forthcoming publication of her new book.[46] In it, she included some passages of the description of the bombing of San Lorenzo which occurred on 19 July 1943 and gave the article its title. Although her name did not appear on the page and she used the third person singular, Morante wrote the tagline and chose the extract, the photograph, and the title, as confirmed in a 1986 article by Aldo Maffey, one of the editors of *Il Messaggero*:

> Ai primi di giugno del 1974, Elsa Morante telefonò a Ruggero Guarini, che era allora responsabile della pagina culturale del 'Messaggero'. *Di sua iniziativa,* proponeva di anticipare ai lettori del nostro giornale alcune pagine del suo nuovo romanzo *La Storia* [...]. Nel proporre l'anticipazione del proprio libro, la *Morante aveva chiesto di poter titolare lei stessa l'articolo* [...]. Elsa *Morante* [...] *in una cartellina aveva tutto*: le pagine scelte per l'anticipazione del libro, il titolo, una fotografia con relativa didascalia e [...] il progettino per l'impaginazione. Ma tutto così curato — e soprattutto, rispettoso della grafica del 'Messaggero' di allora — che a Ruggero Guarini non restò che mandare tutto in tipografia e andarsene a casa.[47]

> [In early June 1974, Elsa Morante phoned Ruggero Guarini, who was then in charge of the Culture page of the 'Messaggero'. *On her own initiative,* she proposed to give the readers of our newspaper a preview of a few pages of her new novel *La Storia* [...]. In proposing a preview of her book, *Morante had asked to write the article herself* [...]. Elsa *Morante* [...] *had everything in a folder*: the pages chosen for the preview of the book, the title, a photograph with its caption and [...] the design for the layout. But all so well-finished — and above all, respectful of the graphics of the 'Messaggero' of the time — that Ruggero Guarini only had to send everything to the printer and go home.]

The following quotation is the tagline which prefaced the extract from the book:

> Fra pochi giorni sarà in vendita nelle librerie e nelle edicole il nuovo attesissimo romanzo di Elsa Morante 'La Storia' che esce in prima edizione assoluta nella collezione economica 'Gli Struzzi' di Einaudi. Pagine di testo 665. Prezzo lire duemila. Tiratura iniziale di centomila copie.
> *Questo romanzo di massimo impegno,* al quale Elsa Morante ha dedicato tutto il suo lavoro degli ultimi tre anni (dal 1971 al 1974) si svolge prevalentemente nella città di Roma — dal quartiere Tiburtino al Testaccio — durante il periodo della guerra e dell'immediato dopoguerra. Per cortese concessione dell'editore, ne offriamo qua in anticipo un estratto ai lettori del 'Messaggero'.[48]

> [In a few days, Elsa Morante's highly anticipated new novel 'La Storia' will be on sale in bookstores and newsstands, which is out in its first edition in Einaudi's cheap imprint, 'Gli Struzzi'. Pages of text 665. Price two thousand lire. Initial circulation of one hundred thousand copies.

This novel of maximum commitment, to which Elsa Morante has dedicated all her work over the last three years (from 1971 to 1974) is set mainly in the city of Rome — from the Tiburtino district to the Testaccio — during the period of the war and the immediate postwar period. By courtesy of the publisher, we offer here an excerpt in advance for the readers of the 'Messaggero'.]

By stating the low price of the book, giving readers a foretaste of the text, and calling her book a 'romanzo di massimo impegno', thus revealing her commitment to its writing, she anticipated the commitment that she was to make explicit only two years later.

In May 1976, Morante presented a paper to a cultural conference in Rome, 'La cultura spagnola fra ieri e oggi' [Spanish Culture Between Yesterday and Today], organised by the Sindacato Nazionale Scrittori and by the Federazione Unitaria dei Poligrafici.[49] Her paper concerned the translation of *La Storia* by Juan Moreno, published by Plaza y Janés in 1976 in Nationalist Spain, and the meaning she attributed to her book.[50] She defended the integrity of her novel and explained its intent. She opened her speech by saying that she had ended her working relationship with Plaza y Janés after they published an incomplete version of *La Storia*, and she noted:

> Considero mio dovere prendere occasione da questo convegno per dare notizia agli amici e compagni spagnoli qui presenti della vertenza che mi ha portato in questi giorni a rompere definitivamente ogni intesa con gli editori Plaza y Janés di Barcellona, in seguito a una loro pubblicazione in lingua spagnola del mio ultimo romanzo *La Storia*.
>
> Dopo aver sottoscritto un preciso e irrinunciabile impegno che mi garantiva una traduzione assolutamente fedele e integrale del romanzo, questi editori ne hanno stampato e diffuso una edizione in cui non soltanto il titolo originale *La Storia* è stato sostituito con un altro che ne riduce e ne svaluta il significato; ma il testo medesimo è stato arbitrariamente alterato e amputato in vari luoghi, e in ispecie in quelli che potevano, a giudizio degli editori stessi, disturbare l'attuale regime politico spagnolo e la ideologia che tuttora lo domina.[51]

> [I consider it is my duty to take the opportunity from this conference to inform Spanish friends and comrades present here of the dispute that has led me in recent days to definitively break all understanding with the Plaza y Janés publishers in Barcelona, after the publication in Spanish of my latest novel *La Storia*.
>
> After having signed a precise and binding commitment that guaranteed me an absolutely faithful and complete translation of the novel, the publishers have printed and distributed an edition in which not only the original title *La Storia* has been replaced with another that reduces and devalues its meaning; but the text itself has been arbitrarily altered and amputated in various places, and especially in those that could, in the opinion of the publishers themselves, disturb the current Spanish political regime and the ideology that still dominates it.]

Morante mentioned the mistranslation of the title, which I think needs to be analysed together with the choice of also replacing the original photo-montage. As shown above, the title and the photo-montage of the first Italian edition reveal Morante's idea of history as a subjective re-elaboration of events and her denunciation of its silences and biases. The 1976 Spanish publication changed the title *La Storia: romanzo* to *Algo en la Historia* [Something in History] and used an image of a pregnant woman with a man in the background as the cover picture.[52] With these changes, the publishers suggested that the novel was about just one story in history, the story of a woman and her child, and thus mispresented the reality of the novel. The cuts limited Morante's condemnation of ideologies and prevented any possible reading of the text as opposition to Fascism, including the Fascism of Nationalist Spain. In the lecture, she gave examples of the changes her text went through and explained the reasons behind the writing of the novel and the message it contains:

> In attesa di un esame più esteso, già fin da un primo sommario controllo limitato alle pagine iniziali, io stessa ho potuto constatare, che circa ogni pagina del testo ha là subito di tali interventi censorii. Mi basta citarne uno solo, operato là dove il testo riassume, in forma cronologica, gli eventi spagnoli del 1936.
>
> Trovandomi alle soglie della vecchiaia, sentivo di non potermene partire da questa vita senza lasciare agli altri una testimonianza dell'epoca cruciale nella quale il destino mi aveva fatto nascere. Prima ancora che un'opera di poesia [...] il mio romanzo *La Storia* vuol essere un atto d'accusa contro tutti i fascismi del mondo e una domanda urgente e disperata per un risveglio comune.[53]

> [Waiting for a more extensive examination, from a first brief check limited to the initial pages, I myself have been able to ascertain that almost every page of the text has undergone such censorial interventions. It is enough for me to mention just one, made where the text summarises, in chronological form, events in Spain in 1936.
>
> Finding myself on the threshold of old age, I felt I could not leave this life without leaving others a testimony of the crucial era in which fate had given me life. Even before being a work of poetry [...] my novel *La Storia* is meant to be an indictment of all Fascism in the world and a pressing and desperate demand for a common awakening.]

Together with the 1974 article in *Il Messaggero* and her talk at the 1976 conference, another document confirms Morante's commitment to writing about the Second World War. In 1977, in the introductory note to the first edition of William Weaver's English translation of *La Storia*, Morante unambiguously states why she wrote *La Storia*:[54]

> Col presente libro, io, nata in un punto di orrore definitivo (ossia nel nostro Secolo Ventesimo), *ho voluto lasciare una testimonianza documentata della mia esperienza diretta*, la Seconda Guerra Mondiale, esponendola come un campione estremo e sanguinoso dell'intero corpo storico millenario. Eccovi dunque la Storia, così come è fatta e come noi stessi abbiamo contribuito a farla.
>
> Però mentre nei trattati a protagonisti della vicenda storica vengono assunti i mandanti o esecutori della violenza (Capi, condottieri, signori), in questo romanzo i protagonisti (gli eroi) sono invece coloro che subiscono, ossia le vittime dello scandalo.[55]

[With this book, *I*, born at a point of definitive horror (that is, in our twentieth century), *wanted to leave a documented testimony of my direct experience of the Second World War*, exposing it as an extreme and bloody example of the entire millennial historical body. So here is history, as it is made and as we ourselves have contributed to making it. But while in the treaties the principals or perpetrators of the violence are hired as protagonists of the historical event (Chiefs, leaders, gentlemen), in this novel the protagonists (the heroes) are those who suffer, victims of the outrage.]

With *La Storia*, she wrote about the reality of the violence and horror she witnessed and experienced herself, and through her fictional characters she re-elaborated the commonly-shared insecurities and worries that gripped her during the war:

E io, guardando con attenzione i miei protagonisti, ho potuto leggere nei loro occhi sempre un'unica domanda, che è la *domanda della vita stessa* [...]. A tale domanda, ormai urgente e disperata, certo io non presumo con questo libro, di dare una risposta: intendo solo di porre la domanda di fronte alla coscienza dei miei contemporanei, così come io l'ho posta di fronte alla mia propria coscienza [...]. Allora io devo avvertire che questo libro, prima ancora che un'opera di poesia, vuol essere un atto di accusa, e una preghiera.[56]

[And looking carefully at my protagonists, I could always read only one single question in their eyes, *which is the question of life itself* [...]. The question is now pressing and desperate, but I certainly do not presume with this book to give an answer to it: I intend only to ask the question in the face of the conscience of my contemporaries, just as I have posed it before my own conscience [...]. So I must give this warning, that this book, even before being a work of poetry, is intended as an indictment, and a prayer.]

By writing *La Storia*, Morante committed to transmitting knowledge and counter-memories across generations. Through the description of the physical, sensory, and emotional experiences of her ordinary characters, she helped readers to take on a more personal, deeply-felt memory of a narrated past and as a result to reflect upon the war in new ways. That is how she transcribed her own consciousness of the past and transmitted her shared consciousness to her readers. In this sense, she prefigured key principles of cultural memory studies as developed in later decades in the concept of prosthetic memory, thus helping readers to assimilate historical notions more easily. Indeed, as noted, in some key passages at the heart of the novel, these principles of commitment and of history and cultural memory are focused on the events of the round-up and deportation of 16 and 18 October 1943, and it is to these pages that we now turn, paying particular attention to Morante's channelling of emotions and what we have called 'prosthetic memory'.[57]

Fear, Hearing, and Sight

In Chapter '1943', the characters through whose eyes readers see the events of 16 and 18 October and through whose bodies readers feel them are Ida and Useppe. The perceptions of Ida and Useppe encourage recollection and understanding of these events and of the process of depersonalisation of the victims as carried out by the Nazis.

The first report of the round-up is made on Sunday 17 October by Tore, a minor character of the novel, who tells Ida what he knows:

> Quella domenica, fra gli altri commenti, [Tore] notò poi che sul 'Messaggero' non c'era traccia di una notizia che pure circolava dentro Roma, e che era stata pure trasmessa, dicevano, dalla Radio Londra-Bari: ieri, Sabato (16 ottobre) tutti i giudii di Roma erano stati razziati all'alba, casa per casa, dai Germani, e caricati su camion verso destinazione ignota. (S, p. 533)

> [That Sunday, among his other comments, [Tore] remarked that in the 'Messaggero' there was no trace of a piece of news that was, however, circulating inside Rome, and that had even been broadcast, they said, by Radio Bari: yesterday, Saturday (October 16th) the Germans had rounded up all the Jews of Rome at dawn, house by house, and loaded them into trucks for an unknown destination.] (H, p. 202)

On that night, Ida is scared that the Germans might come to arrest her and Useppe. She does not sleep, they might have to make their escape:

> S'era coricata vestita [...] per evitare che i Tedeschi, se venivano a cercarla durante la notte, la sorprendessero impreparata. Si teneva stretta a Useppe, avendo deciso che, non appena fuori udisse il passo inconfondibile dei militari e il loro picchiare all'uscio, tenterebbe la fuga per i prati calandosi giù dal tetto col figlioletto in braccio. (S, p. 534)

> [She had gone to bed with her clothes on, [...] so that the Germans, if they came for her in the night, wouldn't catch her unprepared. She held tight to Useppe, having decided that, the moment she heard the soldiers' unmistakable tread outside and their knocking on the door, she would try to escape through the fields, dropping from the roof with her baby in her arms.] (H, p. 203)

The round-up is described through Ida's fear which is reported through her auditory hallucinations of the noise of military boots.[58] Her fear fosters empathy and a sense of identification in the reader:

> Si sapeva che durante la razzia degli Ebrei, i Tedeschi avevano afferrato le creature, pure quelle in braccio alle madri, buttandole nei loro luttuosi furgoni come stracci da immondezza [...] a queste notizie (le quali invero — occorre ripeterlo — furono poi confermate dalla Storia, e anzi rappresentavano solo una piccola parte della realtà) poca gente, allora, dava fede, stimandole troppo incredibili. Ma Ida non riusciva a scacciare quelle visioni. (S, p. 592)

> [It was known that during the round-up of the Jews, the Germans had grabbed children, even babes in their mother's arms, flinging them into their funereal trucks, like rags into a rubbish pile [...]. Few people, at that time, believed these reports, considered too incredible (though, to tell the truth — it must be reported — they were later confirmed by History and, indeed, represent only a small part of the reality). But Ida couldn't dispel those visions.] (H, p. 244)

The language used in this passage shows Morante's interest in reporting what the Roman people could have been aware of during the occupation as well as her re-elaboration of the process of reification. In the quotation, the narrative voice starts the sentence with 'si sapeva', an impersonal form whose subject is undefined. Here it refers to the Roman people, a group to which Ida, the narrator, and Morante herself belong. Phrases such as 'luttuosi furgoni' and 'stracci da immondezza' vividly evoke the process of dehumanisation: 'luttuosi furgoni' immediately brings to mind images of the deportation of those who were captured; and 'stracci da immondezza' echoes the ideas of Hannah Arendt, among others, in suggesting how the Nazis transformed people into superfluous creatures or mere things, so that 'murder is as impersonal as the squashing of a gnat'.[59] The narrative voice addresses readers indirectly within brackets and uses the emphatic 'occorre ripeterlo' to confirm that what is told in the novel has been proved 'dalla Storia'.

In *La Storia*, the nadir of this process of reification comes during the description of 18 October. Morante personalises the experience of the deportation through two main effects: first, as the Nazis depersonalise their victims, so Morante re-personalises them; second, the individual perceptions of the event that she offers, with their counter-memories, details and complexities, become a counterforce to the hegemonic discourse of history that had omitted them.

Ida is with Useppe near Stazione Tiburtina when she recognises Celeste Di Segni, the wife of a Jewish salesman she knew, and starts following her. Celeste is the literary representation of a historical figure: Costanza Calò Sermoneta. As mentioned in Chapter 2, historical records confirm that Costanza was not in Rome at the time of the round-up.[60] She had been visiting the countryside and when she got home she was told that her family was in Stazione Tirbutina, leaving for an unknown destination. She arrived at the railway station and volunteered to get on the same cattle-truck as her husband and children. They all died in Auschwitz. Morante re-elaborates the story of Costanza, transforming it into a narratological representation of the events at Stazione Tiburtina on 18 October. Costanza's experience and the cattle-trucks at the railway station are described through Ida's sense of hearing and Useppe's sense of sight. These sensory perceptions invite readers to be participants in, and even to feel, the suffering of the victims, and Morante's language is particularly powerful on this point.

When Ida arrives at the railway station, she hears an indistinct sound which grows louder as she comes closer to the railway tracks. First, she perceives it as a hum, then it is an animal cry, then it is human:

> Verso la carreggiata obliqua di accesso ai binari, il *suono* aumentò di volume. Non era, come Ida s'era indotta a credere, il *grido di animali* [...]. Era un *vocio di folla umana* [...]. In fondo alla rampa, su un binario morto rettilineo, stazionava un treno [...]. Il vocio veniva di là dentro. (*S*, pp. 540-41, my emphasis)

> [Towards the oblique road leading to the tracks, the *sound's volume* increased. It was not, as Ida had already persuaded herself, the *cry of animals* [...]. It was a *sound of voices, of a human mass* [...]. At the end of the ramp, on a straight, dead track, a train was standing [...]. The voices came from inside it.] (*H*, pp. 207-08)

The voices of hundreds of Jews herded into cattle-trucks, amongst which individual voices cannot be heard, develop from a 'suono' to a 'grido di animali', and finally to a 'vocio di folla umana'. The reader's experience is Ida's experience.

The story of the Di Segnis is also described through the sounds that Ida hears: Celeste runs up and down beside the cattle-trucks, and yells the name of her husband

and children: '"Settimio! Settimio!... Graziella!... Manuele!... Settimio!... Settimio!
Esterina!... Manuele!... Angelino!" [...] minacciosa e inferocita, picchiando i pugni
contro i carri, 'qua c'è la mia famiglia! Chamateli! Di Segni! Famiglia Di Segni!'
['Settimio! Settimio!... Graziella!... Manuele!... Settimio!... Settimio! Esterina!...
Manuele!... Angelino!' [...] threatening and enraged, hammering her fists against
the cars, 'my family's in there! Call them! Di Segni! The Di Segni family!] (*S*, p.
541; *H*, p. 208). Ida is intimately drawn to the voices of the Jews in the cattle-trucks
and among them she recognises that of Settimio Di Segni: 'riconosceva questo
coro confuso. Non meno che le strida quasi indecenti della signora Di Segni [...],
tutto questo misero vocio dei carri la adescava con una dolcezza struggente' [and
Ida recognized this confused chorus. No less than the Signora Di Segni's almost
indecent screams [...], all this wretched human sound from the cars caught her in a
heart-rending sweetness] (*S*, p. 542; *H*, p. 209). The reader witnesses the dialogue
between Settimio and Celeste as she hears it:

> 'Vattene, Celeste.'
> 'No che non me ne vado!! Io puro so' giudia! Vojo montà pur'io so sto
> treno!!'
> 'Resciud, Celeste, in nome di Dio, vattene, prima che *quelli* tornino'.
> 'Noooo! No! Settimio! E dove stanno gli altri? Manuele? Graziella? Er
> pupetto?... Perchè non se fanno véde?' D'un tratto come una pazza, ruppe di
> nuovo a urlare. (*S*, p. 543)

> ['Go away, Celeste.'
> 'No, I won't go away. I'm just as Jewish as you! I want to get into this train
> too!!'
> 'Reschut, Celeste, in the name of God, get out, before *they* come back.'
> 'Nooo! No! Settimio! Where are the others? Manuele? Graziella? The
> baby?... Why can't I see them? Why don't they show their faces?' Suddenly, like
> a madwoman, she burst out screaming again.] (*H*, p. 209)

The sound of the incessant calls in the Roman Jewish dialect guarantees a realistic
representation of the scenes and gives the readers the impression of being able
to hear the characters. Both this auditory dimension and the dialogue between
Settimio and Celeste point to the hypotext, Debenedetti's *16 ottobre 1943*. Morante
extensively underlined her copy of *16 ottobre 1943* which is held at the Biblioteca
Nazionale Centrale, including two words that directly recall the description of the
round-up in *16 ottobre 1943*, 'Resciud' and 'pupetto': "Sterina! Sterina [...] Scappa,
che prendono tutti!" "Un momento, vesto pupetto, e vengo". Purtroppo vestire
pupetto le fu fatale: la signora Sterina fu presa con pupetto e tutti i suoi' ['Sterina,
Sterina [...] Get out. They're taking everyone.' 'In a minute. I'll dress the baby and
be right down.' Unfortunately dressing the baby was fatal. Signora Sterina, her
baby, and entire family were taken], and '"*Resciud*, Enrico!" Ma in quel momento
sette tedeschi sopraggiungono' ['Resciud! Enrico.' But just at that moment seven
German soldiers arrive] (*SO*, pp. 47, 51; *OS*, pp. 43, 48), for example.[61]

Ida is not the only character at the railway station looking at the cattle-trucks,
Useppe is there, too. Ida holds him and hears, and feels, his heartbeats:

Sentì dei colpi forti e ritmati, che rimbombavano da qualche parte vicino a lei; e li credette, lì per lì, soffi della macchina in movimento, immaginando che forse il treno si preparasse alla partenza. Però subitamente si rese conto che quei colpi [...] risuonavano vicinissimi a lei [...]. Era il corpo di Useppe che batteva in quel modo. (*S*, p. 544)

[She heard some deep and cadenced blows, echoing somewhere near her; and she thought at first they were the puffs of the engine starting, and imagined that the train was preparing for its departure. She promptly realized, however, that those blows [...] were resounding very close to her, right against her body. In fact, it was Useppe's heart beating that way.] (*H*, p. 210)

The child is paralysed:

Non s'era più mosso [...] fin dal primo istante [...] seguitava a guardare il treno con la faccia immobile, la bocca semiaperta, e gli occhi spalancati in uno sguardo indescrivibile di orrore [...]. C'era, nell'orrore sterminato del suo sguardo, anche una paura, o piuttosto uno stupore attonito. (*S*, p. 544)

[He hadn't moved [...] since the first moment [...] she saw him still staring at the train, his face motionless, his mouth half-open, his eyes wide in an indescribable gaze of horror [...]. There was, in the endless horror of his gaze, also a fear, or rather a dazed stupor; but it was a stupor that demanded no explanation.] (*H*, pp. 210-01)

As Adriana Cavarero suggests, at the railway station Useppe is paralysed because he is unable to make sense of what he is seeing.[62] People of every age and gender are indiscriminately herded towards deportation. The freezing and paralysing effect that Useppe undergoes 'does not depend on the natural fear of death [...] but rather on disgust for an ontological crime that outrages the human condition'.[63] This is one of those moments when Useppe feels the weight of witnessing historical events; he faces History, capitalised, but his understanding of the world is very limited. Here at Stazione Tiburtina, he is frightened, paralysed, and confused as he was after the bombing of San Lorenzo and as he will be in 1945 when he confronts for the first time the earliest images of victims of the war found in newspaper cuttings.[64]

Through the witnesses' auditory and visual perceptions of the train, Morante represents Stazione Tiburtina as the first place and the first instrument of Nazi bestialisation and reification. She describes two spaces, two worlds, which run along parallel trajectories. One is the train composed of cattle-trucks and the other is the railway platform: '"Vada via! Signora! Non resti qui!" [...] Degli uomini si agitavano a distanza verso di lei [...] però non si avvicinavano al treno. Sembravano, anzi, evitarlo, come una stanza funebre o appestata' ['Go away, Signora! Don't stay here!' [...] Some men [...] were gesticulating to her from a distance, with agitated urging. But they didn't approach the train. They seemed, indeed, to avoid it, like a funeral or infected chamber] (*S*, p. 543; *H*, p. 210). On one side, there are the Aryans: they do not even go near the train. On the other, there are the victims who, as Sophie Nezri-Dufour notes, are intentionally described only through metonym and synecdoche to capture the progressive dehumanisation to which they are subjected.[65] Ida feels she belongs with the Jews, although she is outside the cattle-trucks, on the railway platform. From what she hears, she identifies with the victims and unconsciously recognises herself as one of them, Jewish. She does not recognise herself as an individual, but as an inseparable part of the crowd locked up in the cattle-trucks:

> *S'era quasi smemorata di se stessa. Si sentiva invasa da una debolezza estrema; e per quanto, lì all'aperto sulla piattaforma, il calore non fosse eccessivo, s'era coperta di sudore come avesse la febbre a quaranta gradi. Però, si lasciava a questa debolezza del suo corpo come all'ultima dolcezza possibile, che la faceva smarrire in quella folla, mescolata con gli altri sudori.* (S, p. 544, my emphasis)

> [*She, too, had almost forgotten about herself.* She felt invaded by an extreme weakness; and although the heat wasn't excessive there in the open, on the platform she was covered with sweat as if she had a fever of 40 degrees. However, she abandoned herself to this weakness of her body as if to the *last sweetness possible*, as she became *confused in this throng*, mingling with the sweat of the others.] (H, p. 210)

She feels that she belongs to the confused chorus of sounds, from which 's'accalcavano dei vagiti, degli alterchi, delle salmodie da processione, dei parlotti senza senso, delle voci senili' [babies' cries overlapped with quarrels, ritual chanting, meaningless mumbles, senile voices], and this ancestral sound turns into 'un punto di riposo che la tirava in basso, nella tana promiscua di un'*unica famiglia sterminata*' [it was a place of repose that drew her down, into the promiscuous den of a *single, endless family*] (S, p. 542; H, p. 209, my emphasis).

The destiny of Ida is mirrored by that of the historically-rooted character of Celeste. Celeste is praying to be deported with her children. She hangs on to the train, she wants to board it. She draws attention to herself: '"io so' giudia! So' giudia! Devo partí pur'io! Aprite! Fascisti! FASCISTI!! aprite!" [...] e si accaniva al tentativo impossibile di sforzare le barre di chiusura' ['"I'm a Jew! A Jew! I have to go with them! Open up! Fascists! FASCISTS!! Open the door!' [...] and she insisted doggedly in her impossible attempt to force the bars] (S, p. 543; H, p. 210). Historical records confirm that Celeste/Costanza was indeed put in the same truck and deported to Auschwitz, where she died with her family. Ida eventually runs away in her attempt to protect Useppe: '"Andiamo via, Useppe! Andiamo via!" [...] essa si girava per affrettarsi via di là' ['"We're going, Useppe! We're going away!" [...] she turned to hasten off from there] (S, pp. 544-45; H, p. 211). She leaves the victims and the railway station, and she and her son survive the German occupation. Morante's highly dramatic description of 18 October ends with the image of these two women. Two characters, one historical, the other fictional, two mothers with apparently different destinies but actually both victims of History, with a capital H.

The Roman round-up is mentioned once more in Chapter '1946', the penultimate chapter of the novel. In 1946, after the end of the war, Ida begins to work again and Useppe waits for her in their small apartment. One day, on her way home, Ida recognises Vilma, a Jewish woman whom she thought had been deported on 18 October. Ida flinches when she sees Vilma: 'arretrò come alla vista di un fantasma, avendo subito ravvisato in costei (benché mutata) Vilma, la "profetessa" del Ghetto, che essa credeva deportata e morta in un lager, insieme agli altri ebrei del quartiere' [Ida stepped back as at the sight of a ghost, having immediately recognized her (though changed) as Vilma, the 'prophetess' of the Ghetto, whom she had never seen since and had long believed deported and dead in a Lager, with the other Jews of the quarter] (S, p. 818; H, p. 405). Through the meeting between Ida and Vilma, Morante gives space to another historical figure, Elena di Porto, the woman who had warned the Jews of the ghetto of the forthcoming round-up on the evening of 15 October, the 'Celeste' of Debenedetti's work. Morante gives her the name of 'Vilma' and builds her character on Debenedetti's 'Celeste', whom he depicts through the collective perspective of the people of the ghetto:

> Una donna vestita di nero, scarmigliata sciatta, fradicia di pioggia. Non può esprimersi, l'agitazione le ingorga le parole [...]. Una chiacchierona, un'esaltata, una fanatica: basta vedere come gesticola quando parla, con gli occhi spiritati sotto quei capelli di crine vegetale [...]. E poi si sa che in famiglia sua sono tutti un po' tocchi [...]. Come si fa a dare ascolto alla Celeste? (SO, pp. 29-31)

> [A disheveled, dirty woman dressed all in black [...] drenched in rain, she can hardly speak, agitation chokes back her words [...]. She's a gossipmonger, a hysteric, crazy. It's enough to see her gesticulate as she talks, with her wild eyes and that bird's nest hair. And besides, it's a fact that everyone in her family is a little touched [...]. How can anyone pay attention to Celeste?] (OS, p. 23)

Morante does the same when she describes Vilma/Elena on the evening of 15 October, and through the few passages dedicated to the prophetess of the ghetto,[66] she evokes again the Roman round-up and mentions the ransom of fifty kilos of gold:

> Sabato 16 ottobre 1943. Dicono che alla vigilia di quel giorno, Venerdì 15 ottobre sul far della sera, Vilma fosse accorsa piangente e trafelata nel piccolo quartiere giudio, chiamando a gran voce dal basso le famiglie, che a quell'ora stavano raccolte in casa per le preghiere del Sabato. Come un'aralda stracciona, correndo in pianto per le straducole, essa scongiurava tutti quanti di fuggire, portandosi dietro pure i vecchi e le creature e salvando quanto avevano di meglio, perché l'ora della strage (da lei già preannunciata più volte) era venuta, e sull'alba i tedeschi arriverebbero coi camion: e la sua *Signora* aveva perfino visto le liste dei nomi... Non pochi si affacciarono dalle finestrelle, ai suoi gridi, e alcuni scesero giù dabbasso ai portoni; ma nessuno le credette. Non molti giorni prima i tedeschi (da essi giudicati magari feroci ma 'gente d'onore') avevano firmato il patto della salvezza col popolo ebreo di Roma, ottenendone pure il riscatto voluto: cinquanta chili d'oro! messo insieme miracolosamente, con l'aiuto di tutta la città. Vilma fu trattata come al solito come una povera visionaria dalla mente disturbata; e gli abitanti del Ghetto risalirono in casa a terminare le loro preghiere, lasciandola sola. (S, pp. 818-19)

> [Saturday, October 16th, 1943. They say that on the eve of that day, Friday, October 15th, towards evening, Vilma ran weeping and breathless into the little Jewish district, calling from below in a loud voice to the families, gathered in their homes at that hour for the Sabbath prayers. Like a tattered herald, running in tears through the narrow streets, she begged them all to flee, taking with them the old people also and the babies and saving whatever they had that they

valued, because the hour of the massacre (already announced by her so many times) had come, and at dawn the Germans would arrive with trucks; and her *Signora* had even seen the lists of names... A number of people looked out of the windows at her shouts, and some came down to their front doors; but nobody believed her. Not many days before, the Germans (whom the Jews considered fierce perhaps but 'men of honor') had signed an agreement guaranteeing the safety of the Jewish population of Rome, after receiving the desired ransom: fifty kilograms of gold! Collected miraculously, with the help of the whole city. Vilma was treated, as usual, as a poor crack-brained visionary, and the Ghetto's inhabitants went back up into their homes to finish their prayers, leaving her alone.] (*H*, pp. 405-06)

When in 1946 Ida encounters Vilma, Morante's female narrator explicitly reveals her own presence using the first-person singular tense. She shares the information she found out about Vilma, explaining how she had avoided deportation: 'Vilma [...] era fuggita alla cattura (trovando rifugio nel convento della sua famosa Monaca) e anzi di lei si racconta un episodio, del quale *ho udito* invero diverse varianti' [Vilma instead had escaped capture (finding refuge in the convent of her famous Nun) and indeed a story is told of her, which *I have actually heard* in various versions] (*S*, p. 818; *H*, p. 405, my emphasis). Later she supposes Vilma is still alive:

> *Io ho motivo* di supporre che sia sopravvissuta a lungo. *Mi sembra* infatti di averla riconosciuta, non molto tempo fa, in mezzo a quel piccolo popolo di vecchie che si recano a nutrire i gatti randagi del Teatro Marcello e delle altre rovine. (*S*, p. 820, my emphasis)

> [*I have reason* to believe she survived a long time. In fact, *I think* I recognized her, not long ago, in the midst of that little bunch of old women who go every day to feed the stray cats at the Theater of Marcellus or other Roman ruins.] (*H*, pp. 406-07)

With this last meeting between Ida and Vilma, Morante concludes her reflections on the deportation of the Italian Jews in October 1943, and slowly approaches the end of the novel.

As mentioned, in Chapter '1947', Useppe has his last, fatal attack of epilepsy. Ida sinks into apathy: 'Iduzza ebbe un breve sussulto del capo: e questo fu, sembra, l'ultimo stimolo a cui la donna reagì, finché rimase viva' [Ida's head gave a brief jerk: and this, apparently, was the last stimulus to which the woman reacted as long as she remained alive] (*S*, pp. 1019-20; *H*, p. 547). She dies in 1956, after nine years in an asylum. Her loss of connection to her world becomes a description of the readers' loss of connection to the past: 'coi ciechi, coi sordomuti è possibile comunicare; ma con lei, che non era né cieca né sorda né muta, non c'era più comunicazione possibile' [with the blind, with deaf-mutes, it is possible to communicate; but with her, who was not blind or deaf or dumb, there was no possible communication] (*S*, p. 1020; *H*, p. 548). Morante bids Ida farewell and without Ida's sensory perception, the readers too lose their connection to Morante's world.

Constructing and Observing Cultural Memory

The sensory representation of 16 and 18 October in *La Storia* can in conclusion be read through the lens of cultural memory. As discussed in Chapter 1, literature is one of the media most suited to exploring and explaining the meaning of cultural memory.[67] Considering the Second World War and, more specifically the Roman round-up, *La Storia* can be seen to function as both a medium and an object of recollection and remembrance of episodes of the war in Italy, and it works as a tool for observing the production of previous and later cultural memory.

La Storia, and in particular its passages on the Roman round-up, is a forceful example of Rigney's social-constructivist model of literature as cultural memory.[68] With its literary re-elaborations, it mediates historical understanding of the Italian Holocaust and contributes to the broader discussion of the ways in which Italian society recollects its past. It can be considered a 'memorial medium' work, according to the concept proposed by Erll and Rigney: it is a novel which strives to reactivate and re-embody distant individual and social memories, and mediates them in a familiar form of aesthetic expression.[69]

Morante wrote *La Storia* in what Erll defines as 'experiential' mode. She conveys, as we have seen, embodied, seemingly immediate experiences of the two episodes of October 1943 through sensorial and emotional descriptions. At a personal level, her literary representation makes historical data and facts more knowable and memorable, connects to readers' own archives of experience, and provides them with sensory encounters with a past they did not live through. As noted in Chapter 1, Landsberg's notion of 'prosthetic memory' was first and foremost applied to mass media, more specifically to film. However, the close readings of passages from *La Storia* provided so far show that Landsberg's theories can be profitably applied to Morante's text. The emotional and sensorial descriptions of Ida's and Useppe's lives encourage forms of memories which overlap with Landsberg's definition of prosthetic memories. By empathising and feeling a sense of identification with Morante's characters, readers can establish an intimate relationship with them and broaden the horizon of what they consider to be their own heritage. Furthermore, as Rigney more broadly suggests, 'the sensual and physical experience of war [...] has a role to play in building an imaginative and empathic bridge between past actors and present readers'.[70] The historical frames and literary re-elaborations of past events stimulate the readers' historiographical interest. Descriptions of characters' experience of feelings stimulate the process of identification through theories of emotion: Ida's and Useppe's emotions influence the readers' images of the war and persecution and encourage their recollection. The Roman round-up and the deportation from Stazione Tiburtina become Ida's worries and terrors: 'la paura non tralasciò di percuoterla, simile a un flagello di spini' [fear never stopped thrashing her, like a spiked scourge] (*S*, pp. 533–34; *H*, p. 203). They become Useppe's subconscious horror and shock: 'stava lì a scrutare queste scene, in uno stupore titubante, e ancora confuso' [he was there studying these scenes in a hesitant awe, still bewildered] (*S*, p. 689; *H*, p. 315).

At a collective level, *La Storia*, as discussed in Chapter 2, enacts as many as four of Rigney's five functions of literature, working as a 'relay station', a 'catalyst', a 'stabilizer', and an 'object of recollection', the same four as enacted by Debenedetti's *16 ottobre 1943*.[71] We have seen how Morante wrote her novel by re-elaborating historical events and testimonies too. In this sense, *La Storia* can be seen as a 'relay station', primarily of the stories she read in Debenedetti's *16 ottobre 1943* and Katz's *Black Sabbath*. She represented the heterogeneity of the deportation of the Jews of Rome by including also the personal stories of Celeste/Costanza and Vilma/Elena.[72] The two stories are two tiles in the mosaic of experiences of deportation which Morante made resonate and disseminate through her novel.

La Storia can also be thought of as a 'catalyst' because it describes facts of the Italian Holocaust and of the Roman round-up which were neglected in cultural remembrance, and it establishes them as socially and culturally relevant, now part of a bestselling novel. Furthermore, the thirteen editions of *La Storia* now include one in eBook format; the novel has been translated into twenty-two languages and has been re-published several times abroad as well, thus demonstrating its worldwide appeal: from 1974 to date, there have been a total of nine English-language editions, five each in French and German, four in Spanish, and three each in Norwegian and Danish.

La Storia is also a 'stabilizer', in that it provides a cultural frame for later recollections of 16 and 18 October and is therefore a channel for perpetuating that memory. In the literary field, it has been included in numerous research projects on the Italian Holocaust including those by Risa Sodi, Rosario Forlenza, Stefania Lucamante, and Gabrielle Popoff, for example.[73] With regard to the impact it has had on Italian historiography and later narratives of the Roman round-up and of wider histories, *La Storia* is mentioned in *The Holocaust in Italian Culture* by Gordon, by Garofolo in *16 ottobre 1943* (edited by Baumeister, Guerrazzi and Procaccia), in *Dopo il 16 ottobre* by Antonucci and Procaccia, and in *La matta di piazza Giudia* by Petraglia.[74] The historian Anna Foa comments that *La Storia*, together with *16 ottobre 1943*, is the narrative work she looked to before all others when she wrote *Portico d'Ottavia 13*.

La Storia, finally, is an 'object of recollection' because it was made into both film and television versions, with the homonymous title of *La Storia*, directed by Luigi Comencini.[75] A few months before she died in 1985, Morante met Comencini and chose him to adapt *La Storia* into a film having seen his television mini-series *Le avventure di Pinocchio*.[76] As Giorgio Gosetti notes:

> Elsa Morante, già sofferente e ricoverata in ospedale (morirà durante le riprese) si affida a Comencini dopo avere rifiutato numerose proposte e lo fa per un'istintiva simpatia e per aver visto una cassetta di *Pinocchio* che il regista le porta in ospedale. Proprio questa profonda sintonia con l'autrice fa a lungo riflettere Comencini alle prese con una storia che straripa da tutte le parti, che è fluviale per lucida scelta.[77]

> [Already suffering and hospitalised (she dies during filming), Elsa Morante places her trust in Comencini after having rejected numerous proposals and does so out of instinctive sympathy and because she has watched a cassette of *Pinocchio* that the director takes to her in hospital. Precisely this profound

harmony with the author makes Comencini reflect for a long time on how to deal with a story that overflows from all sides, which is fluvial by lucid choice.]

In 1986, the film premiered out of competition at the forty-third Venice International Film Festival and it was then distributed as a television series on Rai 2, thus guaranteeing free national distribution in Italian households. Today, Comencini's *La Storia* is available on the free national on-demand platform Raiplay. It is divided into three episodes of which the second opens with the scenes dedicated to the Roman round-up and the deportation from Stazione Tiburtina.

Comencini's re-elaboration of the episodes of the night of 17 and the morning of 18 October and the related dialogues differs in significant ways from Morante's plot. In the book, as has been seen, Ida is informed of the round-up on the evening of 17 October; during the night, she does not sleep because she is afraid the Nazis will arrest her and Useppe. The day after, they go toward Stazione Tiburtina to buy shoes for Useppe. Ida recognises Celeste and follows her to the railway station where she sees the train of cattle-trucks destined for Auschwitz. In the film, the description of the round-up occupies only a few minutes: as in the book, Ida is randomly informed by Tore of what happened in the ghetto on 16 October. On that night, SS officers enter the refuge of Pietralata looking for Italian deserters. Ida is paralysed by fear, but as soon as the SS officers go away, she decides to leave Rome. In the early morning of 18 October, she goes with Useppe to Stazione Tiburtina. The scene starts with a foreground shot of Ida with Useppe in her arms as described by Morante, but then the camera turns and frames the train station, which is full of civilians. On the tracks opposite the train full of Jews, there is another train, it is crowded too. This is the train that Ida wants to take. The next shots show Ida as she follows Celeste, who in the film is called 'Amalia', and confesses that she, too, is Jewish. But, Celeste/Amalia does not listen to her as she is trying to get on to the cattle-truck where she has found her husband. In this scene, Comencini maintains a central element of Morante's description, Ida's sense of hearing, by conveying the alienating sounds she hears around her: during the scene, there is a consistent hum, which slowly is transformed into a human cry, as we read in Morante's novel. In the film, however, the cry is interrupted by Useppe's scared questions to Ida, 'è quello il treno che pigliamo noi? [...] Che c'è lì dentro? [...] Perchè gridano?' [is that the train we're taking? [...] What's in there? [...] Why are they crying?]. Ida can only answer with hopeless and repeated 'non lo so' [I don't know]. At that point, she decides to flee. She finds a seat on the other train and together with Useppe she stares speechlessly at the Jews, seeing only their hands from the bars of the cattle-trucks. Comencini depicts two parallel worlds on the rail-track, just as Morante herself does, that of the Aryans and that of the Jews who are to be deported. The scenes dedicated to the deportation of the Roman Jews end with the civilians eager to leave Rome getting off their train and walking along the tracks to leave the train station. Among them are Ida and Useppe. 'A' ma dove andiamo?' [mum, where are we going?], asks Useppe; Ida answers, 'torniamo a casa sei contento?' [we're going back home, happy?]. The travellers of the other train though, the Jews arrested during the round-up, are still locked up in the cattle-trucks. They will be deported soon to an unknown destination, the steam of the train blurs the camera. This is the last shot dedicated to 18 October.

Notes to Chapter 4

1. Lucamante, *Forging Shoah Memories*, p. 160.
2. In 1976, in a discussion of the American translation of her novel, Morante sent a letter to her international editor explaining the antiphrastic and intrinsic meaning of the title: 'sulla soglia del testo, era esibita l'ambizione di affidare alla finzione romanzesca — novel — la testimonianza di verità storica — history' [on the threshold of the text, the ambition of entrusting to fiction — novel — the testimony of historical truth — history]: Milan, Fondazione Arnoldo e Alberto Mondadori, Erich Linder Archive, 26883 Elsa Morante, 36, 61/19.
3. Hayden White, *Metahistory: The Historical Imagination in Nineteenth-century Europe* (Baltimore, MD: Johns Hopkins University Press, 1973).
4. Jean-Noël Schifano and Tjuna Notarbartolo, *Cahiers Elsa Morante* (Naples: Edizioni Scientifiche Italiane, 1993); Mauro Baurelli, 'II dominio della Storia: intorno al romanzo di Elsa Morante', in *La memoria della politica: esperienze e autorappresentazione nel racconto di uomini e donne*, ed. by Fiamma Lussana and Lucia Motti (Roma: Ediesse, 2007), pp. 215-26; Sarah Carey, 'Elsa Morante: Envisioning History', in *Elsa Morante's Politics of Writing: Rethinking Subjectivity, History, and the Power of Art*, ed. by Stefania Lucamante (Madison, NJ: Fairleigh Dickinson University Press, 2015), pp. 69-76.
5. I owe this suggestion to a colleague and dear friend of mine, Erica Bellia, who told me about the work of Taro after I noticed the mistaken attribution of the photograph to Capa. On the attribution to Taro, see, for example, International Centre of Photography <https://www.icp.org/browse/archive/objects/body-la-granjuela> [accessed 20 August 2020].
6. On Gerda Taro see: Jane Rogoyska, *Gerda Taro: Inventing Robert Capa* (London: Jonathan Cape, 2013); Irme Schaber, *Gerda Taro: With Robert Capa as Photojournalist in the Spanish Civil War* (Stuttgart: Axel Menges, 2019); and literary works such as Susana Fortes, *Esperando a Robert Capa* (Barcelona: Planeta, 2009), and Helena Janeczek, *La ragazza con la Leica* (Parma: Guanda, 2017).
7. Pino Levi Cavaglione, *Guerriglia nei castelli romani* (Florence: La Nuova Italia, 1971); Bruno Piazza, *Perchè gli altri dimenticano* (Milan: Feltrinelli, 1959); Nuto Revelli, *La strada del Davai* (Turin: Einaudi, 1966), and *L'ultimo fronte: lettere di soldati caduti o dispersi nella seconda guerra mondiale* (Turin: Einaudi, 1971).
8. See Monica Zanardo, 'La biblioteca della Storia attraverso lo studio dei manoscritti: alcuni esempi di utilizzo delle fonti', in *Le fonti di Elsa Morante*, ed. by Enrico Palandri and Hanna Serkowska (Venice: Edizioni Ca' Foscari, 2015), pp. 111-19, and *Il poeta e la grazia: una lettura dei manoscritti della 'Storia' di Elsa Morante* (Rome: Edizioni di storia e letteratura, 2017), pp. 17-58.
9. Compelling and convincing readings of *La Storia* through feminist theories are for example: Lucia Re, 'Utopian Longing and the Constraints of Racial and Sexual Difference in Elsa Morante's *La Storia*', *Italica*, 70.3 (1993), 361–75; Maria Ornella Marotti, 'Revisiting the Past: Feminist Historians/Historical Fictions', in *Gendering Italian Fiction: Feminist Revisions of Italian History*, ed by Maria Ornella Marotti and Gabriella Brooke (Madison, NJ: Fairleigh Dickson University Press, 1999), pp. 41-70; Maria Gimenez Cavallo, 'Elsa Morante's "La Storia": A Posthumanist, Feminist, Anarchist Response to Power', *Annali d'Italianistica*, 34 (2016), 425–47; Rebecca M. Walker, 'Bringing Up the Bodies: Material Encounters in Elsa Morante's *La Storia*', *Italian Studies*, 76.1 (2021), 82–95.
10. On this see: *Discutendo di storia*, ed. by Società Italiana delle Storiche; *Generazioni*, ed. by Società Italiana delle Storiche; *Questioni di teoria femminista*, ed. by Paola Bono (Milan: La tartaruga, 1993); *Donne tra memoria e storia*, ed. by Capobianco; Marotti, 'Literary Historicism and Women's Tradition' and 'Feminist Historians/Historical Fictions'.
11. Maria Ornella Marotti, 'Introduction', in *Gendering Italian Fiction*, ed. by Marotti and Brooke, pp. 15-27 (p. 19).
12. Tiziana de Rogatis, 'Elsa Morante's *History: A Novel* and Svetlana Alexievich's *The Unwomanly*

Face of War: Traumatic Realism, *Archives du Mal* and Female Pathos', in *Trauma Narratives in Italian and Transnational Women's Writing*, ed. by Tiziana de Rogatis and Katrin Wehling-Giorgi (Rome: Sapienza Università Editrice, 2022), pp. 79-111 (p. 108).

13. On this see, for example, Cristina Della Colletta, *Plotting the Past: Metamorphoses of Historical Narrative in Modern Italian Fiction* (West Lafayette, IN: Purdue University Press, 1994), pp. 117-51.

14. According to Zanardo, the chronicles were written only once the body of the novel had been completed: *Il poeta e la grazia*, pp. 210-12.

15. On this episode see for example Concetta D'Angeli, 'Visioni di sterminio ne *La Storia*', *Cuadernos de Filología Italiana*, 21 (2014), 91-100 (pp. 98-100).

16. A prototype of Blitz appears in the unfinished and unpublished work 'Senza i conforti della religione', which Morante started writing at the beginning on the 1950s, and in which there are no other references to the Jewish persecution. On this see Zanardo, *Il poeta e la grazia*, pp. 63-112.

17. On Morante's Judaism see: Marcello Morante, *Maledetta benedetta* (Milan: Garzanti, 1986), pp. 114-16; Stefania Lucamante, *Quella difficile identità: ebraismo e rappresentazioni letterarie della Shoah* (Rome: Iacobelli, 2012), pp. 268-342; Marina Beer, 'Costellazioni ebraiche: note su Elsa Morante e l'ebraismo del Novecento', in *"Nacqui nell'ora amara del meriggio": scritti per Elsa Morante nel centenario della sua nascita*, ed. by Eleonora Cardinale and Giuliana Zagra (Rome: Quaderni della Biblioteca Nazionale Centrale di Roma, 2013), pp. 165-201. Biographical details for Morante can be found in: Enzo Siciliano, *Alberto Moravia* (Milan: Bompiani, 1982); Marcello Morante, *Maledetta benedetta*; Alain Elkann and Alberto Moravia, *Vita di Moravia* (Milan: Bompiani, 1990); Carlo Cecchi and Cesare Garboli, 'Cronologia', in Elsa Morante, *Opere*, 2 vols (Milan: Mondadori, 1990), I, xvii-xc; Graziella Bernabò, *La fiaba estrema: Elsa Morante tra vita e scrittura* (Rome: Carocci, 2012).

18. Cited in Luca Fontana, 'Elsa Morante: A Personal Remembrance', *Poetry Nation Review*, 14.6 (1988), 20.

19. Katherine Mansfield, *Il libro degli appunti*, trans. by Elsa Morante (Milan: Longanesi, 1941); Elsa Morante, *Il gioco segreto* (Milan: Garzanti, 1941), and *Le bellissime avventure di Caterì dalla trecciolina* (Turin: Einaudi, 1942).

20. Siciliano, *Alberto Moravia*, pp. 58, 57.

21. Fontana, 'Elsa Morante', p. 20.

22. Siciliano, *Alberto Moravia*, p. 58.

23. Ibid.

24. It is still not clear where they spent July 1944.

25. Elkann and Moravia, *Vita di Moravia*, p. 151.

26. Alberto Moravia, *La ciociara* (Milan: Bompiani, 1957). Even though the first pages of *La ciociara* were written in 1944, the book was not completed and published until 1957.

27. Elsa Morante, 'Il soldato siciliano', *L'Europeo*, 1.6 (December 1945); in *Opere*, I, 1509-15; hereafter referenced in the main text as *SS*. Unless stated otherwise, hereafter all references to Morante's works will be to *Opere*.

28. Elsa Morante, *Lo scialle andaluso* (Turin: Einaudi, 1963), pp. 135-44; in *Opere*, I, 1509-15.

29. The biological father of Elsa and her siblings was Francesco Lo Monaco, a Sicilian, and not Augusto Morante, Irma Poggibonsi's husband. On this see: Cecchi and Garboli, p. XIX; Bernabò, *La fiaba estrema*, p. 19.

30. On this see: Lydia M. Oram, 'Rape, Rapture and Revision: Visionary Imagery and Historical Reconstruction in Elsa Morante's *La Storia*', *Forum Italicum*, 37.2 (2003), 409-35; Stefania Porcelli, '"As If He Wanted to Murder Her": Fear, Disgust and Anger in *La Storia*'s Rape Scene', *Close Encounters in War Journals*, 1 (2018), 65-81.

31. See: Gregory L. Lucente, *Beautiful Fables: Self-consciousness in Italian Narrative from Manzoni to Calvino* (Baltimore, MD: Johns Hopkins University Press, 1986), pp. 246-65; Cesare Garboli, *Il gioco segreto: nove immagini di Elsa Morante* (Milan: Adelphi, 1995), p. 188; Vittorio Spinazzola, *L'egemonia del romanzo* (Milan: Il Saggiatore, 2007), pp. 287-330; Stefania Lucamante, 'The World Must Be the Writer's Concern', in *Elsa Morante's Politics of Writing*, ed. by Lucamante, pp. 88-111 (p. 101).

32. Garboli, *Il gioco segreto*, p. 188.

33. Lucamante, 'The World Must Be the Writer's Concern', p. 101.

34. Rome, Biblioteca Nazionale Centrale, Vittorio Emanuele, 1618/1, XVI, fol. 72r (my emphasis).

35. De Rogatis adopts the Derridean expression 'patriarchive' intending it as 'the authoritarian paradigms standing at the core of both national and transnational collective memories connected with the Second World War, the Italian Resistance and, more generally, the teleology of progressive values attached to modernity'. De Rogatis, 'Elsa Morante's *History*', p. 84.

36. Spinazzola, *L'egemonia del romanzo*, p. 292.

37. Sharon Wood, 'Excursus as Narrative Technique in *La Storia*', in *Elsa Morante's Politics of Writing*, ed by Lucamante, pp. 77-87.

38. Elsa Morante, 'Il beato propagandista del paradiso', in *Pro o contro la bomba atomica*, in *Opere*, II, 1555-69 (p. 1568).

39. Interestingly this phrase is not translated in *H*.

40. I investigate this subject in Mara Josi, 'Civil Disobedience: Elsa Morante, the Student Movement and the Years of Lead', in *The Winter of Italy's Discontent*, ed. by Maurizio Rebaudengo and Dagmar Reichdart (Oxford: Peter Lang, forthcoming).

41. On this see: Gregory L. Lucente, 'Scrivere o fare... o altro: Social Commitment and Ideologies of Representation in the Debates over Lampedusa's *Il Gattopardo* and Morante's *La Storia*', *Italica*, 61.3 (1984), 220-51 (p. 231); Elena Rancati, '*La Storia*: il "caso Morante"', in *Libri e scrittori di via Biancamano: casi editoriali in 75 anni di Einaudi*, ed. by Roberto Cicala and Velania La Mendola (Milan: EDUCatt, 2009), pp. 339-446.

42. Nanni Balestrini and others, 'Contro il romanzone della Morante', *Il Manifesto*, 18 July 1974. See: Lucente, 'Scrivere o fare... o altro'; Graziella Bernabò, *Come leggere 'La Storia' di Elsa Morante* (Milan: Mursia, 1991); Hanna Serkowska, 'About One of the Most Disputed Literary Cases of the Seventies: Elsa Morante's *La Storia*', *Italianistica Ultraiectina*, 1 (2006), 372-86; Angela Borghesi, *L'anno della Storia 1974-1975: il dibattito politico e culturale sul romanzo di Elsa Morante* (Macerata: Quodlibet, 2019).

43. Natalia Ginzburg, 'Elzeviri: "La Storia"', *Corriere della Sera*, 30 June 1974, p. 3; Carlo Bo, 'I disarmati', *Corriere della Sera*, 30 June 1974, p. 3; Cesare Garboli, 'Un crocicchio di esistenze', *Corriere della Sera*, 30 June 1974, p. 3.

44. See for example, Marco Bardini, *Morante Elsa. Italiana. Di professione, poeta* (Pisa: Nistri-Lischi, 1999), pp. 555-616.

45. Marco Bardini, 'Esporsi al pubblico: Elsa Morante tra occasioni mondane e impegno civile', *Status Quaestionis*, 3 (2012), 1-29 (p. 8).

46. Elsa Morante, 'Il 19 luglio 1943', *Il Messaggero*, 16 June 1974, p. 3. The manuscript draft of the article is held at the Biblioteca Nazionale Centrale in Rome (see Zanardo, *Il poeta e la grazia*, p. 225).

47. Aldo Maffey, 'Quando venne a trovarci in via del Tritone', *Il Messaggero*, 24 November 1986, p. 5 (my emphasis).

48. Morante, 'Il 19 luglio 1943' (my emphasis).

49. On Morante's paper see: Gloria Guidotti, 'L'intraducibile della *Storia* di Elsa Morante nella Spagna del 1976', *Cuadernos de Filología Italiana*, 11 (2004), 167-76; Flavia Cartoni, 'Narrativa e censura: *La Storia* nella prima edizione spagnola del 1976', in *Santi, Sultani e Gran Capitani in camera mia: inediti e ritrovati dall'Archivio di Elsa Morante*, ed. by Giuliana Zagra (Rome: Biblioteca Nazionale Centrale di Roma, 2012), pp. 139-48; Bardini, 'Esporsi al pubblico'.

50. Elsa Morante, *Algo en la Historia*, trans. by Juan Moreno (Barcelona: Plaza & Janés, 1976).

51. Elsa Morante, 'La censura in Spagna', *L'Unità*, 15 May 1976, p. 3, cited in Bardini, *Morante*, pp. 730-31.

52. According to Guidotti, the man in the background stands for the German soldier who raped Ida, namely Useppe's father: 'L'intraducibile della *Storia* di Elsa Morante nella Spagna del 1976', pp. 168-69.

53. Cited in Bardini, *Morante Elsa, italiana*, p. 730.

54. On this see, for example, Zanardo, *Il poeta e la grazia*, pp. 238-44.

55. From the original text: typescript of the introductory note to the American edition of *La Storia* published for the members of the First Ed Society, Pennsylvania 1977, cited in Cecchi and

Garboli, 'Cronologia', in Elsa Morante, *Opere*, I, lxxxiv (my emphasis).

56. Cited in Cecchi and Garboli, 'Cronologia', in Elsa Morante, *Opere*, I, lxxxiv-v (my emphasis).

57. On prosthetic memory see Chapter 1.

58. Walker compellingly analyses Ida's bodied fear of being Jewish: 'in Morante's fictionalised account, Ida's fear is that her concealed half-Jewishness is what Hannah Arendt terms a "physical stain"': 'Bringing Up the Bodies', pp. 91-92. On Ida's fear and shame of being Jewish also see Porcelli, '"As If He Wanted to Murder Her"', where she suggests that Ida's fear and shame are inherited from her mother's obsession with her Jewish identity.

59. Hannah Arendt, *The Origins of Totalitarianism* (San Diego, CA: Harcourt Brace Jovanovich, 1979), pp. 442-43. Arendt's works do not appear in the list of Morante's books stored in the Biblioteca Nazionale Centrale; probably they have been passed on to Morante's heirs. Siriana Sgavicchia, 'Fonti storiche e filosofiche nell'invenzione narrativa della *Storia*', in *'La Storia' di Elsa Morante*, ed. by Siriana Sgavicchia (Pisa: ETS, 2012), pp. 101-24 (p. 114).

60. See for example, Katz, *Black Sabbath*, p. 234.

61. The friendship between Morante and Debenedetti helps us to understand some aspects of the intertextual bonds between their two works and the nature of the tribute Morante was paying to Debenedetti's text when she re-elaborated facts and testimonies included in *16 ottobre 1943* in her own account. Debenedetti and Morante met in 1936 and in 1937, when Debenedetti had moved definitively to Rome, their friendship grew closer. In the first years of the war, they met frequently; in the summer of 1942, daily. When the Nazis occupied Rome Debenedetti decided to leave the capital with his family and go to Cortona. On 14 September, on their way to Stazione Termini, the Debenedettis bumped into Morante and Moravia: 'Il vero saluto, quello più caldo e cordiale, lo rivolse Elsa a papà [...]. Le cerimonie di saluto fra Elsa e Giacomino posso aggiungere, avendo assistito ad altri loro incontri, tendevano ad escludere gli altri presenti, privilegiando una complicità che affondava le sue radici in qualcosa di notturno, forse di un po' ebraico e soprattutto di intellettuale fino all'insopportabilità, allo scandalo di un cerebralismo nemico dell'aria, del sole e della vita' [The true greeting, the warmest and most cordial, was addressed by Elsa to dad [...]. The greeting ceremonies between Elsa and Giacomino, I can add, having witnessed their other meetings, tended to exclude others present, favouring a complicity that had its roots in something nocturnal, perhaps a little Jewish and above all intellectual to the point of the unbearable, to the outrage of a cerebralism that is the enemy of air, sun and life] (A. Debenedetti, *Giacomino*, p. 70). This was the last time Morante and Debenedetti met before the end of the war. There is no information about the correspondence and meetings between the two authors until 1948 when Debenedetti was on the jury of the Premio Viareggio and supported Morante's *Menzogna e sortilegio* which won the award jointly with *I fratelli Cuccoli* by Aldo Palazzeschi. Again, there is no relevant information about subsequent contact between the two before February 1957, when Debenedetti presented Morante's *L'isola di Arturo* at Einaudi in Rome; their correspondence about *L'isola di Arturo* is intense. In March 1957, Debenedetti and Morante went together to the Soviet Union; however, the correspondence between 1957 and 1967 has not yet been made public. But the words Morante wrote to Debenedetti's wife Renata on 22 January 1967, two days his death, confirm the long-lasting mutual respect, admiration, and friendship that existed between Debenedetti and Morante, who maintained regular contact with Renata and her children after his death. On this see: A Debenedetti, *Giacomino*. Also see M. E. Debenedetti, 'Cronologia', pp. lxix-lvxx; Elsa Morante, *L'amata: lettere a e di Elsa Morante*, ed. by Marcello Morante and Giuliana Zagra (Turin: Einaudi, 2012), pp. 173-94.

62. Adriana Cavarero, 'Framing Horror', in *Concentrationary Imaginaries*, ed. by Griselda Pollock and Max Silverman (London: I. B. Tauris, 2015), pp. 47-58 (pp. 56-57).

63. Ibid., p. 50.

64. For compelling analysis of Useppe's traumatic experience when he sees pictures of the extermination camps, the war, and Mussolini's dead body, see Tiziana de Rogatis and Katrin Wehling Giorgi, 'Traumatic Realism and the Poetics of Trauma in Elsa Morante's Works', *Allegoria*, 83 (2021), 169-83, and Katrin Wehling Giorgi, '"Come un fotogramma spezzato": Traumatic Images and Multistable Visions in Elsa Morante's *History: A Novel*', in *Trauma Narratives*, ed. by de Rogatis and Wehling-Giorgi, pp. 55-78.

65. Sophie Nezri-Dufour, 'La Figure du juif dans *La Storia* d'Elsa Morante', *Cahiers d'études italiennes*, 7 (2008), 65-74 (p. 72).

66. According to Lucamante, Vilma 'rappresenta quella voce eterna del popolo ebraico che preconizza le sue stesse sorti' [represents that eternal voice of the Jewish people that predicts their own destiny]: *Quella difficile identità*, p. 341.

67. Erll and Rigney, 'Literature and the Production of Cultural Memory', p. 112.

68. Ann Rigney, 'Portable Monuments: Literature, Cultural Memory and the Case of Jeanie Deans', *Poetics Today*, 25.2 (2004), 361-96 (p. 369).

69. Erll and Rigney, 'Literature and the Production of Cultural Memory', p. 112.

70. Ann Rigney, 'All This Happened, More or Less: What a Novelist Made of the Bombing of Dresden', *History and Theory*, 47 (2009), 5-24 (p. 19).

71. Rigney, 'The Dynamics of Remembrance', pp. 350-51.

72. On this see: Sgavicchia, 'Fonti storiche e filosofiche nell'invenzione narrative della *Storia*', pp. 99-122; Zanardo, *Il poeta e la grazia*, pp. 49-52.

73. Risa Sodi, 'Whose Story? Literary Borrowings by Elsa Morante's *La Storia*', *Lingua e Stile*, 33.1 (1998), 141-53, and *Narrative and Imperative: The First Fifty Years of Italian Holocaust Writing (1944–1994)* (New York: Peter Lang, 2007), pp. 190-206; Rosario Forlenza, 'Sacrificial Memory and Political Legitimacy in Postwar Italy: Reliving and Remembering World War II', *History and Memory*, 24.2 (2012), 73-116; Lucamante, *Quella difficile identità*, pp. 268-342, and *Forging Shoah Memories*, pp. 153-97; Gabrielle Elissa Popoff, '"Once Upon a Time there was an S.S. Officer": The Holocaust between History and Fiction in Elsa Morante's *La Storia*', *Journal of Modern Jewish Studies*, 11.1 (2012), 25-38.

74. Gordon, *The Holocaust in Italian Culture*, p. 101; Garofalo, '"Non dimenticarlo il nostro ottobre"', p. 159; Silvia Haia Antonucci and Claudio Procaccia, 'Introduzione', in *Dopo il 16 ottobre*, ed. by Antonucci and Procaccia, pp. 7-34 (p. 9); Petraglia, *La matta di piazza Giudia*, pp. 169 and 202.

75. *La Storia*, dir. by Luigi Comencini (Rai 2, Antenne 2, SACIS, 1986). Then *La Storia*, dir. by Luigi Comencini (Rai 2, December 1986). On this see: Giorgio Gosetti, *Luigi Comencini* (Milan: Il Castoro Cinema, 1988), pp. 94-100; Tiziana Jacoponi, '*La Storia*: un libro, un film', *Narrativa*, 17 (2000), 117-22; Antonio Costa, '*Cuore, La Storia*', in *Luigi Comencini: il cinema e i film*, ed. by Adriano Aprà (Venice: Marsilio, 2007), pp. 222-30; Hanna Serkowska, 'La Storia morantiana sullo schermo', *Cuadernos de Filología Italiana*, 21 (2014), 173-83; and Mara Josi, 'From Book to Screen: Images of the Fascist Dictatorship in Elsa Morante's *La Storia*', *Annali d'italianistica*, 41 (forthcoming).

76. *Le avventure di Pinocchio*, dir. by Luigi Comencini (Rai 1, April 1972).

77. Gosetti, *Luigi Comencini*, p. 95.

CHAPTER 5

❖

Rosetta Loy,
La parola ebreo

An Introduction

Published by Einaudi in 1997, *La parola ebreo* by Rosetta Loy narrates personal, family, and public memories of the years between 1936 and 1943 in Rome. It describes the life of the 'narrated I', the child Rosetta, during the war and her relationship with the Jews who lived in the building on via Flaminia where she also lived.[1] Rosetta is the youngest child in a Catholic upper-middle-class family. She goes to private schools in Rome and is raised by a German governess, Anne Marie. Some of those around her are Jews: her neighbours, Signora della Seta and the Levis, her family doctor, Professor Luzzatti, and a child, Regina, who plays with her at Villa Borghese. She is fascinated by Jews, because both Anne Marie and the nuns at school consider them to be different. Yet, she cannot see the difference. The plot, in general terms, revolves around the life of the young Rosetta. The 'narrating I' is the literary construction of the adult Loy, who reflects on her childhood indifference. She frequently intervenes in the narrative, so that her readers add another point of view to the child's perception of the war, that of an adult who knows the historical events of that time and later comments on them.

La parola ebreo reports on how the perception of the Jews in Italy changed during the period of Fascism and on how the Racial Laws of 1938 and after took root in Italian society. It analyses Italian culture, tradition, history, and politics with references to the international, transnational, and macro-historical picture of persecution and deportation of Jews in Europe. It looks at the complex relationship between Pius XII, Fascism, and Nazism. At the beginning of the book, for example, the 'narrating I' reflects on the process of the persecution of the Jews in Italy and considers the influence of Nazi Germany on Fascist Italy:

> Il primo, tragico appuntamento per gli ebrei italiani è stato infatti l'ascesa al potere di Hitler, nel 1933. Qualcosa di profondamente nuovo si è fatto strada nell'immaginario degli oltre 40 milioni di abitanti della penisola. All'olio di ricino e al manganello del fascismo, ha cominciato a sovrapporsi la coreografia mortuaria e sacrificale della croce uncinata.[2]

> [For Italian Jews, the first step on the road to tragedy is in 1933 with Hitler's rise to power, when a profound shift occurs in the mind of Italy's forty million

citizens. With his appointment to the chancellery, the emblems of Italian
Fascism, its discipline and fervor, are conflated with the deathly racial program
of the Nazi swastika.][3]

These reflections on Italian society culminate in the description of the Roman
round-up and the deportation of the Jews from Rome. The book ends with the
child Rosetta's blurred memories of the evening of 16 October and with the
accurate reconstruction of the round-up that the adult narrative voice provides by
retracing the vicissitudes of her Jewish neighbours. Through narrative and historical
research, girlhood, pale, and blurred memories of that day become a vivid portrait
of discrimination, persecution, and deportation in Rome.

La parola ebreo combines the genres of autobiography, historiography, and
reportage in a hybrid form of narrative, and has been defined variously as an
autobiography, a memoir, an essay, and a philological study.[4] Each genre is then
adjusted, even deformed, to create a narrative space where the child and the adult
meet, and through which Loy reflects on the Italian Holocaust and the processes of
remembering history. In the text, Rosetta's childhood is retraced alongside the flow
of history. In 1940, Rosetta has not yet realised how the war is changing the world:
'la guerra è ancora qualcosa che non mi riguarda e in certi momenti mi appare
addirittura esaltante' [the war still does not concern me and sometimes even find it
thrilling]. Similarly, between the end of 1941 and the beginning of 1942, nothing
seems to change in Rosetta's childhood, and yet in July 1942 the child's life is about
to change: 'noi traslochiamo. È luglio [...]. La guerra ha cambiato diverse cose nella
nostra vita, anche se ancora non molte' [we're moving [...]. It's July [...] the war has
made some changes in our lives, still not that many]. In 1943, during summer, 'la
fame è entrata con prepotenza nei nostri giorni; io non ho più scarpe e indosso i
sabot [...]. Sono cresciuta e i vestiti mi vanno corti e stretti' [hunger has barrelled
his way into our daily lives. I no longer have shoes and instead wear clogs [...]. I've
grown and my clothes are all short and tight on me] (*PE*, pp. 88, 106, 115; *FW*, pp.
105, 127, 137–38).

Loy merges autobiographical elements with historiographical sources, moving
between childhood memories and the historical reflections and thoughts of the
adult she became. The narrative she thus creates is not a recollection of her lived
experience of persecution, nor of memories that were passed down to her through
her family, but is a reflection on her childhood indifference and lack of awareness,
and on the wider responsibility of the Italians for the massacre of the Jews. The
intertwining of historical documents with childhood memories forms, as the basis
for her text, a close link between fading memories, past responsibility and lack
of awareness, and present awareness, and brings a public perspective to private
memories. Millicent Marcus notes:

> Loy puts into play two forms of cognition — one lodged in the consciousness of
> the child, experiencing fragmentary perceptions of persecution history without
> awareness of their significance, and one lodged in the consciousness of the
> adult, whose knowledge of the genocidal future of the Roman Jews compels
> her to insert passages of straightforward historical reportage amidst the annals
> of childhood.[5]

This hybrid autobiographical memoir shares aspects of postmodern cultural forms prevalent in this period, which, as Linda Hutcheon suggests, foster 'the evolution of private experience to public consciousness [to] create a new critical and communal awareness of past and present errors of oppression, omission, and commission'.[6] The textual collage of *La parola ebreo* represents fragmented images of the Holocaust in Italy through the use of historical data, archival sources, and personal testimonies.

In *La parola ebreo*, as in *La Storia,* macro-history retroactively governs the narrated micro-histories: Loy's selection of memories depends on the historical events she wants to discuss. There is, though, a difference between these two works. In *La Storia*, the chronicle forms of historical data are confined to the beginning of the chapters. Loy, instead, places a constraint on her literary creativity in an attempt to report historical facts and events as part of the plot, weaving them into story of her childhood. As the quotation below shows, there is a continuity between the private and the public realms:

> Nel 1937 Hitler è al potere da quattro anni e in Germania i primi campi di concentramento hanno accanto alla sezione per i politici anche quella per ebrei [...]. Il 1937 vede anche una nuova edizione a cura di Julius Evola dei *Protocolli dei Savi di Sion* [...]. Le bambine fotografate nell'estate di quel 1937 sulla terrazza del signor Stuflesser a Ortisei [...] festeggiano il 15 agosto il ritorno di papà e mamma da un viaggio attraverso la Germania. (*PE*, pp. 17-19)

> [In 1937 Hitler has been in power for four years. In Germany the first concentration camps have areas for political prisoners and a section for Jews [...]. The same year a new edition of *The Protocols of the Elders of Zion* appears in Italian [...]. A picture taken in August 1937 on Signor Stuflesser's terrace in Ortisei shows three little girls [...] are celebrating the return of their mother and father from a trip across Germany.] (*FW*, pp. 21-23)

As mentioned, the book ends with a description of the Roman round-up, but this description works in a different way from the previous representations of 16 October analysed so far. Loy's text does not directly and centrally address the round-up. It is not a detailed chronicle, unlike *16 ottobre 1943* by Debenedetti. It does not picture the lives of ordinary fictional characters overwhelmed by the Second World War, unlike *La Storia* by Morante. Rather, Loy's text is a reflection on Italian anti-Semitism and a consideration of its path and development in society, with 16 October as the representative event of the Holocaust in Italy, but also of the moral-historical crisis of Fascism and anti-Semitism. Like the rest of the historical events described in the text, 16 October is pictured through a contrapuntal play of childhood memories and historical chronicles, which is supported by the documents and the sources Loy had gathered. It is described through quotations from history books and testimonies. The narrative is interrupted by long extracts from *Storia degli ebrei italiani sotto il fascismo* by Renzo De Felice, by depositions from the trial of Friedrich Bosshammer, and by the testimony of a young girl, Alberta Termin Levi, who managed to hide from the SS troops on 16 October. These sources are introduced by insertions such as 'racconta Renzo De Felice' [Renzo De Felice gives the following account], 'questa è parte della deposizione resa al processo di Friedrich Bosshammer' [this is part of the deposition he gave at the trial of Friedrich

Bosshammer], and 'Alberta, così si chiamava, [...] è lei a raccontare di quella mattina' [her name is Alberta [...] this is her account of that morning] (*PE*, pp. 123, 144, 138; *FW*, pp. 147, 172, 164-65).

Loy provides a range of details on the events and protagonists of the round-up, such as the 365 SS troops under the command of Captain Dannecker arriving the evening before (*PE*, p. 122; *FW*, p. 146). Other details are accompanied by her own observations within parenthesis:

> Svegliati con forti colpi alla porta [...] hanno avuto venti minuti di tempo per vestirsi e radunare il cibo per otto giorni, fare una sommaria valigia e prendere il denaro che avevano in casa (denaro che lestamente i tedeschi provvederanno a portargli via fino all'ultima lira). (*PE*, p. 122)

> [Awakened by heavy pounding on their doors, men, women, and children are given twenty minutes to get dressed and pack food for eight days, throw their things into a suitcase and take all the money they have in the house (money that the Germans will swiftly arrange to take from them, down to the last lira).] (*FW*, p. 146)

She describes how some Italians helped the Jews: 'oggi conosco storie meravigliose di persone che hanno nascosto intere famiglie dividendo per mesi il miserabile scarsissimo cibo delle tessere annonarie e sentendosi gelare le ossa a ogni scampanellata sospetta' [I know some wonderful stories of people who hid entire families, sharing for months the miserable amounts of food available from the rationing program and feeling their blood freezing at every unexpected ring of the door-bell] (*PE*, p. 131; *FW*, p. 157). Some families were warned by Catholics and were able to flee before and during the round-up: 'il pomeriggio del 15 ottobre uno stornellaro di quartiere [...] avvertì [...] di alcune voci che giravano in questura secondo cui i tedeschi quella notte sarebbero andati a prendersi gli ebrei' [on the afternoon of October 15, 1943, a neighborhood street singer [...] warned [...] he had heard talk at the police station that the Germans were planning to come that night to take away the Jews] (*PE*, p. 131; *FW*, p. 157). She notes that 237 people were set free because they were recognised by the Germans as 'non ebrei, coniugi ariani o figli di matrimonio misto, o perché appartenenti a Stati neutrali' [non-Jews, Aryan spouses, or children of mixed marriage or because they are citizens of neutral countries] (*PE*, p. 122; *FW*, p. 146).[7] She refers to Costanza Calò Sermoneta, as Morante did through the literary re-elaboration of Celeste: 'al momento dell'arresto non era in casa e raggiunse disperata la Stazione Tiburtina dove ottenne di salire sullo stesso convoglio del marito e dei figli' [was not at home when her family was arrested and ran desperately to Statione Tiburtina where she asked and was permitted to climb aboard the car that was carrying her husband and children] (*PE*, p. 123; *FW*, p. 146). She summarises diplomatic relations between the Church and Nazi Germany as they stood on 16 October:

> Il 16 ottobre, quando l'operazione *Judenrein* è avvenuta, si può dire, sotto gli occhi del Papa, a poche centinaia di metri in linea d'aria da San Pietro in Vaticano c'è stata molta agitazione e il Segretario di Stato ha convocato l'ambasciatore Weizsäcker. (*PE*, p. 123)

[The roundup operation is carried out right in front of the pope, as it were, just a few hundred meters from Saint Peter's. There is considerable agitation in the Vatican. Secretary of state Luigi Maglione summons Ambassador Weizsäcker.] (*FW*, p. 147)

At this point, out of sequence with the events of October, there is a reference to the ransom of the fifty kilos of gold:

Il 26 settembre Herbert Kappler, comandante delle SS a Roma, aveva chiesto alla comunità israelitica cinquanta chili d'oro, pena la deportazione immediata di 200 ebrei. Cinquanta chili che era stato possibile mettere insieme con grandi sacrifici tra gente che era già stata spremuta in tutti i modi dalle leggi razziali e dalla miseria della guerra, e alla cui raccolta contribuirono anche diversi 'ariani' che si presentarono al Tempio offrendo chi un anello, chi una catenina o un braccialetto (Pio XII si offrì di prestarne 12, di chili, che la comunità avrebbe potuto restituire con comodo. Ma non ce ne fu bisogno). E se l'odio antisemita dei nazisti era tristemente noto, non sembrava attribuibile ai tedeschi una frode tanto maramalda e disonorante. La crudeltà sì, ma la mancanza di parola no. (*PE*, p. 127)

[On September 26, 1943, Herbert Kappler, the SS commander in Rome, demands that the Jewish community hand over fifty kilograms of gold, lest he proceed with the immediate deportation of two hundred Jews. With great sacrifice, people who have already been squeezed in every conceivable way by the racial laws and by the suffering of war manage to put together the fifty kilos, some of which is contributed by 'Aryans' who show up at the synagogue where the gold is being collected to offer a ring, a necklace, or a bracelet. (Pius XII offers to make a loan of twelve kilos that the Jewish community can give back at a later date. But there is no need). The dastardly and shameful fraud of the gold ransom that fails to buy Jews' freedom seems too much even for the Germans. Everyone expects cruelty, but not the failure to keep their word.] (*FW*, pp. 151-52)

Loy's thoughts and comments on the event recall those of Debenedetti. Both said that the Jews considered the Germans honourable people and did not expect them to deport anyone after the payment of fifty kilos of gold. That was one of the reasons why the Jews did not leave their homes or look for refuge. Loy, like Morante, does not mention the plundering of the Jewish community and rabbinical libraries on 11 October.

Loy's depiction of the Roman round-up culminates in the documentation of the minimal information that she had found about two characters who link the history of the Holocaust to her private realm: Eva Della Seta and Giorgio Levi, her Jewish neighbours, who were both deported and died in Auschwitz. She recounts their stories and with them concludes the description of the victims of 16 October. As Maurice Actis-Grosso notes: 'alla cronologia storica [...] subentra la cronologia intimistica individuale di alcuni destini [...] che incarnano e simboleggiano con esempi umanamente tangibili i dati spaventosi della Shoah' [historical chronology [...] is replaced by the individual, intimate chronology of some destinies [...] which embody and symbolise the frightening facts of the Shoah with tangibly human examples].[8]

Engaging with History

Before considering in further detail the representation of the Roman round-up in *La parola ebreo* and its implications for the history of its literary representation which I am tracing, it is useful to briefly consider three earlier works by Loy: *La bicicletta*, *La porta dell'acqua*, and *Cioccolata da Hanselmann*.[9] They all provide interesting points of discussion for a better understanding of themes developed later in *La parola ebreo*, where we find the culmination of Loy's reflections on the Holocaust and of her research into it.

In 1974, Loy published her first novel, *La bicicletta*, and with it won the Premio Viareggio. *La bicicletta* revolves around the lives of a wealthy, upper-middle-class family at the end of the Second World War. As Sharon Wood suggests, the main characters are either disinterested in the past or, in rare cathartic moments, dazed by the precarious and yet extraordinary nature of the present which seeks to erase the past.[10] In this novel, Loy considers memory in various phases, from the necessity of bearing witness to the processes of recollection and their failure. She discusses in a very veiled manner the indifference of the social class she came from, the Italian Catholic bourgeoisie, when she describes, for instance, an empty cinema screening a documentary on the Bergen-Belsen concentration camp. In 1974, even if in purely fictional terms, she examines, and at the same time quietly denounces, a public and collective act of ignoring and forgetting the traumas of the Second World War, especially those concerning persecution. This indifference of the Italians, as will be analysed later in the chapter, is unequivocally represented and investigated in *La parola ebreo*.

In 1976, Loy published *La porta dell'acqua*, an autofiction in which she briefly depicts the Jews who populated her childhood. According to Lucamante, 'in *La porta dell'acqua* Loy aveva trattato in modo del tutto inconsapevole del dramma degli ebrei come facente parte della propria infanzia' [in *La porta dell'acqua* Loy treated the drama of the Jews in a wholly unconscious way as part of his own childhood].[11] It is only in *La parola ebreo* that Loy turns the Jewish figures represented in *La porta dell'acqua* into fully-embodied characters. In *La porta dell'acqua*, the child is both narrator and protagonist. She presents her own life and delves into her relationships with her mother, whom she feels is an absent figure, and with her nanny, Anne Marie, a young and strict woman from Alto Adige who raised her. In her presentation of the people around her, she briefly depicts some Jews because she is intrigued by them. She tells of an infant who is about to be circumcised, of Regina with whom she plays, of her neighbours the Della Seta family, and of her family doctor. In *La parola ebreo*, these Jewish characters all reappear. In the 2000 edition of *La porta dell'acqua*, Loy makes clear the kinship with *La parola ebreo* and explained that the autobiographical elements of the two texts coincide: 'questo [*La porta dell'acqua*] l'ho saccheggiato, quando ho voluto scrivere *La parola ebreo*, perchè mi servivano alcuni elementi autobiografici, così gliel'ho sottratti senza tanti scrupoli' [I ransacked this [*La porta dell'acqua*] when I wanted to write *La parola ebreo*, because I needed some autobiographical elements, so I stole it from it without scruples].[12]

Cioccolata da Hanselmann, published in 1995, revolves around the dramas of an

Italian-Swiss Catholic family during the Second World War from the perspective of the oldest daughter, Lorenza. It is divided into two parts, the first of which is set during the war: Lorenza, the narrator, is a child and has a partial understanding of what is happening to some of her relatives in Rome and in Switzerland. The second part is set after the end of the war: Lorenza has grown up and starts digging into her family affairs and reconstructs the story of a friend, the lover of her mother, Arturo, who was of Jewish origin. During the war, Arturo was persecuted but he evaded deportation because he obtained false documents and reached Switzerland. There, he hid for several months at Lorenza's family's house, before running off again one day. Only in the second part of the novel do readers get to know that Arturo left Switzerland because he had murdered the man who wanted to denounce him to the police. Loy describes in fictional terms the story of persecution and deportation by following the wanderings around Europe and the USA of her fictional character and, through him and his vital impulse for self-preservation, also deepens the kaleidoscope of images of Jews during the war.[13] She discusses phases of the history of the Second World War as experienced, interpreted, and relived within the most intimate psychological realms of her fictional characters, and uses a narrator with a partial understanding of what surrounds her and who, eventually when grown up, provides a more detailed and accurate picture of the story. Similar, but altered, narrative strategies return in *La parola ebreo*.

Loy reworked themes, characters, and narrative strategies of *La bicicletta*, *La porta dell'acqua*, and *Cioccolata da Hanselmann* in *La parola ebreo* and published it in a particularly crucial moment in Italian collective and cultural memory. Together with *Lezioni di tenebra* by Helena Janeczek and *Campo di sangue* by Eraldo Affinati in the literary field, and *La vita è bella* by Roberto Benigni and the film of *La tregua* by Francesco Rosi in cinema,[14] *La parola ebrea* contributed to the perception of 1997 as a landmark in the history of Holocaust memory and culture in Italy.[15] That year became a cardinal point for reading the cultural and cinematic sensitivities of that moment thus showing a new way of thinking, and re-thinking, about the Holocaust. In broader terms, from the mid-1990s, the theme of the Holocaust began to spread widely within culture in elusive and multi-coded forms. As Jeffrey K. Olick points out, the trauma of Auschwitz does 'not disappear with the death of the last survivor; nor is it carried through those — mainly their children — who suffered its personal ripple effects: Auschwitz remains a trauma for the narratives of modernity and morality, among others'.[16]

According to Loy, the Holocaust is an event which concerns all Europeans and indelibly stamps their lives, perspectives, and growth. In 2001 interview dedicated to *La parola ebreo*, she defined it as the tragedy 'qui a marqué l'Europe [...], un événement terrible qui nous concerne et nous interpelle tous, juif ou non. Personne ne peut se considérer étranger à cette horreur. Nous sommes tous concernés parce que nous avons tous laissé faire' [which marked Europe [...], a terrible event which concerns and challenges us all, Jews and non-Jews. No one can consider themselves a stranger to this horror. We are all implicated because we all let it happen]. She revealed a shared sense of guilt, which originates in the indifference shown during the time of discrimination against the Jews and their persecution. Talking of her text, she commented: 'je [...] voulais [...] seulement exprimer de réflexions auxquelles je tenais particulièrement' [I [...] just wanted [...] to express reflections which I particularly cared about].[17] She felt the need to share her belated awareness of the Italian Holocaust and her own research into it:

> Pendant de nombreuses années j'avais comme effacé ce souvenir dramatique de ma mémoire mais il a fini par resurgir et maintenant je ne peux plus l'oublier. C'est la lecture [...] qui m'a réveillée de cette espèce de léthargie er poussée à m'intéresser à l'horreur de l'antisémitisme. Ensuite, cette thématique est enracinée en moi, c'est comme si je m'étais arrêtée à cette époque-là.[18]

> [For many years I had somehow erased this dramatic memory from my own memory, but it ended up resurfacing and now I can no longer forget it. It was the act of reading [...] that woke me up from this sort of lethargy and prompted me to take an interest in the horror of anti-Semitism. Then, this theme rooted itself in me, it's as if I had stopped at that time.]

Literature is the means by which she re-appropriated her past and forgotten memories, and assumed the burden of memory and recollection, thus becoming a 'vicarious witness', as defined by Froma Zeitlin.[19] Her obsessive quest for knowledge about the Holocaust turns into a need to share her belated historical research through the medium of literature. *La parola ebreo* is her farewell to Signora della Seta and the Levis and the means of retelling the stories of them and of all those who died, forgotten, in Auschwitz.

Loy's desire to represent a past of discrimination, persecution, and deportation can be seen as a belated second-generation coming to the Holocaust, therefore falling into Hirsch's category of 'postmemory' even though Loy was not born after the war and, most importantly, was not Jewish. Unlike Debenedetti and Morante, who had lived through the war in their adulthood and had been discriminated against by the Fascist regime and persecuted by the Nazi occupiers, Loy did not live through the trauma of discrimination, persecution, and deportation and, as a child, did not perceive the war until it had begun to undermine her world. And yet, she felt the need to tell, through her tangential perspective of a Catholic, of the experiences and stories of those Jews whom she knew.[20]

As a work of postmemory, *La parola ebreo* is an inter- and trans-generational act of transfer, as will be discussed later on in this chapter in relation to Rigney's categories. Loy wrote about her parents' generation for both her own generation and younger ones: 'J'ai décidé de raconter toute cette triste histoire pour les jeunes générations qui ne la connaissent pas' [I decided to tell this sad story for the younger generations who do not know it].[21] Once again, narrating becomes a means of remembering and of inviting people to reflect upon the past and change their perception of it. Loy's commitment to recounting the Holocaust can be read as a political, civic, and ethical endeavour shared with writers of the late 1990s. It is social and cultural, in the conventional sense of passing on a message. However, it also needs to be read in relation to the evolution of the perception that Loy had of herself as a writer. When she decided to become a writer, she defied the expectations of her family. As she confessed in an unpublished interview to Sharon Wood: 'non era cosa concepita nella mia famiglia una donna che scrive' [a woman who writes was inconceivable in my family].[22] As Wood suggests, 'the rebellion was for a long time accompanied by a deep sense of doubt and guilt about her activity as a writer'; she points out that Loy found it difficult 'letting the world know that she wrote, [and therefore] seeking public recognition'.[23] Following this argument, Ursula Fanning refers to the evolution of peritextual elements in Loy's books and indicates that, before *La parola ebreo*, Loy always entrusted to other scholars and critics the peritext of her publications. Fanning convincingly suggests that such a 'pattern might well indicate Loy's early discomfort with the role of woman writer [...] which is overcome only slowly [...]. By the time [of] *La parola ebreo* [...], Loy seems comfortable directly addressing the reader in her postscript'.[24]

In the postscript to *La parola ebreo*, a bibliographical note, Loy guides her readership in the interpretation of her work, explaining that:

> Questa memoria autobiografica non è un saggio ma neppure un racconto di fantasia e chiama specificatamente in causa fatti e avvenimenti storici realmente accaduti. Mi sono trovata quindi nella necessità di *sottoporre a continue verifiche la mia narrazione*, e per obbligo filologico ma soprattutto *per rendere un servizio al lettore*, mi limito a dare notizia dei principali testi da cui sono state tratte le notizie riguardanti gli avvenimenti raccontati. (*PE*, p. 149, my emphasis)

> [This autobiographical memoir is not an essay but not even a fictional story and it specifically calls into question facts and historical events that really happened. I, therefore, found myself needing *to subject my narration to continuous checks*, and, out of philological obligation but above all *to render a service to the reader*, I limit myself to giving notice of the main texts from which the information concerning the events narrated was taken.][25]

The bibliographical note helps us to understand Loy's evolving perspective of her role as a writer, of her role as a writer within society. This evolution coincides, I think, with her willingness to write unequivocally about the Holocaust and to create with her book a conduit for information about it. With the expression 'rendere un servizio al lettore', for example, she demonstrates her need to inform people about the Holocaust by providing stories of discrimination and persecution from the unexpected perspective of a Catholic child and a Catholic woman.

With her acknowledgments and bibliography, Loy emphasises the trustworthiness of her text. The works cited in the bibliography contextualise and corroborate Loy's memories within a historical panorama, as well as providing further scope for her readers to widen their knowledge of the past events. The list of thirteen books is divided into five groups. The cited volumes represent her starting-point for an approach to the themes of the Racial Laws in Italy, the Second World War, Italian Jews between 1933 and 1945, the encyclical *Humani Generis Unitas*, and the protests of the Dutch bishops in 1942. Her research is not limited to Italian historiography. It includes several foreign works.[26]

By turning away from fiction and confining her writing to memories and historical facts and documentation, Loy draws her readers into the debate around literary narratives dedicated to the discussion, exploration, and representability of the Holocaust. Her stylistic and narrative techniques reveal to her readers the complexity of contemplation and representation of the Holocaust. The back-and-forth movements between the periods before, during, and after the war until the present-day transport readers from a personal to a historical perception of the events. In the autobiographical passages, readers are projected into the re-elaboration of her childhood memories, into her apartment in via Flaminia, for example. In the the historical passages, they become aware of the process of her writing, which employs dispassionate accounts of historical data glossed by the personal thoughts, doubts, and concerns of the 'narrating I' and so invites them to ask collective questions such as: 'cosa si aspettavano da noi?' [What did they expect from us?] (*PE*, p. 130; *FW*, p. 156). 'Noi' represents the collectivity to which Loy belongs and to which she dedicates her text.

From the very beginning of her book, Loy is acutely conscious of her readers. The text starts, as already noted, with the narrator's recollection of the first time she heard the word *ebreo*: 'se vado indietro nel tempo e penso a come la parola "ebreo" è entrata nella mia vita, mi vedo seduta su una seggiolina azzurra nella camera dei bambini' [if I go back in time and think of when I first heard the word *Jew*, I see myself sitting on a little blue chair in the nursery] (*PE*, p. 3; *FW*, p. 3). Readers are invited to approach the story they will be told and the memories the narrator will share with them, entering Loy's 'camera dei bambini', a real as well as a metaphorical place. The child is looking out of the window, the family she sees in the opposite building attracts her, she asks her governess if they are celebrating a baptism. She is told that they are Jews: 'sono ebrei aggiunge accennando con il mento al di là della finestra, loro i bambini non li battezzano, li circoncidono. Ha detto "beschneiden" con una smorfia di disgusto' ['they are Jews', she adds, gesturing towards the window with her chin. 'They don't baptize their babies, they circumcise them', she explains, using the German, *beschneiden*, with a grimace of disgust] (*PE*, p. 3; *FW*, pp. 3–4). From that moment, the child starts thinking of the Catholic and Jewish worlds as separate and distinct. The German word *beschneiden* and its root *schneiden* become the embodiment of the supposed Jewish otherness, a dichotomy between 'us' and 'them' as if these two worlds were incomparable and inassimilable. The child unconsciously but constantly questions this dichotomy and otherness for the rest of the book: 'Al di là di quelle finestre vedo passare bambine con i fiocchi in testa *simili* al mio, signore con perle al collo e i corpi fasciati da morbidi vestiti di maglia *come* quelli della mamma' [Inside the apartment across the street I can see little girls with bows in their hair *just like* mine, and ladies wearing pearl necklaces, draped in soft knit dresses *like* the ones my mother wears] (*PE*, p. 4; *FW*, p. 4, my emphasis). With 'simili' and 'come', she starts to compare the two worlds and silently wonders about the difference between them, even doubts if there is one. And so, Loy leads her readers to understand the gradual process of 'othering' that the Jews were subjected to at this point, to reflect on how their stories of discrimination and persecution have been forgotten, and to consider the responsibility that Italians bear for the deportations. These three phases are also three lenses through which her text reads this history: otherness, oblivion, and responsibility.

Otherness, Oblivion, and Responsibility

The 'narrating I' describes the victims of the round-up as fading in her childhood memories. Imagine a void which engulfs the victims of the Holocaust in darkness and oblivion. It represents the abyss into which the Roman Jews metaphorically fall and their stories vanish, where individuality is erased, and the victims become a nameless mass. Imagine silences, the silence the Jews left behind with their death, and the silence of the non-Jewish Italians, their sense of guilt and indifference. The void is the picture of the fading memory of both the child and the Roman collectivity.

The 'narrating I' plumbs the depths of this void and recognises among the victims those Jews who were constant figures during her childhood. She retraces the fluctuations in the lives of two of her neighbours: Signora Della Seta, a middle-aged woman, and Giorgio Levi, a young boy who loved playing Chopin. Her voice and her words become instrumental in giving expression to their stories. While the young Rosetta is slowly forgetting them as their images disappear from her memory, and the reader in turn sees them vanishing, it is the 'narrating I' who retrieves them from oblivion and creates a space for their stories. It is through her description of these two characters that Loy confronts the themes of otherness, of oblivion, and of Italian responsibility for the persecution of the Jews.

At the beginning of the narrative, the 'narrating I' introduces both Signora Della Seta and the Levis as Jews. She suggests a sort of otherness: 'La signora Della Seta è ebrea. Abita accanto a noi' [Signora Della Seta is Jewish. She lives next door] (*PE*, p. 4; *FW*, p. 4). The child sees Signora Della Seta as old; she describes her kindness and caring:

> La signora Della Seta [...] è vecchia, così almeno sembra a me. Quando sono malata viene a trovarmi, io ho la febbre e il mio corpo scompare nel grande letto matrimoniale in camera della mamma. La signora Della Seta ha i capelli grigi raccolti in una retina. Mi porta un regalo [...]. Mi sembra un regalo bellissimo [...]. Adoro la signora Della Seta, *anche se* è ebrea. (*PE*, p. 4, my emphasis)

> [Signora Della Seta [...] is old, or at least she seems to me. One day when I'm sick she comes to visit. I have a fever and am lying in my mother's room in the huge double bed, where my body is all but swallowed up. Signora Della Seta's gray hair is rolled up in a net. She has a present for me [...]. I love Signora Della Seta, *even though* she's Jewish.] (*FW*, pp. 4-5)

The child is torn: she is influenced by the idea of Jewish otherness that her governess, her parents, and the nuns at her schools have instilled in her, yet she grows fond of this Jewish woman. The adversative conjunction 'anche se' reveals the child's unresolved perception of Signora Della Seta, a confusion of feelings: from the child's perspective, it seems that Signora Della Seta should be loved, and yet should not be loved because of her Jewishness. Loy considers the influence of nurture in several of her other works,[27] and in an interview in 1988 she explained:

> Ritengo di grande importanza la piattaforma da cui si parte [...]. Il punto di partenza, la visuale che si ha dalla propria 'camera della nascita', mi sembra sia determinante. Come se noi iniziassimo a guardare con un asse ottico nel fondo

della pupilla e l'inclinazione iniziale condizionasse poi l'angolazione dello sguardo.[28]

[I believe the platform from which we start everything is of great importance [...]. The starting-point, the view from one's 'birth room', seems to me to be decisive. As if we started looking, on an optical axis, into the depth of the pupil and the initial inclination influenced the angle of the gaze.]

In *La parola ebreo*, the 'narrated I' distances herself from her own 'camera della nascita' when she reveals her affection for Signora Della Seta. From that point, she starts to compare her world with the unknown and intriguing Jewish world. She is fascinated by Regina, one of the Jewish characters from *La porta dell'acqua*. Rosetta meets her at Valle Giulia, a playground in the centre of Rome:

> Poco lontano dalle panchine c'è a volte un'altra bambina destinata *come* me alla solitudine che rimesta la ghiaia con una paletta colorata, accovacciata sulle gambe. Vedo le sue mutandine bianche, delle mutandine Petit bateau *uguali* a quelle che Anne Marie mi infila ogni mattina. Anche io mi piego sulle gambe e la guardo. È bionda e i capelli le scendono giù ondulati intorno al viso dalla pelle chiarissima. Mi piacerebbe avere la sua paletta. Al collo porta una stella d'oro [...]. *Sono affascinata* da quella stella che dondola al sole sprizzando scintille [...]. Quella stella adesso mi sembra piena di *mistero*. *Invidio* quella bambina che la porta invece della mia ispida mediettina. (PE, pp. 6-7, my emphasis)

> [Sometimes there's another little girl on her own, crouched near the benches, stirring the gravel around with a colored shovel. I can see her underpants, the large white kind we call petit bateau, *just like* the one Anne Marie slips on me every morning. I squat on the gravel as well and look at her. She is blond and her wavy hair falls down around her very fair skin. I'd like to have her shovel. Around her neck she wears a gold star [...]. *I am fascinated* by her star as it dangles in the sun [...]. Now the star seems full of *mystery*. *I am jealous* of the girl who can wear that instead of my plain old medallion.] (FW, pp. 7-8)

The child, who in this passage is the narrator, stresses the similarities between herself and the other child with words such as 'come' and 'uguale'. She sees the Jews as different but not as others and finds both similarities and differences between these two worlds.

The Levi family lives in the same building as Rosetta, on via Flaminia: 'al piano di sopra abitano i Levi. Loro sono più rumorosi della signora Della Seta, si sente spesso suonare il pianoforte [...]. Ci incontriamo [...] sulle scale o in ascensore [...]. Anche loro, dice Anne Marie, sono ebrei' [our upstairs neighbors are the Levis. They are noisy. Sometimes I can hear them playing the piano [...]. We see them only on the stairs or on the elevator [...]. Anne Marie says they are Jewish as well] (PE, p. 4; FW, p. 5). Their lives cross, she hears them and meets them. She describes them as a bourgeois family, fully integrated in the society around them. Giorgio Levi and her brother play together:

> Suona alla porta e chiama mio fratello per andare a giocare a pallone a Villa Borghese. Giorgio ha un anno in più, è alto e ha i capelli scuri e ondulati, lo sguardo allegro di chi è impaziente di precipitarsi giù dalle scale per raggiungere i compagni di gioco. (PE, pp. 4-5)

[[He] rings our doorbell and asks my brother to play soccer with him in the Villa Borghese. Giorgio is a year older than my brother. He has dark wavy hair and the cheerful face of a boy who lives to race down the stairs to play outside with his friends.] (*FW*, p. 5)

The promulgation of the Racial Laws makes this family formally different and isolated. Initially, the 'narrated I' does not realise it: 'niente in quell'inverno del 1939 viene a turbare l'ordine di via Flaminia [...]. Neanche mi sono accorta che Giorgio Levi ha smesso di suonare alla porta per andare con mio fratello a giocare a pallone' [nothing in that winter of 1939 disturbs the orderly course of life in via Flaminia [...]. I haven't noticed that Giorgio Levi has stopped ringing our bell to go to play football with my brother] (*PE*, p. 57; *FW*, p. 69). Nonetheless, her perspective on the world is about to change:

> Urla nell'androne: il contendente è l'ascensore. La portiera Elsa [...] urla [...]. Ha gli occhi azzurro scuro Elsa, limpidi e feroci [...]. Non l'ho mai sentita gridare così, la sua voce è acuta, aggressiva. Giorgio Levi è appena entrato reggendo la bicicletta e fermo sul pianerottolo aspetta l'ascensore. Lei gli urla che la bicicletta non può metterla nell'ascensore, e neanche nella guardiola o da qualsiasi altra parte, e ancora urla che comunque sarebbe meglio che l'ascensore, lui, non lo prendesse per niente [...] perché *non ne ha diritto* [...]. Senza parlare il ragazzo solleva allora la bicicletta e comincia faticosamente a salire le scale. (*PE*, p. 58, my emphasis)

> [Screaming in the foyer, a fight over the elevator. Elsa, the concierge's wife, [...] is screaming [...]. Elsa's deep blue eyes are fierce [...]. I've never heard her yell like this; her voice is shrill and aggressive. Giorgio Levi has just come from outside, carrying his bicycle, and he's standing on the landing waiting for the elevator. She screams at him that he mustn't put the bicycle in the elevator, or in the concierge's office, or anywhere else for that matter, and screams again that it would be better if he didn't use the elevator at all, first because *he has no right* to use it [...]. Without saying a word the boy picks up the bicycle and starts to struggle up the stairs.] (*FW*, p. 70)

In Elsa's shouts and screams lies Italian responsibility for the exclusion and segregation of the Jewish population. Awakening the young Rosetta, they reveal to her for the first time acts of discrimination and of persecution. She does not understand these acts and starts to wonder, for the first time, whether she sees Jews as different because they are literally marked as such by those around her, or whether, rather, between Jews and Catholics there is no difference: 'se i neonati vengono lasciati in un cesto davanti alla porta, chi mi può assicurare che mi abbiano lasciato davanti alla porta giusta e non fossi destinata invece a quella subito accanto, la porta dei Della Seta?' [if newborn babies arrive in basket outside the door, who can assure me that I was left outside the right door, that I wasn't meant for the Della Seta's?] (*PE*, p. 59; *FW*, p. 71). She has no answer but, with this thought, keeps reflections on Jewish otherness in the reader's mind.

Loy calls upon historical data to explain how the Racial Laws removed the Jews' civil rights and so othered them:

> In pratica 48032 italiani di religione o di famiglia ebraica, che nel mese di ottobre
> erano ancora *cittadini* a pieno diritto, a novembre si ritrovano trasformati in
> 'persone di razza ebraica' e come tali, oltre che schedati, privati di quello 'status'
> garantito a tutti i loro connazionali [...]. Isolati dal resto della popolazione
> queste 48000 'persone' si ritrovano da un giorno all'altro alla mercé della
> benevolenza dei loro ex concittadini che non di rado cederanno alla tentazione
> di approfittarne. Nell'arco di un mese, senza alcuna colpa, sono diventati *merce*
> di scambio con il glorioso alleato tedesco. (*PE*, p. 48, my emphasis)

> [For all practical purposes, 48,032 Italians of the Jewish religion or from
> Jewish families who in the month of October were still full *citizens* with all
> their civil rights intact now find themselves in November transformed into
> 'persons of Jewish race', and as such, besides being recorded on a separate list,
> they are deprived of the status enjoyed by the rest of their fellow Italians [...].
> Isolated from the rest of the population, these 48,000 'persons' find themselves
> from one day to the next at the mercy of their former fellow-citizens, who not
> infrequently will give in to the temptation to take advantage of the situation. In
> the space of one month, through no fault of their own, the Jews have become
> bargaining *chips* in negotiations with the country's glorious German ally.] (*FW*,
> pp. 58-59)

They are transformed from 'cittadini' into 'persone' and then into 'merce'. In the
choice of these words, Loy implicitly invites readers to reflect upon how the Jewish
people began to be considered as things. By the end of the book, the 'narrating I'
questions the dichotomy between Jews and non-Jews:

> I Levi non si sono difesi e non sono riusciti a immaginare l'inconcepibile [...].
> Per troppo tempo avevano condiviso con *noi* giornate tristi e felici, paure, viltà,
> speranze. Erano saliti e scesi per le medesime scale, avevano bevuto lo stesso tè
> e girato il cucchiaino nella tazza parlando la medesima lingua: in senso lessicale,
> ma anche nel senso dei sentimenti. Troppo tempo, per sentirsi *altri*. (*PE*, pp.
> 135-36, my emphasis)

> [The Levis did not defend themselves and were unable to imagine the
> inconceivable [...]. For too long they had shared with *us* happy days and sad,
> fears, cowardice, hopes. Going up and down the same stairs, drinking the
> same tea, stirring the spoon in the cup, they had spoken the same language, in
> the lexical sense but also in the emotional sense, for far too long to think of
> themselves as *other*.] (*FW*, p. 162)

The Levis specifically and the Italian Jews more broadly had shared with the rest
of the Italians a sense of belonging to their own nation, social history, and culture.
Loy transmits this in her choice of words: 'condiviso', 'medesime', 'stesso', and
'medesima' show that they are not other. She bridges the distance between 'us' and
'them' so that the otherness to which the Jews had been confined collapses.

   To the notion of 'otherness', Loy then progressively adds the theme of 'oblivion'.
When the child admits that 'i Levi e Della Seta si erano [...] impalliditi nel mio
ricordo' [the Levis and Della Setas have already become pale memories], the
'narrating I' intervenes and explains that 'dovranno accadere cose terribili perché io
torni a visitare quel tempo e guardi nel pozzo dove la signora Della Seta, i Levi [...]
stanno scivolando giù senza che ne arrivi il minimo fruscio' [some terrible things

will happen to make me go back and visit that time, to look down into the well that Signora Della Seta, the Levis [...] are sliding into with not the slightest sound] (*PE*, pp. 121, 57; *FW*, pp. 145, 69).

The child Rosetta's fleeting memories of Signora Della Seta and Giorgio Levi are transformed by the 'narrating I' into a chronicle of their lives once they have been captured by the SS officers. Their vanished figures re-assume clear profiles only after historiographical research.

During the war, Signora Della Seta becomes more and more evanescent, turning into an opaque image of an old woman with grey hair, increasingly ill-defined:

> L'aria che entra dalle finestre spalancate fa appena ondulare la sua gonna di seta plissé, solleva qualche capello grigio sulla sua fronte pallida. I tratti del suo viso *si cancellano* nella grande luce di luglio, *si perde* il contatto delle sue mani e il timbro della voce nel grande silenzio che la circonda. Questa è l'ultima volta che la vedo e appoggio le labbra sulla sua guancia rugosa. (*PE*, pp. 107-08, my emphasis)

> [The light breeze coming in through the wide-open windows makes her pleated silk skirt flutter just slightly and lifts a few grey hairs off her pale forehead. The features of her face *are erased* by the bright light of July, the touch of her hands and the timber of her voice *are lost* in the great silence that surrounds her. This is the last time I will see her, and I rest my lips on her wrinkled cheek.] (*FW*, p. 128)

When the 'narrating I' intervenes and looks back on these childhood memories, she feels a sense of guilt and starts to ask herself questions:

> In quella giornata di luglio *la sua immagine si è dissolta* lasciando nella memoria un'impronta quasi fosse stampata in trasparenza su una garza, senza che sia possibile, mai più ritrovarne il corpo [...]. Senza sospettare che quell'immagine [...] si insinuava inavvertita nella nostra coscienza [...]. Presenza tenace e inoppugnabile che ripropone ancora oggi senza risposta possibile quella domanda: 'Perché lei? Perché quell'interminabile atroce viaggio verso la morte?' Perché non si è messa al sicuro e non ha alleggerito di questo ingombrante fardello noi, cattolici, apostolici, romani, battezzati in San Pietro. (*PE*, pp. 108-09, my emphasis)

> [*Her image dissolves* on that July morning, leaving its marks on my memory as if silk-screened onto fabric [...]. Without our suspecting it, the figure left behind [...] is insinuating itself in our memory [...]. Its tenacious, irresistible presence poses its question even today, with no possible response: Why her? Why that terrible journey toward death? Why didn't she seek safety sooner and relieve us of this unbearable burden, we Roman apostolic Catholics, baptized in Saint Peter's, raised in the love of Christ, in the memory of his Passion?] (*FW*, p. 130)

In October 1943, Signora Della Seta's flat was empty. The child does not wonder where she might have gone, it is the adult who tries to reconstruct her story. She gathers very little information; she does not mention her sources:

> *A lungo ho cercato* di conoscere la sorte della signora Della Seta. Nessuno era tornato e l'appartamento di via Flaminia era stato venduto, i Della Seta deportati a Auschwitz erano stati molti e io non conoscevo il suo nome. Alla fine, quando non ci speravo più, *l'ho ritrovata*. In quell'ottobre del'43 *Eva Della*

> *Seta* si era rifugiata insieme al fratello in una villa che avevano a Chianni [...].
> Qualcuno del paese li ha traditi, o forse venduti [...]. Non ci sono superstiti a
> raccontare. Il 20 aprile del 1944 [...] sono stati prelevati e portati in carcere a
> Firenze [...]. Il treno composto da numerosi vagoni merci su cui era stata stesa
> della paglia, è partito da Firenze il 16 maggio [...]. Eva Della Seta Di Capua è
> presumibilmente entrata nella camera a gas appena scesa dal treno il 23 maggio
> 1944. (*PE*, pp. 144-47, my emphasis)

> [I tried *for a long time* to find out about the fate of Signora Della Seta. Nobody
> returned to the apartment in via Flaminia and it was sold. The Della Setas
> deported to Auschwitz were quite numerous and I didn't know her first name.
> At last, when I'd lost all hope, *I found her.* In that October of 1943 *Eva Della
> Seta* found refuge together with her brother in a villa they had in Chianni [...].
> Someone in the town betrayed them or perhaps sold them [...] There are no
> survivors to tell the story. On 20 April, 1944 [...] they were picked up and taken
> to a jail in Florence [...]. The train, made up of a large number of freight cars
> with straw spread on the floor, left Florence on May 16 [...]. Eva Della Seta di
> Capua presumably entered the gas chamber immediately after getting off the
> train on May 23, 1944.] (*FW*, pp. 172-75)

The 'narrating I' brings back from the void a memory of one of the many Jewish
victims of Fascism and Nazism.

Giorgio's disembodiment starts at the end of 1941. Rosetta has a blurred, remembered image of him on his bicycle. She sits on the bus with her schoolmates. Giorgio
is isolated and alone. He has been excluded from school and goes to a Jewish school
in Trastevere: 'qualche volta, ancora assonnata, lo vedo dai vetri del piccolo autobus
che ci porta a scuola mentre pedala veloce verso Lungotevere, la bicicletta che
sobbalza sulle rotaie del tram' [sometimes as I ride, still sleepy-eyed, on our school
bus I can see him pedalling quickly along the river road, his bicycle bouncing
over the tram tracks] (*PE*, p. 98; *FW*, p. 117). He too is slowly falling into the void
of oblivion. On 16 October, Rosetta is informed that the Levi family have been
captured that morning, but in a few hours she forgets about them. She is indifferent,
innocently so:

> A informare papa è il portiere: i Levi sono stati portati via dalle SS quella
> mattina alle sei. Dei Della Seta, Domenico non sa niente; da alcuni giorni
> hanno lasciato la casa senza avvisare nessuno. Ma i Levi e i Della Seta erano già
> impalliditi nel mio ricordo. (*PE*, p. 121)

> [It was the concierge who informs Papa: the Levi family was taken away by the
> SS that morning at six. As for the Della Seta family, Domenico knows nothing.
> They left the house a few days ago without telling anybody.] (*FW*, p. 145)

It is the 'narrating I', again, who retraces the story of the Levis, and brings it back
from the void. Loy had found a testimony which refers to Giorgio's experience. It is
a long quotation composed of a first-hand testimony to his capture from his cousin
Alberta Termin Levi. It interrupts the narrative:

> La storia del 'ragazzo dei Levi' la conosco bene perché in seguito a una di
> quelle circostanze impreviste che di colpo aprono un buco sulla storia, ho
> potuto vederla attraverso gli occhi di una ragazza che era con lui la mattina che
> vennero a prenderlo. (*PE*, pp. 137-38)

[The story of Giorgio Levi is one I know well. By one of those unforeseen coincidences that suddenly opens up a piece of history I was able to hear it from a girl who was with him the morning they were deported.] (*FW*, p. 164)

While it is intrinsically impossible to offer complete attestations of Eva's and Giorgio's stories, Loy is committed to providing at least a snapshot of their lives. Here we can draw a contrast with Debenedetti and Morante, neither of whom describe the lives of the victims of the round-up before or after 16 October. Loy instead gives a more detailed account of the lives of Signora Della Seta and the Levis because of the role they played in her childhood. By remembering them, she admits her innocent complicity in anti-Semitism and her indifference towards the victims of the Holocaust as a child. By recollecting, writing, and publishing the stories of Signora Della Seta and Giorgio Levi, she encourages readers to reflect on what non-Jewish Italians, they themselves, did not see or do. Their responsibility towards the victims of the Holocaust is the third lens through which we can view her representation of the Roman round-up. Actis-Grosso comments that:

> Una *maturazione etica* si è dunque concretizzata in questo volume, non in termini di *liberazione interiore* propriamente detta poiché la riconoscenza del peccato in questo caso preciso non lo cancella ma ne perpetua il ricordo, ma in termini di *pacificazione intima*.[29]

[An *ethical maturation* has therefore materialised in this volume, not in terms of proper *inner liberation* because the acknowledgement of sin in this specific case does not cancel it but perpetuates its memory, but in terms of *intimate pacification*.]

The retrospective consideration of the 'narrating I' explicitly narrates her own childhood indifference and implicitly deals with the collective one:

> E la sera del 16 ottobre, *l'allieva di seconda media che corrisponde all'autrice di queste righe*, chiamata per recitare il Rosario, aveva sbuffato di noia come tutte le altre sere lasciando che le palpebre le calassero giù nel cantilenare delle ave marie e dei paternoster; senza che le passasse per la mente di supplicare *il suo Dio, che era anche quello dei Levi e dei Della Seta*, perché mandasse in loro soccorso l'Angelo Sterminatore. Senza avvertire alcun impulso di gridare, di fare qualcosa per quel ragazzo dallo sguardo allegro che suonava alla porta, il pallone di cuoio stretto sotto il braccio. Di preoccuparsi del destino di quella signora dai capelli grigi che entrava nella stanza tappezzata di verde simile a una foresta dove mi perdevo, calda di febbre, nel grande letto matrimoniale [...]. I pensieri di quella bambina non più bambina (sono un metro e sessanta e porto il 38 di scarpe) non sono in quella sera di ottobre molto diversi dal solito, in massima parte occupati dai bigliettini che attraverso un sistema di carrucole e di spaghi si scambia attraverso il balcone con le bambine Calcagno al piano di sotto. (*PE*, 136-37, my emphasis)

[And on the evening of October 16, *the student this writer once was*, recites the rosary, sighing with boredom as she does every evening, letting her eyelids drop amid the singsong of the Hail Marys and Our Fathers. She does not give the slightest thought to supplicating *her God, who after all is also the God of the Levis and the Della Setas*, to send the avenging angel down to help them. She feels no impulse to scream, to do something for that boy with the cheerful face who used to ring their bell, his leather ball tucked tightly under his arm. No need to concern herself with the fate of the woman who came into the semi dark room where a child lay, hot with fever in a big double bed [...]. On that night of October 16, the thoughts of that girl who was no longer little (by now five foot three and wearing size 8 shoes) aren't much different from usual, focused mainly on the notes she exchanges, by way of an elaborate system of pulleys and strings, with the Calcagno girls, who live in the apartment under hers.] (*FW*, pp. 163-64)

This passage is near the end of the book and is crucial to our analysis. The 'narrating I' explicitly states that the God she carelessly prays to is the same as the God of Signora Della Seta and Giorgio Levi. She definitively denies the otherness of Jews. Then she reveals for the first and only time within the narrative her autobiographical pact. The 'narrating I' never mentions either her first or her last name, but in this passage she describes the protagonist as 'l'allieva di seconda media che corrisponde all'autrice di queste righe'. Her autodiegetic narration has so far been implicit. This revelation of her identity only at this point can be read as a means by which Loy makes her family and herself part, and representative, of the Roman collectivity. She pictures vicissitudes with which everybody can identify, the episodes describing her family could be describing anyone in the collective, their indifference and blindness epitomise those of Catholic Italians in general:

> Nessuno ha trovato il coraggio per impedire agli uomini di Dannecker di far rimbombare i loro stivali su per le scale di via Flaminia 21 e irrompere nelle loro stanze. Nessuno ha fermato i camion che si allontanavano con uomini e donne, bambini svegliati orrendamente dal sonno. Pio XII non è comparso bianco e ieratico alla stazione di Trastevere per mettersi davanti al convoglio fermo sul binario e impedirne la partenza [...]. È rimasto chiuso dietro le finestre della sua stanza dove si alzavano in brevi voli i canarini Hänsel e Gretschen. Neanche mio padre e mia madre, che di sicuro avranno provato pietà per il destino dei Levi, hanno dimenticato per un giorno i fogli di francobolli e la carne e il pane, le uova. (*PE*, p. 136)

> [Nobody summons the courage to stop Dannecker's men from thundering up the stairs in their boots at 21 via Flaminia and bursting into the Levis' apartment. Nobody stops the trucks that drive away loaded with men and women and children awakened so horribly from their sleep. Pius XII does not appear, white and solemn, at the Trastevere station to stand on the tracks in front of the convoy and block its departure [...]. Pius XII stays closed behind the windows of his room, where the canaries Hansel and Gretel take off into the air on their brief flights. My father and mother, who surely must feel compassion for the Levis, do not forget, even that day, the sheets of stamps and the meat, and the bread, and the eggs.] (*FW*, pp. 162-63)

The 'narrating I' shows the child in a position of non-knowledge and partial blindness. She denounces her own near-sightedness and simultaneously reports that of the collectivity. She moves from her private realm to the collective, showing that people were only able to focus on their own lives and that they perceived the rest of the world, farther away, as a blur. They should share her sense of guilt. She excludes nobody, not even her own parents, not even Pius XII.

Constructing and Observing Cultural Memory

Rosetta Loy's work of recovery and memory in *La parola ebreo* can be fruitfully analysed through cultural memory studies and thus may usefully be compared to the texts of Debenedetti and Morante. Equally, as we saw in Part I, *La parola ebreo* can be said to have been written in a style which reflects Erll's categorisations of 'experiential' and 'reflexive' modes and assumes the connotations and functions of what Rigney's categories of 'catalyst', 'relay station', 'calibrator', and 'stabilizer'.

Loy represents the past by combining two approaches, effectively mixing what Erll defines as 'experiential' and 'reflexive' modes.[30] From the beginning of the book, there are two parallel layers of action and thought: that of the adult and that of the child. Everything happens as if the story were happening contemporaneously with the narration. Readers perceive the whole narrative in one vast and deep present where both the 'narrated I' and the 'narrating I' both use the present tense. As Gianluca Cinelli suggests, 'avviene una fusione fra i due io con l'interpolazione dei pensieri e dei sentimenti propri della scrittrice nel suo presente, consapevole a posteriori di una verità del passato che il personaggio non possiede' [a fusion occurs between the two selves with the interpolation of the writer's own present thoughts and feelings, aware a posteriori of a truth from the past that the character does not possess].[31] This simultaneity is clear from the beginning of the book, as the 'narrating I' re-elaborates the experience of the 'narrated I' and reflects on the word *ebreo* and the different connotations it has taken on, from integration to segregation to persecution:

> Se *vado* indietro nel tempo e *penso* a come la parola 'ebreo' *è entrata* nella mia vita, *mi vedo* seduta su una seggiolina azzurra nella camera dei bambini [...]. *Posso* guardare nell'appartamento al di là della strada dove dai vetri aperti le tende *dondolano* all'aria [...]. In quella casa da poco è nato un bambino, quella festa è per lui. 'Un battesimo?' *chiedo*. (*PE*, p. 3, my emphasis)

> [If I *go* back in time and *think* of when I *first heard* the word Jew, I *see* myself sitting on a little blue chair in the nursery [...]. I *can* look into the apartment on the other side of the street and see the curtains there *swinging* in the breeze [...]. Just a few days ago, the family had a new baby and the party is for him. [...] 'Is it a baptism' I *ask*.] (*FW*, p. 3)

Loy pictures the past by re-elaborating her personal experience, building on memories and observations. Although she does not stage episodic memory as the main source for her writing, the narrative relies on the specific narrative strategies of the transmission of experience. She uses modes of re-enactment and reanimation: the shift between 'experiential' and 'reflexive' modes is manifest when the narrator's voice shifts from the first-person reminiscence of the 'narrated I' to the third-person chronicle of persecution of the 'narrating I' who draws attention to the process and the problems of remembering: 'brucia dirlo ma un orlo nero segna i nostri giorni incolpevoli, senza memoria e senza storia' [there is a black border around those guiltless days of ours] (*PE*, p. 135; *FW*, p. 162). As Giuliana Minghelli suggests:

> Contained by a black rim of guilt, the ahistorical time of childhood is, from
> the beginning, transformed into a gaping hole, a well from which the path of
> memory takes its point of departure and to which it endlessly returns.[32]

In this sense, with *La parola ebreo*, the reader experiences a cognitive journey from
obliviousness to fully-fledged awareness through historical hindsight as provided
by Loy.

The passages dedicated to the Roman round-up are a clear example of the
combination of the 'experiential' and 'reflexive' modes. The 'narrated I' remembers
16 October as 'il nostro secondo giorno di scuola' [our second day [of school]] (*PE*,
p. 121; *FW*, p. 145). The few images of this personal memory project readers into
Rosetta's apartment, from where any perspective of the event is limited or made-up:

> La mamma andava raccontando di una donna che aveva appena partorito e
> ancora in camicia da notte era stata costretta dalle SS a salire su un camion
> [...]. E mentre la mamma parla *mi sembra di vederla* quella donna, disperata e
> spettinata, così come deve averla vista chi si trovava a passare di lì e ha assistito
> impietrito alla scena. (*PE*, pp. 121-22, my emphasis)

> [My mother is telling me about a woman who had just given birth when, still
> in her nightgown, she had been forced by the SS to climb onto a truck [...]. As
> my mother is talking I *can see* that woman, desperate and unkempt, just as she
> must have looked to the eyes of those who had been passing by and watched,
> petrified.] (*FW*, p. 145)

It is through historical documentation of the 'narrating I' that readers are made
aware of what happened in the middle of the ghetto — 'era sabato (sempre il sabato
sceglievano i tedeschi perché sapevano che era più facile trovare le famiglie riunite)
[...] dalle quattro del mattino avevano cominciato a sparare fra le strade del ghetto
per impedire a chiunque di uscire' [it is a Saturday (the Germans always choose
Saturday because they know it will be easier to find families together) [...] at four
o'clock in the morning they begin shoooting in the streets of the ghetto to prevent
people from leaving their houses] — and in the Vatican, 'in Vaticano c'è stata molta
agitazione' [there is considerable agitation in the Vatican] (*PE*, pp. 122, 123; *FW*,
pp. 146, 147). By parenthetically explaining the events, the 'narrating I' establishes
a relationship with her readers and draws them in.

Loy meditates on the way in which the Holocaust has been transmitted and
perceived, making her text part of the Italian cultural memory of the Holocaust,
and at the same time prompts reflections upon the processes of representation and
commemoration of it. Thus, *La parola ebreo* can be included in four of Rigney's
overlapping and permeable categories of literary text.[33]

La parola ebreo is a 'catalyst' because since 1997 it has played its part in intensifying
public interest in the Italian Holocaust.[34] It has been reprinted four times (including
an eBook) and has also been translated into seven languages: Catalan, French (to
date reprinted four times), German (reprinted three times), Dutch, Hebrew, English
(reprinted four times), and Czech. Among the authors who endorsed *La parola ebreo*
was the politician and intellectual Vittorio Foa, the father of Anna Foa, the last of
the writers to be analysed in this book. In 1997, Vittorio Foa was interviewed by
Eleonora Martelli: their discussion of *La parola ebreo* and the concept of memory

corroborates the analysis offered here. Foa felt that the particular contribution of *La parola ebreo* to an understanding of the history of the time lies in Loy's demonstration of how discrimination against the Jews, and the persecution of them, grew within Italian society:

> [Loy] costruisce, nel doppio registro di un'infanzia protetta posta accanto ad una tragedia collettiva, un punto di riferimento, una sponda, la quale ci permette di capire la tragedia proprio perché si può confrontare con una vita tranquilla [...]. Allora questo libro è tante cose: è la dimostrazione di una tragica inadempienza sociale e nazionale, della responsabilità di aver lasciato passare quella tragedia [...]. E poi c'è la rappresentazione della tragedia, che diventa comprensibile perché è posta a confronto con realtà diverse. E c'è la scrittura della Loy, che è così dolce e discreta, e allo stesso tempo avvolgente.[35]

> [[Loy] builds, in the double register of a protected childhood placed next to a collective tragedy, a point of reference, a shore, which allows us to understand the tragedy precisely because it can be compared with a peaceful life [...]. So, this book is many things: it is the demonstration of a tragic social and national failure, of the responsibility of having let that tragedy happen [...]. And then there is the representation of the tragedy, which becomes understandable because it is placed beside different realities. And there is Loy's writing, which is so sweet and discreet, yet all-embracing at the same time.]

La parola ebreo, consequently, gives new insight into the representation and recollection of 16 October and represents a benchmark for reflection on the involvement of the Catholic Church in the war, in the Holocaust, and specifically in the Roman round-up. In this sense, it can also be seen as a 'calibrator'. Furthermore, because it gives space to private, unrecorded, or little-known stories of the victims of the Jewish persecution in Italy, and because it provides an unusual, Catholic perspective on the Roman round-up, it can also be thought as a 'relay station'. Finally, it is also a 'stabilizer' because, since its publication, it has become an object of scholarly interest and cultural debate. In 1997, it won the nineteenth Premio Fregene in the category of 'Storia e civiltà contemporanea'. In 1999, Enzo Forcella included some reflections on *La parola ebreo* in *La resistenza in convento*, his book dedicated to the German occupation of Rome, in which, as we saw in Chapter 2, he reflects on the Church's involvement in the Holocaust and the deportation of the Roman Jews. Among the literary works concerning the Pope and the Holocaust, he quotes and comments on Loy, especially her condemnation of the Pope — 'Pio XII non è comparso bianco e ieratico alla stazione Tiburtina' [Pius XII does not appear, white and solemn, at the Trastevere station] — which Forcella criticises as a stereotypically common perception of Pius XII: 'un'immagine poetica quanto incongrua' [an image that is as poetic as it is incongruous].[36] In the literary field, numerous critical works have included *La parola ebreo* in their analyses of Italian literature of the Holocaust.[37] With regard to the impact it has had on Italian culture and memory of the Roman round-up and of the Holocaust, it is considered in *The Civilization of the Holocaust in Italy* by Wiley Feinstein and in *The Holocaust in Italian Culture* by Gordon.[38] Finally, in the historiographical field, it has been cited in books which in the last few years have developed new perspectives and sources on the historical knowledge of the round-up, such as *16 ottobre 1943* by Pezzetti and *L'interprete di Auschwitz* by Rigano.[39]

At the threshold of the new millennium, Loy's text represented a new attempt to reflect upon the past, and a new means of transmitting historical knowledge. By describing the processes of discrimination and persecution, it encouraged readers to take an interest in the Italian responsibility for the events of the Second World War. Before the publication of Loy's work, *16 ottobre 1943* by Debenedetti and *La Storia* by Morante were the major literary texts which represented the Roman round-up.[40] By describing the people of the ghetto and inviting his readers to enter the ghetto before and during the round-up, Debenedetti encouraged an understanding of the Jewish community and an identification with the victims of Portico d'Ottavia. In *La Storia*, Morante stimulated an identification with overwhelmed characters and placed the round-up at the heart of a vast canvas of the history of the war and suffering. She re-elaborated sensory and emotional perceptions of the war and of the deportation. They both attempted to make people empathise with the story of the Jews. Loy's work, in contrast, because of its hybrid structure, does not foster a sense of identification between the reader and the protagonist, or between the reader and the victims. The back and forth between the autobiographical and the essayistic form, and between a merging of the past and present, prevents prosthetic memory from engendering itself in the reader's mind. However, Loy does evoke the lived lives of the characters before the round up, even if at a remove. She shares Morante's attempt to give space to the memories of those who fell into the void of indifference, but she does so for a collective and generational need to dig into the Italian Holocaust and Italian responsibility for it. She shows how the Roman collectivity reacted to the persecution and deportation of their Jewish fellow citizens. She invites a new generation of readers to remember that 'c'è chi gli ha voltato le spalle con stolida indifferenza e c'è chi li ha traditi e venduti per cinquemila lire' [there are those who turn away from the Jews with stolid indifference and there are those who betray them for five thousand lire]. Nonetheless, Loy leaves a glimmer of light. Between indifference and collaboration, some families were saved: 'c'è anche chi non ci ha pensato due volte a rischiare la vita per salvarli' [there are also those who don't think twice about risking their own lives to save them] (*PE*, p. 131; *FW*, p. 156). She shows how an act of recovery and responsibility in the present, such as her book, is possible.

Notes to Chapter 5

1. Key bibliography regarding Rosetta Loy's *La parola ebreo* includes: Enrico Elli, 'Storia e memoria nella narrativa di Rosetta Loy', *Vita e Pensiero*, 2 (1996), 135–44; Maurice Actis-Grosso, 'La colpa degli innocenti: una psicanalisi romanzesca: *Cioccolata da Hanselmann* e *La parola ebreo* di Rosetta Loy', *Narrativa*, 16 (1999), 35–62; Giuliana Minghelli, 'What's in a Word? Rosetta Loy's Search of History in Childhood', *MLN*, 116.1 (2001), 162–76; Stefania Lucamante, 'The "Indispensable" Legacy of Primo Levi: From Eraldo Affinati to Rosetta Loy between History and Fiction', *Quaderni d'Italianistica*, 24.2 (2003), 87–104; Luciano Parisi, 'I collage di Rosetta Loy', *Romance Studies*, 22.1 (2004), 75–82; Cesare Segre, *Tempo di bilanci* (Turin: Einaudi, 2005), pp. 279–81; Gianluca Cinelli, 'Silenzi e verità ne *La parola ebreo* di Rosetta Loy', *MLN*,

123.1 (2008), 8-21; Judith Lindenberg, 'La Religion juive ou la découverte de l'altérité dans *La parola ebreo* de Rosetta Loy', *Cahiers d'études italiennes*, 7 (2008), 45-51; Silvia Marchetti, 'Private Memory, Public History, and Testimony in Rosetta Loy's *La parola ebreo*', in *Memoria collettiva e memoria privata: il ricordo della Shoah come politica sociale*, ed. by Stefania Lucamante, and others (Utrecht: Utrecht Publishing and Archiving Services, 2008), pp. 111-22; Robert S. C. Gordon, 'Postmodernism and the Holocaust', in *Postmodern Impegno: Ethics and Commitment in Contemporary Italian Culture*, ed. by Pierpaolo Antonello and Florian Mussgnug (Bern: Peter Lang, 2009), pp. 167-88; Lucamante, *Quella difficile identità*, pp. 223-38.

2. Rosetta Loy, *La parola ebreo* (Turin: Einaudi, 1997), pp. 12-13; all further Italian quotations are taken from this edition (hereafter referenced in the main text as *PE*).

3. Rosetta Loy, *First Words: A Childhood in Fascist Italy*, trans. by Gregory Conti (New York: Metropolitan Books/ Henry Holt, 2000), p. 15; all further English quotations are taken from this edition (hereafter referenced in the main text as *FW*).

4. See for example: Cinelli, 'Silenzi e verità ne *La parola ebreo* di Rosetta Loy', pp. 17-19; Minghelli, 'What's in a Word?', p. 165.

5. Millicent Marcus, *Italian Film in the Shadow of Auschwitz* (Toronto: University of Toronto Press, 2007), p. 22.

6. Linda Hutcheon, *A Poetics of Postmodernism: History, Theory and Fiction* (New York: Routledge 1988), pp. 93-94.

7. The number of people set free is inaccurate, but that figure was still uncertain when Loy was writing her book.

8. Actis-Grosso, 'La colpa degli innocenti', p. 52.

9. Rosetta Loy, *La bicicletta* (Turin: Einaudi, 1974), *La porta dell'acqua* (Turin: Einaudi, 1976), and *Cioccolata da Hanselmann* (Milan: Rizzoli, 1995).

10. Sharon Wood, 'Rosetta Loy: The Paradox of the Past', in *The New Italian Novel*, ed. by Zygmunt Baranski and Lino Pertile (Edinburgh: Edinburgh University Press, 1993), pp. 121-38.

11. Lucamante, *Quella difficile identità*, p. 225.

12. Rosetta Loy, 'Nota', in *La porta dell'acqua* (Milan: Rizzoli, 2000), pp. 101-02 (p. 102).

13. A compelling reading of Arturo appears in Actis-Grosso, 'La colpa degli innocenti', pp. 40-51.

14. Helena Janeczek, *Lezioni di tenebra* (Milan: Mondadori, 1997); Eraldo Affinati, *Campo di sangue* (Milan: Mondadori, 1997); *La tregua*, dir. by Francesco Rosi (3 Emme Cinematografica, Stephan Films, UCG Images, Dazu film); *La vita è bella*, dir. by Roberto Benigni (Cecchi Gori Group, Melampo Cinematografica, 1997).

15. Gordon, 'Postmodernism and the Holocaust', p. 170.

16. Jeffrey K. Olick, 'Collective Memory: The Two Cultures', *Sociological Theory*, 17.3 (1999), 333-48 (p. 345).

17. Rosetta Loy, 'La Tentation autobiographique', *Magazine littéraire*, 404 (2001), 98-103 (p. 102).

18. Ibid.

19. Froma Zeitlin, 'The Vicarious Witness: Belated Memory and Authorial Presence in Recent Holocaust Literature', *History and Memory*, 10.2 (1998), 5-42.

20. Hirsch, 'The Generation of Postmemory', p. 106.

21. Loy, 'La Tentation autobiographique', p. 102.

22. Wood, 'Rosetta Loy', p. 122.

23. Ibid., pp. 121, 122.

24. Ursula Fanning, *Italian Women's Autobiographical Writings in the Twentieth Century* (Madison, NJ: Fairleigh Dickinson University Press, 2017), p. 205.

25. Interestingly this passage is not included in *FW*.

26. The foreign texts Loy cites are: Raul Hilberg, *The Destruction of the European Jews* (New Haven, CT: Yale University Press, 1961); Winston Churchill, *The Second World War*, 6 vols (Boston, MA: Houghton Mifflin Harcourt, 1948-53); and George Bensoussan, *Histoire de la Shoah* (Paris: Presses universitaires de France, 1996).

27. In *La porta dell'acqua*, for example, Rosetta's perspective is strongly influenced by the milieu in which she lives.

28. Rosetta Loy, 'Confessione d'autore', *Paragone*, 39.12 (1988), 116-21 (p. 118).

29. Actis-Grosso, 'La colpa degli innocenti', p. 62.

30. Erll, *Memory in Culture*, pp. 158-59.

31. Cinelli, 'Silenzi e verità ne *La parola ebreo* di Rosetta Loy', p. 18.

32. Minghelli, 'What's in a Word?', p. 169.

33. See Chapters 1 and 2. Rigney, 'The Dynamics of Remembrance', pp. 350-51.

34. See, for example, the following reviews: Annalisa Capristo, '*La parola ebreo*', *La Rassegna Mensile di Israel*, 63.3 (September 1997), 134-38; Patricia M. Gathercole, '*La parola ebreo*', *World Literature Today*, 72.2 (January 1998), 351; Maria Grazia Parri, '*La parola ebreo*', *Rivista di Studi Politici Internazionali*, 65.1 (January 1998), 156; Renede Ceccatty, '*Madame della Seta aussi est juive*', *Biography*, 22.3 (1999), 447.

35. Eleonora Martinelli, 'E la parola "ebreo" divenne insulto: dialogo sulla memoria con Vittorio Foa', *L'Unità*, 10 June 1997, p. 4.

36. Forcella, *La resistenza in convento*, pp. 102, 103.

37. See n. 1 above.

38. Wiley Feinstein, *The Civilization of the Holocaust in Italy: Poets, Artists, Saints, Anti-Semites* (Madison, NJ: Fairleigh Dickinson University Press, 2003), pp. 300, 333, 386; Gordon, *The Holocaust in Italian Culture*, p. 102.

39. Pezzetti, *16 ottobre 1943*, p. 123; Rigano, *L'interprete di Auschwitz*, p. 90n.

40. As noted in Chapter 2, there were at least two literary writings on the topic of the Roman round-up published between 1994 and 1996: *Il treno di piazza Giudia* (1995) by Gianni Campus, and *Gli anni rubati* (1996) by Settimia Spizzichino. See Cavaglion, 'Il grembo della Shoah'.

CHAPTER 6

❖

Anna Foa,
Portico d'Ottavia 13

An Introduction

Portico d'Ottavia 13: una casa del ghetto nel lungo inverno del '43 by Anna Foa was published in 2013 on the seventieth anniversary of the Roman round-up by Laterza, a leading publisher of both academic and popular history. In nine chapters, the book recounts the round-up on the night of 15-16 October, the subsequent deportations during the German occupation of Rome, mainly from January 1944, and the trials of the Fascist collaborators such as Celeste Di Porto, Vincenzo Antonelli, and Remo Canigiani after the war. The title and the subtitle suggest that Foa's representation of 16 October, and of the past more broadly, is confined to one building, which stands on the edge of the former ghetto: via del Portico d'Ottavia 13. On 16 October, thirty-four Jews from this building were arrested. Foa herself lived in the same building for twelve years, from 2000-12, many decades after the events of 1943. The photomontage of the book's cover shows in gloomy colours the internal courtyard of that building, introducing Foa's use of spatiality to re-elaborate the Roman round-up, examining place and micro-histories. She takes readers into the building, which she calls 'la Casa', and into its apartments. She names each resident, describes the eighteen households which lived there on 16 October, seeks to obtain information on the destiny of each family, and narrates their stories.[1]

In *Portico d'Ottavia 13*, the triangular relationship between history, memory, and literature explored throughout the book is not particularly obvious, but a close reading of it nevertheless reveals that its structure lies in the combination of historical sources, individual memories, and literary narrative techniques. Foa looks at the sources of 16 October tangentially, focusing mostly on the historical sources that related to the residents of 'la Casa' and on their testimonies and reworks them into a narrative which is easily accessible to any reader.

Foa's narrative, peritext, and paratext all reveal her approach to the representation of 16 October: the kinship between historical data and individual memories is traceable in the plot, the premise, the bibliographical note, and the acknowledgments, as well as in the interviews that Foa gave after the publication of the book.[2] As Bruno Bonomo suggests, 'il libro è basato sull'intreccio tra fonti archivistiche (carte dell'Archivio storico della Comunità ebraica romana e fascicoli processuali conservati presso l'Archivio di Stato di Roma) e fonti dell'io: diari e memorie pubblicati in tempi diversi e testimonianze orali' [The book is based on the interweaving of archival sources (papers from the Historical Archive of the Roman Jewish Community and procedural files held in the State Archive of Rome) and ego-documents: diaries and memoirs published at different times and oral testimonies].[3] Throughout the book, Foa explains that she retraced the story of 'la Casa' mainly through testimonies and archival sources, gathering statements given to the Comunità Ebraica di Roma and the Shoah Foundation, the non-profit organisation dedicated to making and collecting audio-visual interviews with survivors and witnesses of the Holocaust, and consulting the files of the trials of the Roman fascist collaborators. The trial of the Jewish woman Celeste Di Porto, for example, was particularly interesting because Di Porto's life was intertwined with those of the residents of 'la Casa':

> Il verbale dell'istruttoria in cui sono riportate molte testimonianze di ebrei romani è particolarmente ricco di particolari e significativo: è infatti quello di Celeste Di Porto, detta Stella e soprannominata, dopo la Liberazione, Pantera Nera, la giovane ebrea che denunciò molti correligionari ai fascisti e ai tedeschi e le cui vicende si intrecciano con la storia degli abitanti della Casa.[4]

> [The minutes of the investigation in which many testimonies of Roman Jews are reported are particularly rich in details and significant: indeed, it is those of Celeste Di Porto, who was also called Stella and known, after the Liberation, as Black Panther, the young Jewish woman who denounced many co-religionists to the fascists and Germans and whose history is intertwined with the history of the dwellers of la Casa.]

As discussed in Chapters 4 and 5, in Morante's *La Storia* historical events shape and direct the plot so that macro-history governs the narrated micro-histories, and in *La parola ebreo* Loy's selection of memories is determined by the historical events that she chose to discuss. In *Portico d'Ottavia 13*, it is different: it is the particular, the everyday, and the ordinary that are used to explore the macro-topics of persecution and deportation, and the involvement of the Pope and the Church. The role played by the Church, for example, is analysed at two points in the text. Foa introduces it in the third chapter when she describes what happened on 16 October to Attilio Di Veroli's family, who lived in a top-floor apartment in 'la Casa': they escaped by way of a window onto via di Sant'Angelo and found refuge in the Parrocchia di San Benedetto where Don Gregorini, a local parish priest, hid them for months:

> A piedi, evitando i blocchi, anche con l'aiuto della gente intorno, arrivarono anche loro ore dopo, intorno alle 11.30 del mattino, nella parrocchia di San Benedetto in via del Gazometro e bussarono alla porta. Rosina ricorda la risposta del parroco, don Giovanni Gregorini, quando li vide: 'Entra Attilio, che *abbiamo avuto adesso l'ordine di farvi entrare*'. (*PO13*, p. 43, my emphasis)

> [On foot, avoiding the roadblocks, also with the help of the people around, they too arrived hours later, around 11.30 in the morning, in the parish of San Benedetto in via del Gazometro and knocked on the door. Rosina remembers the response of the parish priest, Don Giovanni Gregorini, when he saw them: 'Attilio come in, *we have just been told to let you in*'.]

Foa does not immediately comment on the reported testimony, but waits until the last chapter, entitled 'Dalla microstoria alla storia' [From Micro-history to History], in which she recalls the episode and gives it more space. She interpretes Don Gregorini's phrase as possibly referring to a rescue attempt by the Church during the round-up: '"abbiamo avuto adesso l'ordine di farvi entrare", *frase molto significativa perché indica un coordinamento da parte ecclesiastica dei primi soccorsi* già subito dopo la razzia' ['we have just been told to let you in', *a most significant sentence because it indicates that the Church coordinated assistance* straight after the round-up'] (*PO13*, p. 116, my emphasis). She mentions other religious institutions which hid Jews, to corroborate the hypothesis that the Church helped the Jews of Rome during the round-up and in the months following October 1943. However, she still limits these examples to the personal memories of the residents of Portico d'Ottavia 13: 'le donne ebree rifugiate a Santa Francesca Romana mantengono i rapporti con le suore anche nel dopoguerra, le vanno a trovare, serbano vivo il loro ricordo' [Jewish women refugees in Santa Francesca Romana maintain relations with the nuns even after the war, they go to visit them and keep their memory alive] (*PO13*, p. 117). This brief but telling reference to the question of the Church and its role in protecting the Roman Jews demonstrates that in this book Foa's historical reflections on the Italian Holocaust are examined deliberately only through the personal stories of the residents of Portico d'Ottavia 13.

Portico d'Ottavia 13, in this sense, can be said to be a book of popular history, in which historical understanding comes from the account of individual experiences and vividly-narrated life stories.[5] At a book launch in 2013, Foa explained why she had revised her historical approach in order to build on ideas that have arisen in debates around the public use of history.[6] She said that she had re-evaluated her method of historical research and of writing history books because she sees individual and collective memories as essential parts of history, and the boundaries between private and public spheres as blurred. She, generally, believes in the pedagogical value of literary re-elaborations of private stories for the transmission of historical knowledge and in the perception and understanding of the public sphere through the perception and understanding of the private. According to Foa, readers develop deeper historical understanding when the characters of history have names and when life experiences, of war for example, are personalised: 'una memoria riempita di fatti, di nomi, di luoghi, di sapori, di odori, di emozioni, questo loro [i lettori] interessa e lo percepiscono come qualcosa che serve a costruire la loro cultura e il loro sapere' [a memory filled with facts, names, places, flavours, smells, emotions, this interests them [the readers] and they perceive it as something that serves to build on their culture and their knowledge].[7]

After the publication of *Portico d'Ottavia 13*, Foa continued to publish non-specialist, popular works of history in which her historical approach is combined with personal memory and narrative forms, as is evident in her family history *La famiglia F.* (2018) and in *Anime nere* (2021, co-written with Lucetta Scaraffia), which is dedicated to two women who lived in occupied Rome and were denounced as collaborators when Rome was liberated, Elena Hoehn and the above-mentioned Celeste di Porto.[8]

In *La famiglia F.* there is an interesting passage which helps with an understanding of the roots and nature of Foa's fascination with the Holocaust and more specifically with the literature dedicated to it:

> Ai campi e alla Shoah [...] ho il ricordo netto di essermi accostata ed immersa da sola, verso i sette-otto anni, quando leggevo voracemente tutto quello che trovavo in casa [...]. A catalizzare tutte queste memorie e a farmi piombare a capofitto nella Shoah fu, credo, *Il diario di Anna Frank*, che lessi avidamente quando uscì, che vidi a teatro con la scuola [...] piangendo calde lacrime da quando si alzò il sipario. A casa mia madre diceva con ironia che mi identificavo con Anna Frank anche perché avevo le stesse iniziali, A.F. Poi molto più tardi sarebbero venute le letture da storica, i libri di Primo Levi, Lanzmann, il lavoro sulla memoria.[9]

> [The camps and the Shoah [...] I have the clear memory of having approached them and immersed myself into them alone, at the age of seven or eight, when I was voraciously reading everything I could find at home [...]. What catalysed all these memories and plunged me headlong into the Shoah was, I believe, *The Diary of Anne Frank*, which I read avidly when it came out, and which I saw in the theatre with the school [...] crying hot tears from the moment the curtain went up. At home my mother said with irony that I identified with Anne Frank also because I had the same initials, A.F. Then much later, came my readings as a historian, the books of Primo Levi, Lanzmann, the work on memory.]

To herself and many of her generation and after, Anne Frank's diary became the first 'catalyst' of an intimate understanding of the Holocaust. As a young girl, Foa felt a sense of identification with Frank's experience, which triggered her interest before any other reading. She acknowledged the value of testimonies reworked in literary narratives and recognised that literary or narrative forms of writing are powerful media in fostering personal memory and in transmitting historical knowledge. In this sense, she implicitly explained her choices of writing about 16 October in more literary terms. Her representation of the Roman round-up from an alternative, ex-centric historical perspective challenges the predominant historical interpretation of the event and, as we will see, offers a new understanding and a new process of memorisation of it.

In the bibliography of *Portico d'Ottavia 13*, we can see Foa's entanglement of historical sources, personal memories, and literary influences, as well as her perception of the book as a literary work. The bibliography is not in chronological or alphabetical order. Rather, it is composed of bullet-points divided into eleven topics. Foa comments on each volume she cites, thus showing her pedagogical intent to help her readers understand her different uses of the cited volumes. The section of the bibliography dedicated to 16 October shows the texts, the diaries, and the testimonies on which Foa based her narrative, starting with Debenedetti's *16 ottobre 1943*, whose importance is made clear in her accompanying comment:

> Il *primo e indispensabile testo di riferimento per la razzia del 16 ottobre* è [...] *16 ottobre 1943* [...]. Il testo, un vero e proprio capolavoro, è stato scritto nel 1944 quando ancora non si sapeva con certezza il destino dei deportati, ed è stato pubblicato per la prima volta nel dicembre 1944 nella rivista romana 'Mercurio'. (*PO13*, p. 126, my emphasis)

[The *first and foundational reference text for the round-up of 16 October* is [...] *16 ottobre 1943* [...]. The text, which is a masterpiece, was written in 1944 when the fate of the deportees was not yet known with certainty; it was published for the first time in December 1944 in the Roman magazine 'Mercurio'.]

It is striking that *16 ottobre 1943* appears as the first text to be examined, even before any historiographical work, but in a 2019 interview in the Rai Radio3 series *Un giorno nella storia* she emphasises how deeply influenced by it she was:

> La coralità del libro di Debenedetti mi ha molto suggestionata, forse gli devo molto perché anche io ho pensato di ricostituire una coralità che non era la coralità di tutto il ghetto, di tutti gli ebrei romani, ma era la coralità di questa grande casa in cui abitavano un centinaio di persone e di cui una cinquantina sono morte durante l'occupazione.[10]

> [The polyphonic nature of Debenedetti's book impressed me greatly, perhaps I owe him a lot because I too thought of reconstituting the voices that were not the voices of the whole ghetto, of all the Roman Jews, but were the voices of this large house in which about a hundred people lived and about fifty of whom died during the occupation.]

Her book, she continues, 'si inserisce in un filone che è soprattutto un filone narrativo, penso a *La Storia* di Morante e a *16 ottobre 1943* di Debenedetti' [it is part of a thread which is above all narrative, I'm thinking of *La Storia* by Morante and *16 ottobre 1943* by Debenedetti].[11] Neither *16 ottobre 1943* nor *La Storia* provide scientific descriptions of the Roman round-up, and yet Foa suggests that both guarantee an historical understanding and an intimate perception of the event, achievements which are repeated in a different way in *Portico d'Ottavia 13*. In another interview in 2013, she said that, *Portico d'Ottavia 13* 'è quasi un romanzo, ma non c'è nulla di finto. Piuttosto [esso] ricostruisce la realtà di quella casa raccontando cioè usando un tono narrativo' [is almost a novel, but nothing has been invented. Rather [it] reconstructs the reality of the house as a narrative, that is, by using a narrative tone].[12] Foa does not mention Loy's *La parola ebreo* either in the bibliographical note or in interviews. She does not include it among the literary texts which have influenced her perception of the Roman round-up, even if, as we have seen in the previous chapter, her father, Vittorio Foa, appreciated Loy's text deeply for its transmission of historical knowledge. Elsewhere she comments that:

> Il libro di Rosetta Loy, che ho molto apprezzato, l'ho letto in un altro modo, al suo apparire, come una riflessione identitaria, della sua identità cattolica rispetto a quella ebraica. È un libro in cui gli ebrei non sono davvero protagonisti.[13]

> [I greatly appreciated Rosetta Loy's book, but, when it appeared, I read it in another way: as reflection on identity, on her Catholic identity compared to the Jewish one. It is a book in which the Jews are not really the protagonists.]

Yet, Loy's and Foa's works bear interesting comparisons. As seen in Chapter 5, even though Loy is not of Jewish origin and anchors *La parola ebreo* in autobiography rather than in what her family might have told her, we are able to include her in the second generation of postmemory by stretching the boundaries of Hirsch's definition. But when it comes to Foa, who is of Jewish origin and whose only experience of war, persecution, and deportation has been through what her parents told her and her own readings, there is no stretching of Hirsch's definition. Both *La parola ebreo* and *Portico d'Ottavia 13* are works of postmemory in that they foster an inter- and trans-generational dialogue about the Holocaust in Italy and the German occupation of Rome by constructing their works on a bed of interwoven testimonies, historiographical research, and personal reflections. Both, too, consider the processes of commemoration of 16 October. Like Loy, Foa wrote a hybrid text in which historical facts and personal stories are re-elaborated in a narrative form of writing which includes her own perceptions of the deportation of the Roman Jews: 'Ho voluto mettere insieme le mie emozioni e la mia razionalità storica: chiudere un circolo che metteva insieme il mio mestiere di storica e le emozioni che sentivo rispetto al Nazismo e allo sterminio degli ebrei' [I wanted to bring together my emotions and my historical rationality: to close a circle that brought together my profession as a historian and the emotions I felt about Nazism and the extermination of the Jews].[14] Foa's historical method are based on both her empathy with the subject and her historical research. It, therefore, seems to be in line with the ideas of feminist historians, among whom is Anna Rossi-Doria, who believed in the need for carrying out historical research through a combination of the subjective, historicism, and scientific methods of historiography.[15] For Foa, that which most clearly links her personally and empathically to the Roman round-up is the building, Portico d'Ottavia 13. 'La Casa' is not only the frame and the common thread of the reported microhistories but also the means by which she identifies with the victims.

Engaging with History

Anna Foa was born in 1944 in Turin. Her father was Vittorio Foa, an intellectual and politician who, despite his Jewish origin, considered himself to be an atheist. Her mother was Lisa Giua, an activist in the Resistance. From the early 1930s, Vittorio and Lisa's family were part of antifascist circles in Turin. Vittorio joined the antifascist movement Giustizia e Libertà (GL) and in 1935 was arrested and sentenced to prison for antifascist activities. After the promulgation of the Racial Laws in 1938, some members of his family chose exile. In 1943, he took part in the Resistance and joined the political party that grew out of GL, the Partito d'Azione. In 1946, he was elected a deputy of the Partito d'Azione and, after its dissolution in 1947 he joined the Partito Socialista Italiano, of which he became the national leader and, for three legislatures (1953-68), a deputy. In 2007, he was one of the founders of the Partito Democratico. His political career continued until his death in 2008.[16]

Anna Foa grew up in a highly educated, political family. She was brought up as an atheist but converted to Judaism in adulthood. She became a modern historian and taught at the University of Rome from 1974 to 2010. She herself sees a connection between her conversion and her career:

> Mi sembra che il mio diventare ebrea per i rabbini (che poi questa è la mia
> 'conversione', recuperare un ebraismo che credevo mi appartenesse e che scopro

non essere così) ha certo influito sulle mie ricerche di storica, ma forse è vero anche il contrario, che le mie ricerche hanno influito sulla mia volontà di 'diventare ebrea'.[17]

[I think that my becoming Jewish through the rabbis (which is my 'conversion', the recovering of a Judaism that I believed belonged to me and which I discovered did not) has certainly influenced my research as a historian, but perhaps the contrary is also true, that my research has influenced my willingness to 'become Jewish'.]

Her research ranges from social and cultural history during the Renaissance to modern and contemporary Jewish history. Her publications on Jewish history include *Ebrei in Europa: dalla peste nera all'emancipazione XVI–XIX secolo* (1992), *Diaspora: storia degli ebrei nel Novecento* (2009), *Eretici: storie di streghe, ebrei e convertiti* (2011), *Andare per ghetti e giudecche* (2014), and *Donne e Shoah* (2021); and she co-edited volumes such as *Ebrei, minoranze, Risorgimento: storia, cultura, letteratura* (2013), and *Ebrei, una storia italiana: i primi mille anni* (2017).[18]

In *Diaspora*, one of her earlier works of general history, Foa includes a brief account of 16 October which makes a useful precedent for *Portico d'Ottavia 13*. In it, Foa re-constructs the history of the Jews from the end of the nineteenth century to the 1970s by starting with a question: 'Chi sono gli ebrei del Novecento?'[Who are the Jews of the Twentieth century?].[19] She dedicates a few pages to 16 October in the chapter entitled 'La Shoah', in which she examines the Roman round-up following an account of the origins of Nazism, the Italian Racial Laws, the persecution of Jews from a European perspective, Auschwitz as the emblem of the extermination camps, and the Nuremberg trials. By including the Roman round-up in this chapter — describing the German occupation of Rome, the episodes which preceded the round-up, the ransom demand of fifty kilos of gold on 26 September, and the plunder of the Jewish Community and Rabbinical Libraries on 11 October — she presents it within the context of the wider national and international genocide. She directly quotes Debenedetti's *16 ottobre 1943*, and she includes it in the bibliography among her sources, thus affirming the value she already attributed in 2009 to non-historical works in the transmission of historical data.

Foa briefly goes on to describe the round-up itself: 'alle cinque di mattina, i tedeschi circondano le case, pongono sentinelle armate agli angoli, salgono nelle case, portano via tutti [...]. I rastrellati vengono ammassati dentro il fossato di fronte a Portico d'Ottavia' [at five in the morning, the Germans surround the houses, they post armed sentries at the corners, go up into the buildings, take everyone away [...]. Those rounded-up are gathered together in the ditch in front of Portico d'Ottavia]. She numbers the victims and traces the stages of their journey to Auschwitz. She reflects on the presence of the Vatican in Rome and alludes to the sense of protection created in the community by the proximity of the Pope: 'a pochi passi dal Vaticano, nulla poteva accadere agli ebrei [...]. Anche i nazisti condividevano quest'idea, almeno in parte, tanto è vero che si mossero con una certa cautela' [a few steps from the Vatican, nothing could happen to the Jews [...]. Even the Nazis had this sense, at least in part, so much so that they operated with some caution]. She ends the section by referring to the Church's initiatives to protect as many Jews as possible: 'dopo il 16 ottobre, si moltiplicarono le iniziative vaticane di solidarietà concreta' [after 16 October, the Vatican multiplied its initiative of solidarity] (*D*, pp. 158, 159).

If in *Diaspora* Foa offered a relatively neutral overview of the Roman round-up as an event in the twentieth-century history of the Jews, in *Portico d'Ottavia 13* she reconsiders her way of transmitting historical knowledge through a revision of her method of research:

> Possiamo ricorrere alla memoria e interrogare i testimoni rimasti, che allora erano giovanissimi, oppure in mancanza di essi i loro figli, sperando che i racconti che hanno ascoltato siano accurati e che li ricordino senza troppe confusioni o orpelli. Ancora, possiamo trovare delle risposte nelle pieghe degli atti dei processi del dopoguerra contro spie e collaborazionisti. Le testimonianze sugli arresti, infatti, sono spesso dettagliate e ci dicono sempre se essi avvennero ad opera dei fascisti oppure dei tedeschi e se anche le donne e i bambini furono portati via. (*PO13*, p. 85)

> [We can go back to personal memories and question the remaining witnesses, who were very young at the time, or in their absence their children, hoping that the stories they have heard are accurate and that they will remember them without too much confusion or misapprehensions. Again, we can find answers in the folds of the documents of the post-war trials of spies and collaborationists. The testimonies of the arrests, in fact, are often detailed and always tell us if they were carried out by [Italian] fascists or by Germans and if women and children were also taken away.]

She adapts her mode of writing too: it becomes more accessible in terms of narrative forms, thus reaching out to a heterogeneous and non-specialist readership. This approach is triggered, I think, by her desire to tell the story of the building she lived in: Portico d'Ottavia 13.

In the foreword of *Portico d'Ottavia 13*, Foa gives points of reference for her readers to by which to understand and interpret her book, explaining why she started re-reading the Roman round-up through 'la Casa'. In the beginning, when she moved into 'la Casa', she was not particularly interested in what had happened there on 16 October 1943: 'nel 2000 andai ad abitare nella Casa [...]. Talvolta, mi domandavo cosa fosse successo su quelle scale il 16 ottobre del 1943, ma non mi ci si soffermavo troppo a riflettere' [in 2000 I went to live in 'la Casa' [...]. Sometimes, I wondered what had happened on those stairs on 16 October 1943, but I did not dwell on it too much] (*PO13*, p. xi). Then, she found an undated photograph of 'la Casa':

> Scoprii inaspettatamente una fotografia del cortile della Casa, scattata chissà in che anno ma certo dopo il 1943: degradato, scuro e tetro il cortile appariva come nelle descrizioni degli anni successivi alla guerra [...]. La didascalia, suggerendo che la foto risalisse alla razzia del 16 ottobre, diceva: 'Un'immagine spettrale del ghetto di Roma deserto' [...]. Fu allora, credo, che cominciai a rimuginare sulla storia della Casa durante i mesi dell'occupazione nazista e su chi ne fossero allora gli abitanti, nessuno dei quali vi abitava più [...]. La storia della Casa cominciò ad assillarmi ma non trovavo il modo di iniziare a scriverne. (*PO13*, p. xii)

[I unexpectedly found a photograph of the courtyard of la Casa, taken who knows in what year but certainly after 1943: the courtyard, degraded, dark and gloomy, looked reminiscent of the descriptions of the years following the war [...]. The caption, suggesting that the photo dated back to the round-up of 16 October, said: 'An image of the deserted ghetto of Rome' [...]. It was then, I believe, that I began to think about the history of 'la Casa' during the months of the Nazi occupation and about who its inhabitants, none of whom lived there any more, were then [...]. The history of 'la Casa' began to haunt me but I could not find a way to start writing about it.]

Having had her interest in the events of 16 October sparked by a photograph, she then met a witness, Gianni Di Segni, who had lived through that day when he was a child:

Poi incontrai un testimone, che all'epoca era un bambino ma aveva conosciuto tutti nella Casa e che per primo mi raccontò. Dopo di lui altri racconti emersero ad illuminare un poco quei mesi e la vita nella Casa sotto l'occupazione. E allora decisi che avrei ricostruito quella storia, che non avrei più salito quelle scale senza sapere i nomi di quanti in quei giorni vi avevano abitato, senza conoscerne almeno un poco la storia. È proprio l'immagine delle scale che mi assilla, quella degli ebrei che le scesero quel 16 ottobre per andare verso la morte: tanti, troppi. (*PO13*, pp. xii–xiii)

[Then I met a witness, who at the time was a child but had known everyone in 'la Casa' and who was the first to tell me what happened. After him, other stories emerged to illuminate, a little, those months and the life in 'la Casa' under occupation. At that point, I decided that I would reconstruct that story, that I would never again climb those stairs without knowing the names of those who had lived there in those days, without knowing at least a little of their history. It is precisely the image of the stairs that haunts me, that of the Jews who went down those stairs on 16 October and towards their death: many, too many].

Foa started collecting the first-hand testimonies of those who had escaped and re-assembled the stories of those who were deported from a range of sources. She explains: 'di alcuni ho saputo di più, di altri di meno, di altri ancora nulla, tranne che i nomi e le date di nascita e di deportazione. Ma la Casa si è riempita di abitanti, di nomi, di vite vissute' [of some I learned more, of others less, of others almost nothing, except their names and dates of birth and deportation. But 'la Casa' started to be filled with its inhabitants, with names, with lived lives] (*PO13*, p. xiv). She tells their individual stories, which become the tools for reflecting on 16 October and for leading her readers to an intimate understanding of the persecution. She sees her book turning into:

Un tentativo di riparazione, forse. Un riconoscimento verso quelle persone che il 16 ottobre hanno sceso dietro la spinta dei fucili tedeschi quei gradini che tante volte, sessant'anni dopo, ho salito inconsapevole, attenta solo alla mia realtà quotidiana. Restituire anima e volto a quelle persone, a cui la vita di ogni giorno è stata strappata brutalmente, in un attimo. (*PO13*, p. xv, my emphasis)

[*An attempt at reparation*, perhaps. Recognition of those people who on 16 October behind the thrust of German rifles went down those stairs that many

times, sixty years later, I climbed unaware, only attentive to my everyday life.
[I want to] restore body and soul of those people, those whose everyday life was
brutally torn from them, in a moment.]

Her commitment is surely pedagogical, but the phrase 'tentativo di riparazione' also
implies a different moral relationship with her characters and attributes a reparative
value to literature. Hence, her perception of *Portico d'Ottavia 13* in literary terms is
even more significant because, through her words, Foa tries to '*ridare l'anima alle
persone* che la [la Casa] abitavano in quei giorni terribili dell'occupazione [...] questo
il mio proposito' [*to restore the soul of the people* who lived there in those terrible
days of the occupation [...] this is my purpose] (*PO13*, p. xiii, my emphasis). This
reparation can be made possible by her book, by her readers, by her generation, by
the later Jewish community, and by the later Italian nation.

Stairs and Names

Portico d'Ottavia 13 is structured by and narrated around the place of Portico
d'Ottavia 13 and the names of the residents of 'la Casa'. Throughout the chapter, the
terms 'space' and 'place' are used according to Tim Cresswell's definitions: 'place'
meaning the ideas of significant location and of possession, and 'space' indicating a
more abstract concept.[20]

The names and the place that appear in the book are the elements that distinguish
Foa's representation of 16 October from the texts examined so far. Foa makes a
monument of the building and of the book in which the names of its residents are
engraved. Her writing is powerfully commemorative: at the end there is a list of
the families and households of 'la Casa'. With this, she provides a visual scheme to
clarify for her readers the family relationships and the events of her characters' lives.
The eighteen families are graphically separated on the page, each name is followed
by a date of birth. Those names with no asterisk are the people who managed to
avoid deportation, sixty-eight of these. Those with an asterisk were deported on 16
October and did not come back, thirty-four of them. Those with two asterisks were
deported after that Saturday and died in Auschwitz, six of them. Those with three
asterisks were victims of the Fosse Ardeatine massacre, six of them.

In the narrative, the residents are introduced by their first and last names; their
stories are described through a quantity of information which might easily become
confusing for readers, but Foa helps them by moving from one family to another
and from one apartment to another at a time so that each story becomes a tile in
a mosaic, a voice in a choir, gradually building up a picture of the round-up. The
effect is cumulative:

> Sempre al pianterreno, subito a sinistra del cancello, abitava Angelo Di Segni,
> sfasciacarrozze, figlio di Giovanni Di Segni ed Emma Sabatello che abitavano
> al numero 9. Angelo si era trasferito là al momento di sposarsi, come aveva fatto
> anche suo fratello Rubino, che abitava al piano superiore. Era nato nel 1906 e
> viveva con la moglie Ines Pavoncello e le due figlie Emma e Rina. Sua moglie
> [...] si era molto spaventata quando i nazisti avevano fatto richiesta dell'oro e
> aveva convinto il marito ad andarsene e a nascondersi fuori Roma [...]. Il 16

ottobre i Di Segni non erano quindi a Roma e per molti giorni non seppero nulla di quello che era successo [...]. Nella deviazione che si apre al pianterreno, sulla sinistra, in cima a una scaletta di pietra ad angolo, abitava una famiglia che fu completamente distrutta nella razzia del 16 ottobre, quella di Marco Di Veroli: una famiglia numerosa con ben nove bambini fra i due e i diciassette anni. Tutti furono arrestati quel giorno, tutti perirono ad Auschwitz. Il padre aveva quarant'anni e faceva il facchino, la madre, Fortunata Di Porto, ne aveva quarantatré e faceva la cucitrice. (*PO13*, pp. 30-32)

[Angelo Di Segni, who was a car-breaker and the son of Giovanni Di Segni and Emma Sabatello, lived at number 9 on the ground floor, immediately to the left of the gate. Angelo had moved there when he got married, as had his brother Rubino, who lived upstairs. He was born in 1906 and lived with his wife Ines Pavoncello and their two daughters Emma and Rina. His wife [...] was very frightened when the Nazis asked for gold and she persuaded her husband to leave and hide outside Rome [...]. On 16 October the Di Segnis were therefore not in Rome and for many days they knew nothing of what had happened [...]. In the return that opens on the ground floor, on the left, at the top of an angled stone staircase, lived Marco Di Veroli's family that was completely destroyed in the round-up of 16 October; a large family with nine children between two and seventeen years old. All were arrested that day, all died in Auschwitz. The father was forty and was a porter, the mother, Fortunata Di Porto, was forty-three and was a seamstress.]

Although the residents are poignantly described, Foa's accounts of them are too brief to foster a sense of individual identification, there is too little time for the reader to identify with them. Foa's purpose, I think, is rather to involve readers through the 'place' of 'la Casa' by picturing the places where the round-up occurred and conjuring the atmosphere of the morning of 16 October. She zooms in from the wider round-up across Rome and the ghetto to the intimacy of 'la Casa'. She transforms the building into the core of, and the means to achieve, her historical reconstruction.

Foa in fact defines 'la Casa' as the protagonist of her book: 'di questo libro, il primo protagonista è la casa, con le sue colonne, le sue mura spesse, le sue deviazioni inaspettate' [in this book, the main protagonist is 'la Casa', with its columns, its thick walls, its unexpected returns] (*PO13*, p. xiii). She describes the building in detail:

Al numero 13 di via del Portico, nel tratto fra vicolo di Sant'Ambrogio e il passaggio che conduce a via di Sant'Angelo di Peschiera, a fianco dei ruderi romani del Portico, c'è un vecchio portone di legno che si apre inaspettatamente su un vasto cortile circondato di logge rette da colonne antiche, simile più a un chiostro che ad un cortile d'abitazione.
    Era una casa suggestiva e piena di bizzarrie, una casa in cui ci si poteva perdere. Salendo le scale, tra il pianterreno e il primo piano, trovavi sulla sinistra un piccolo corridoio che si apriva all'improvviso su un altro slargo, che conduceva verso via di Sant'Angelo in Pescheria, con una scala che saliva all'aperto verso un altro appartamento. Al pianterreno c'era un'altra deviazione, che sbucava in due cortiletti che prendevano luce dall'alto, quasi sprofondati in un pozzo, su cui si affacciavano altre porte finestre. E fin l'ingresso delle cantine era misterioso. (*PO13*, p. ix)

[At number 13 via del Portico, in the stretch between vicolo di Sant'Ambrogio and the passage that leads to via di Sant'Angelo di Peschiera, beside the Roman ruins of the Portico, there is an old wooden gate which opens unexpectedly onto a vast courtyard surrounded by loggias and supported by ancient columns, it looks more like a cloister than a residential courtyard.

It was a charming house full of oddities, a house in which you could get lost. By climbing the stairs, between the ground floor and the first floor, you found on the left a small corridor which suddenly opened onto a wider space, which led towards via di Sant'Angelo in Pescheria, with a staircase that went up outdoors towards another apartment. On the ground floor, there was another turn, which emerged in two courtyards that were lit from above by the sun, almost sunk into a well, onto which other French windows looked. And even the entrance to the cellars was mysterious.]

It is the detail of the description of the building which leads readers into intimate contact with 'la Casa' and it is through 'la Casa' that they can have an understanding of the everyday life of its residents:

> Era una vita in comune, facilitata dall'affacciarsi degli appartamenti sul cortile interno, dalle logge coperte che invitavano a stringere i legami fra le varie famiglie. Le case erano insufficienti o sovraffollate, ma quegli spazi esterni favorivano lo stare insieme e le porte degli appartamenti restavano sempre aperte [...]. Le donne lavoravano insieme sotto le logge e nel cortile, dove sistemavano le loro macchine da cucire. [...] Le bambine si sedevano a chiacchierare sui gradini, fra un'incombenza e l'altra, e si arricciavano i capelli. I bambini andavano a prendere l'acqua fresca alla fontanella in piazza. (*PO13*, pp. 19-20)

> [It was a life in common, facilitated by face-to-face apartments in the internal courtyard, by covered loggias that invited the forging of ties between the various families. The apartments were inadequate or overcrowded, but the outdoor spaces favoured being together and doors were always open. Women worked together under the loggias and in the courtyard, where they set up their sewing machines. [...] Girls sat chatting on the steps, between one task and the next, and curled their hair. Children went to get fresh water from the fountain in the square.]

Foa's representation of the quotidian, which up to then had been either neglected or purposefully omitted by the traditional historiography of 16 October, significantly adds to what had already been imparted about that date. She provides therefore an *effet de mémoire*, an *effet de réel*. Although her writing is not experiential — she is unable to add to the experience of those she writes about — she nevertheless is able to create the effect of memory and of reality. Her depiction of Portico d'Ottavia 13 is so detailed that readers find themselves there, in 'la Casa' at dawn on 16 October, and read of the arrests that morning by going up and down the stairs: 'Entrando sulla destra, c'era la casa della portiera [...]. Più avanti [...] nell'appartamento sulla destra prima del porticato abitava [...] Sara Moscati [...]. Di fianco all'abitazione di Sara Moscati, sotto il porticato, abitava la famiglia Terracina' [Entering on the right, there was the apartment of the caretaker [...]. Further on, Sara Moscati lived [...] in the apartment on the right before the portico [...]. Next to Sara Moscati's house, under the portico, there were the Terracinas] (*PO13*, pp. 28-29). Foa projects the reader into that morning and into that place among the Jews and the SS: 'ce lo immaginiamo, il vasto cortile con le sue colonne di marmo, pieno di nazisti armati, che iniziano a bussare impazienti alle porte, usando il calcio del fucile quando non c'è risposta' [we can imagine it, the vast courtyard with its marble columns, full of armed Nazis, who start knocking impatiently on doors, using the butt of their rifles when there is no answer] (*PO13*, p. 27). She provides readers with the perception of witnessing those moments from the inside, inviting them to read and imagine the event within the domestic place, and it is the domestic place which stirs their sense of identification, a process that Gaston Bachelard describes in *Poetics of Space*. According to Bachelard, a house has a double function: it provides a material and psychological shelter for the imagination of the dweller and, at the same time, becomes an essential element of that imagination. As soon as readers read about a domestic place, they start to feel a sense of intimacy which projects them into their own intimate places:

> At the very first word, at the first poetic overture, the reader who is 'reading a room' leaves off reading and starts to think of some place in his own past [...]. The values of intimacy are so absorbing that the reader has ceased to read your room: he sees his own again.[21]

Readers are brought to re-imagine the round-up in their own home, threatened by the gunshots and shouts of the Germans of which they read in Foa's book. The connotations of protection and safety that they unconsciously attribute to their own home collapse; they start to imagine their house as susceptible to violation, and themselves as susceptible to displacement and loss; they identify with the victims' feelings of anxiety and fear. Through the description of an intimate and domestic place, Foa triggers a form of Landsberg's prosthetic memory, thus not simply fostering historical understanding, but also inviting readers to take on a more deeply-felt memory of the narrated event. To do so, Foa collocates the round-up with the building of Portico d'Ottavia 13 and principally uses two communicative strategies: verbal forms of the first-person plural and photo-portraits.

First-person plural narratorial verbal forms are both pedagogical and narrative.[22] They allude to a kinship between issuer and receiver. They involve readers in turning-points of the narrative and engender an empathetic relationship with the author when readers are invited to share the former's opinions. Foa uses these verbal forms when she wants her readers to participate in the deportation of 'la Casa' in person, ground floor to top floor, room by room:

> *Vediamo* che cosa è successo nella Casa all'alba di quel 16 ottobre, *entriamo* nel portone e *risaliamo* le scale come devono aver fatto i nazisti di Dannecker, cominciando dal pianterreno, da quelle porte che si aprono dal cortile [...]. Entrando alla destra, c'era la casa della portiera [...]. *Sappiamo* che molti sono stati i portieri che quel giorno e anche successivamente hanno avvisato gli inquilini ebrei di scappare e li hanno aiutati a nascondersi. (*PO13*, p. 27, my emphasis)

> [*Let's see* what happened in 'la Casa' at the dawn of that 16 October, *we enter* the

gate and *go up* the stairs as Dannecker's Nazis must have done, starting from the ground floor, from those doors that open from the courtyard [...]. Entering on the right, there was the apartment of the caretaker [...]. *We know* that, on that day and even later, many caretakers warned the Jewish tenants to escape and helped them to hide.]

She goes up the stairs to describe the arrests of 16 October and she comes back down the same stairs to report the arrests which occurred after 16 October:

> *Avevamo lasciato* la Casa vuota dei suoi abitanti dopo il 16 ottobre, ma *avevamo anche detto* che altre quattordici persone che vi abitavano sarebbero state arrestate nei nove terribili mesi dell'occupazione, prima della liberazione di Roma il 4 giugno 1944. *Vediamo* chi erano, riscendendo le scale che *avevamo salito* con le SS, dall'ultimo piano verso il cortile. (*PO13*, pp. 49-50, my emphasis)

> [*We had left* 'la Casa' empty of its occupants after 16 October, but *we also said* that fourteen other people who lived there would be arrested in the terrible nine months of the occupation, before the liberation of Rome on 4 June 1944. *Let's see* who they were by going down the stairs that *we had climbed* with the SS, from the top floor towards the courtyard.]

In both passages, Foa describes 'la Casa' as if she is a camera recording, and as if her readers are viewers. Here, with the first-person plural forms, Foa exhorts her readership to go up and come down the stairs with her. Together, they grow familiar with the place, with the stories of those who were arrested, and those who managed to escape. She also uses first-person plural narratorial forms to include questions in the narrative: 'Stranamente, non *abbiamo* nessuna fotografia della razzia del 16 ottobre [...]. Eppure *sappiamo* che era usanza dei nazisti prendere immagini delle loro azioni [...]. Le foto c'erano e sono state successivamente smarrite? Emergeranno [...]? *Vedremo*, allora, il portone numero 13?' [Oddly, *we do not have* any photographs of the round-up of 16 October [...]. Yet *we know* that taking pictures of their actions was a Nazi habit [...]. Were the photos there and were they subsequently lost? Will they emerge [...]? *Will we see*, then, gate number 13?] (*PO13*, pp. 8-9, my emphasis). Through the first-person plural forms, Foa describes current shared knowledge of the past, and at the same time prompts reflections on the value of photographs, which can be examined as another way of capturing readers' attention, as Marianne Hirsch suggests in several of her works.[23]

Photographs are a compelling means through which readers empathise with victims and see intimate aspects of events and places. They are part of an aesthetic strategy of identification, projection, and mourning. They bridge distances of time and space and close gaps between the separate destinies of those who are reading and of those who are in the picture. Froma Zeitlin agrees that the image 'is a tangible, visual emblem, which might serve as a primary focus for the retrieval (or re-imagining) of an absent memory and as an uncanny means of personal self-identification with victims'.[24] Pictures link past with present, memory with postmemory, and individual remembrance with cultural recall. They are points of memory because, Hirsch and Leo Spitzer suggest, they strike the readers' imagination by signalling 'a visceral material connection to the past'.[25] Pictures are also a disturbing effect which allow readers to see Holocaust victims; they unsettle readers' emotional responses by being a present glimpse into a traumatic past reality.[26] According to Susan Sontag, they are a physical representation which collides with 'a pseudo-presence and a token of absence'.[27] They not only show a traumatic past and those who lived it, but, because of the emotional disturbance they produce, they also have an impact on the readers' process of recollection.

Foa recognised the importance of a visual perception of historical events, but she found no pictures of the round-up. She saw this lack as a limitation, a downside as it meant that her readers were unable to benefit from the insights which are produced by images that traverse temporal, spatial, and experiential divides. In the book, therefore, she included seven pictures of Jews who lived in the ghetto and three graphic aids which help readers to picture the round-up in the building of Portico d'Ottavia 13.

To trigger her readers' empathy, Foa includes three photographs of two families of 'la Casa'. They show three women, three children, and one infant. The captions give their first and last names: Speranza Sonnino with her two children Giuditta and Leone and her sister Costanza Sonnino are in the first picture; Ester Tagliacozzo and her two children Italia and Umberto are in the second and in the third. They were all deported on 16 October and killed as soon as they arrived in Auschwitz. The four other photographs show: Celeste di Porto, the Jewish woman who denounced many co-religionists to the Fascists and whose trial, as mentioned, is analysed in the text; a woman sewing in one of the courtyards of 'la Casa', dated 1947; and two images of 1948 which, the caption says, represent orphans getting off a truck in the centre of the ghetto, in front of 'la Casa'. These photographs help readers picture the place and people, combining with Foa's verbal descriptions to greater effect than alone to help us connect more intimately with the round-up and so recall it more readily.

In the first half of the book, there are three further images that aid understanding of the round-up: two maps of the neighbourhood and the floor plan of 'la Casa'. Through them, Foa shows how the deportation was strictly defined by the area, the neighbourhood, the building, the apartments, and the rooms in which it occurred, and how the ability of the Jews to escape during the round-up depended on the exact place where they lived:

> Quanti sono riusciti a scappare attraverso i suoi anfratti e a trovare in quel labirinto una strada per la fuga? [...] possiamo immaginarci che dalle finestre ci si sia molto parlato e che di quei solai e quei tetti molti abbiano approfittato per fuggire. (*PO13*, p. xiii)
>
> [How many people have managed to escape through its clefts and have found a way to escape in that labyrinth? [...] we can imagine that much was said from the windows and that many took advantage of those attics and roofs to escape.]

The three images intensify the process of memorisation of the event through an alternative perspective of the place. They help readers locate the building in the ghetto and follow Foa's description of the round-up within Portico d'Ottavia, 13.

Although it is a very different form of book, these same narrative and visual strategies were maintained, though changed in interesting ways, in a children's edition of *Portico d'Ottavia 13* that Foa wrote in collaboration with Carola Susani.

★   ★   ★   ★   ★

In 2014, a year after the publication of *Portico d'Ottavia 13*, Giovanni Carletti of Laterza asked Foa to adapt her work for children, for publication in their new 'Celacanto' series of books for children and young people.[28] She agreed and worked in collaboration with Carola Susani, an established children's author who helped her with the text for the new readers, and Matteo Berton, an illustrator and comic artist.[29] In 2015, Foa and her collaborators published what was her first book for children and the first book for children about the Roman round-up, *Portico d'Ottavia*.[30]

The entire plot of this children's version is based on the adaptation of historical data and individual memories into a narrative accessible to children: a time-travel story. Foa, together with Susani, decided to narrate only the morning of the round-up, did not mention the deportation, and never used the word 'Auschwitz'. Foa noted:

> Con Carola Susani abbiamo avuto una stretta collaborazione. All'inizio, abbiamo deciso insieme che taglio dare al testo, e abbiamo scelto di concentrare tutto nel giorno della razzia del 16 ottobre e di trattarla con delicatezza, data l'età dei lettori, senza indulgere a racconti troppo angosciosi.[31]
>
> [Carola Susani and I collaborated closely. From the beginning, we decided on the format, and we chose to concentrate the plot on the day of the round-up of 16 October and to narrate it with delicacy, given the age of the readers, without dwelling on overly distressing stories.]

Foa again reconstructs the event through places and micro-histories. In the plot, the major characters are a seven-year-old child, Costanza, and an old lady who narrates the story of 16 October. In 2019, Foa described how these characters functioned in the following way:

> Alla fine, piano piano, è venuto fuori una sorta di viaggio nel tempo, in cui il racconto di Costanza Fatucci vecchia, che mi mostra la casa e mi spiega la razzia, si trasforma in un viaggio nel tempo in cui lei bambina mi tiene per mano durante la razzia.[32]
>
> [In the end, little by little, there was a sort of time-travel: the story of the old woman Costanza Fatucci, who shows me 'la Casa' and explains the round-up to me, turns into a time-travel journey in which she, as a child, holds my hand during the round-up.]

Foa did not explicitly say how older children should read this book. However, she suggested that younger ones should be supported by an adult: 'i bambini fino a dieci anni [...] hanno bisogno di una mediazione [...] di qualcuno che spieghi loro il contesto, insomma la guerra e quello che successe' [children up to ten years [...] need a sort of mediation [...] someone who explains the context to them, in short, the war and what happened].[33] From the beginning of the book, they read that the round-up took place in Rome on 16 October 1943. They are encouraged to identify with the child characters and to share their fears and concerns.

There is an extensive body of work — diaries, novels, short stories, picture books — that attempts to make the Holocaust accessible and meaningful to children, beginning, as we saw for Foa herself, with *The Diary of Anne Frank* in June 1947 and reaching forward to John Boyne's 2006 novel *The Boy in the Striped Pyjamas*, for example.[34] *Portico d'Ottavia* is among the works aiming to reach a younger readership. It adapts and reshapes historical facts in order to awaken in children an awareness of Jewish history during the German occupation and personalises the event of the round-up through characters with whom children can identify.

Children's literature uses distinctive mechanisms and communicative strategies to represent the Holocaust.[35] In broad terms, these books typically have children as protagonists, convey an optimistic rather than a more negative worldview, and present a clear moral framework; they use action and dialogue rather than description and introspective perception. The primary narratological tool which characterises Holocaust stories for children is what Joanne Pettitt calls 'reduction': the most extreme elements of Nazism are omitted or hidden in signifiers. According to Pettitt, 'such symbols allow the text to represent without actually showing the true horror of the atrocities and by extension they facilitate the necessary juxtaposition of appropriateness and didacticism'.[36] Concentration and extermination camps are most often situated on the periphery of the narrative, an unseen area outside the frame. In this sense, children's literature creates narratives in which meaning is both created and obscured by a sustained semiotic system. Pettitt comments that 'conceptual integration thus allows, in the narratological space that it creates, a perception of meaning that remains linguistically obscured at least insofar as such meanings are not explicitly expressed on the page'.[37] There is a constant rebounding between the said and the not-said, so that young readers are not directly shown the horrors of deportation, extermination, and death.

Like many works in the tradition of children's picture books about the Holocaust, *Portico d'Ottavia* re-formulates the events it describes, in this case the Roman round-up, in terms which are simultaneously protective and didactic. The event is presented truthfully but without denying the child the possibility of an optimistic and life-affirming outcome to the story. In an interview with Rai Scuola, Foa discusses the difficulties of telling children about the Holocaust more broadly and about the Roman round-up specifically, but is enthusiastic about reaching children and sees the importance of starting a dialogue with them, because although they might not be aware of the detailed historical context, they are able to perceive and identify with the fears and the insecurities that grip the characters in the book.[38]

Most of the pages of *Portico d'Ottavia* are written entirely in graphic text, that presupposes a high level of both attention and time from children to absorb all the information. The pages are all laid out to link Foa and Susani's words closely to Berton's illustrations, illustrations that were much admired by Foa, as she commented in 2019:

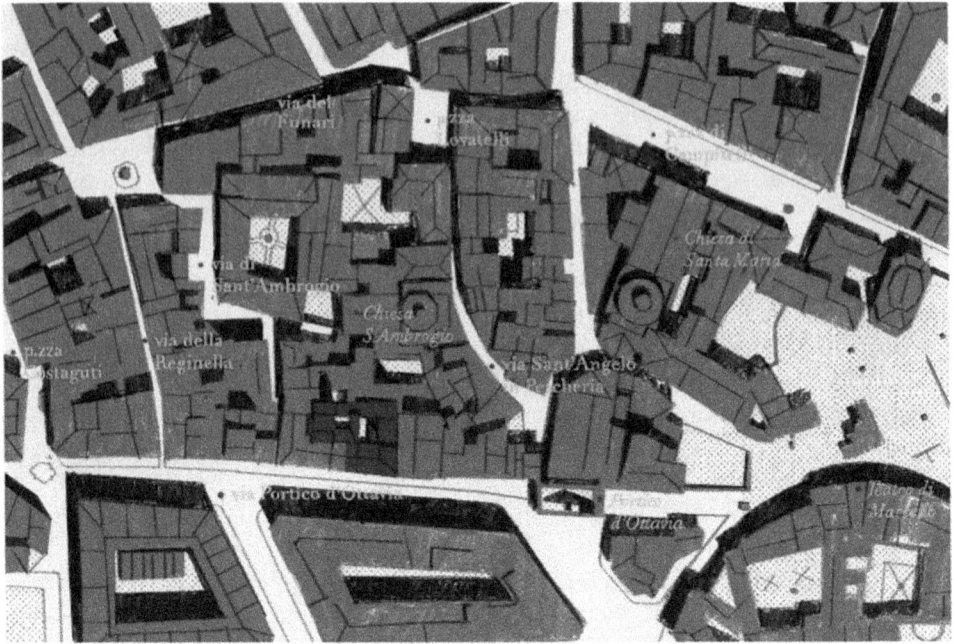

FIG. 6.1. The ghetto streets seen from above with Portico d'Ottavia 13 in red
(*PO*, pp. 2–3).

Con Matteo Berton abbiamo visitato insieme un paio di volte la casa, poi lui
ci è tornato più volte da solo cercando di capire la casa, rendersela famigliare.
Il risultato è stato ottimo, i suoi disegni sono davvero molto belli e rendono il
clima della casa.[39]

[Matteo Berton and I visited 'la Casa' a couple of times, then he went back there
several times by himself trying to understand it and familiarize himself with
it. The result was excellent, his drawings are extremely beautiful and catch the
atmosphere of 'la Casa'.]

As in the adult version of the book, the cover of the children's version depicts 'la
Casa'. The perspective changes, though: while in the adult edition the photomontage
shows the internal courtyard of 'la Casa', on the cover of the children's version there
is an aerial view of Portico d'Ottavia 13 and the adjacent buildings. The endpapers
of the book show a blue map of the ghetto on which 'la Casa' is clearly identified
as a red building (see Fig. 6.1). Generally, colours and perspectives conform to the
narrative, that is to say that, in the first part of the book, when Foa frames the story
she is going to tell and introduces the girl at the heart of the book, the images are
painted in warmer colours. The readers observe these particular scenes head on, as
if standing directly in front of what is happening (see Fig. 6.2). As the Nazis enter
the building, the atmosphere changes. Pictures and atmosphere become gloomy,
painted in mainly cold colours: light and dark blue, grey, and black. Berton also
changes the perspective, so that the readers now view the scene from an indirect
angle as if they are hidden (see Fig. 6.3).

FIG. 6.2. Costanza Fatucci and Anna Foa in their apartment in
Portico d'Ottavia 13 (*PO*, pp. 8-9).

FIG. 6.3. An SS officer entering via del Portico d'Ottavia 13
(*PO*, pp. 22-23).

The story is set in the present and Foa represents herself in the narrative and becomes part of the plot: 'la storia che sto per raccontare mi è capitata l'inverno scorso, mi ero da poco trasferita nella Casa' [the story I'm about to tell happened to me last winter, when I had recently moved into la Casa] (*PO*, p. 7). In the plot, the fictional character of Anna Foa is in her top-floor apartment in via del Portico d'Ottavia 13 when a child, Costanza, appears to her. The Roman round-up is narrated from Costanza's perspective and through her feelings. Costanza is not a fictional character, she is real: she was seven years old in 1943, the youngest daughter of Alberto Fatucci and Rosa Anticoli, and had five siblings — Angelo, Giuseppe, Giacomo, Lazzaro, and Ernesta. They lived all together in the top-floor apartment of Portico d'Ottavia 13, where Foa herself lived almost sixty years later, and all managed to escape the SS troops. When Foa started gathering testimonies about the residents of 'la Casa', Costanza shared her childhood memories with her.[40] Foa re-elaborates Costanza's childhood memories in a time-travel tale in which the ghost of a woman warns the dwellers of Portico d'Ottavia 13 of the forthcoming round-up. 16 October is described in the form of a tale in order to elicit a response from young readers, what Hamida Bosmajian defines as 'enabling rhetoric'.[41]

Costanza invites Anna to travel back in time to see what happened on 16 October 1943: 'se vuoi sapere com'è andata, te lo racconto io: io c'ero' [if you want to know what happened, I will tell you: I was there] (*PO*, p. 10). The modern-day Anna is transported into the past, and a significantly eye-opening experience allows her a new appreciation of the past and an intimate understanding of it. It is this new appreciation and intimate understanding together with a new sense of memory that Foa aims to pass on to children. As Sarah Jordan suggests, the communicative strategy of the journey back in time is a way to make history immediate and accessible to children: 'present-day readers can become a witness to the Holocaust vicariously through [others'] experience[s] and can themselves understand the importance of remembering'.[42]

Anna and Costanza re-experience the arrival of the SS officers through the memories of the child: 'i nazisti entrano senza bisogno di bussare [...] erano le cinque e mezza del mattino [...] sparavano, sparavano nel vuoto e io mi ero agitata' [the Nazis enter without knocking [...] it was five-thirty in the morning [...] they were shooting, they were shooting into the void, and I got nervous] (*PO*, p. 7). The child accompanies Anna around the building, and they witness the escapes and the arrests of the Jews. Neither Costanza nor Anna ever mentions Auschwitz nor refers to it. The narrative tells the stories of those families who escaped, conveying a partly optimistic view of the world; it encourages heroic imaginings and privileges episodes of resistance in a language which does not reveal the reality of the fate of the arrested characters. It describes clear-cut moral characters.

Through Costanza's memories, Foa also tells of the ghost of a woman who warned families to run away:

> La donna fantasma, che si muoveva come una pazza per tutta la Casa e gridava a tutti quelli che incontrava: Scappa, scappa. Si racconta che quella mattina la si incontrasse sulla soglia degli appartamenti vuoti, nei quadri delle finestre, sui

tetti. Arrivava in un fruscio e si dice sussurrasse: Presto, fate presto. (*PO*, pp. 24-27)

[The ghost of a woman, who was moving like crazy throughout 'la Casa' and was shouting to everyone she met: Run away, run away. Some say that on that morning you might have met her on the threshold of the empty apartments, in the window frames, on the roofs. She came with a rustle and some say that she whispered: Hurry, hurry.]

The ghost is a benign figure, in contrast to the SS officers, who protects as many residents as possible. Given that she 'si muoveva come una pazza' and 'gridava', she may be compared to the doomsayers seen in *16 ottobre 1943* and *La Storia*, namely Celeste and Vilma, both literary re-elaborations of Elena di Porto. In *Portico d'Ottavia*, many residents of 'la Casa' listen to the ghost's warnings and thus manage to get to safety. People run across the roofs to escape; others block the door to their apartments and escape through the window. The fantasy of the ghost functions in a book for children to persuade them that they are reading an adventure story with a happy ending. Foa noted: 'molto apprezzata dai piccoli lettori è stata la storia della fantasmina, su cui mi sono state fatte molte domande in ogni presentazione' [the story of the ghost was much appreciated by young readers, I have been asked many questions about that story at each presentation].[43] But the ghost, as we will see, can also be read in terms of cultural memory. Through it, Foa offers a challenge to the dominant realist, documentary mode of other testimonies.

Costanza is the protagonist of this story for two main reasons. First, by the end of the book, young readers have re-experienced the round-up through her memories and point of view. They can more easily identify with Costanza's fears and feelings of powerlessness, bewilderment, and dismay when she sees her friends lined up:

Uscimmo dal portone e non ci fermò nessuno, ma non è vero che tirammo il fiato, non ci calmammo neanche un poco. Anzi forse solo in quel momento davvero ci rendemmo conto di quel che stava succedendo. Dietro di noi c'erano le mie amiche, radunate con le loro famiglie; io lo sapevo, ne sentivo la presenza, ne avvertivo il pianto, la richiesta d'aiuto silenziosa, mi era chiarissimo che non le avrei riviste, volevo salutarle [...]. Combattevo l'istinto di voltarmi indietro. Forse le mie amiche mi guardavano. Mio padre mi strinse il braccio, con un leggero movimento del volto mi fece segno di andare avanti. (*PO*, pp. 44-46)

[We went out of the gate and nobody stopped us, but to be honest we didn't catch our breath, we didn't calm down even a little. Indeed, perhaps it was only at that moment that we really understood what was happening. Behind us there were my friends, gathered with their families; I knew it, I felt their presence, I felt their tears, the silent plea for help, it was very clear to me that I would not see them again, I wanted to greet them [...]. I was fighting the instinct to look back. Probably my friends were looking at me. My father squeezed my arm, with a slight movement of his face he made me go on.]

Readers are led to an emotional involvement with her experience that then prompts their own responses to 16 October.

Second, Costanza's experience is a life-affirming outcome to the story. She and her family survived — her family was one of the two who found refuge at the church of San Benedetto, as recorded in Foa's adult edition. It is not a coincidence that the story ends when Costanza returns to being an old lady who has lived a long life since 1943:

> 'Così mi salvai'. Costanza sorride. 'Ed è per questo che io oggi non ho più questo aspetto'. Senza smettere di sorridere, ma è un sorriso dolce e saggio dove mi sembra in controluce anche il dolore, davanti ai miei occhi la ragazzina di un tempo si trasforma nella signora anziana che è adesso. È la stessa persona, lo si vede dagli occhi, dalle labbra, dall'ironia e dal distacco affettuoso con cui mi guarda [...]. Siamo sedute sul mio divano, Costanza porta alle labbra una tazza di tè fumante, guardiamo insieme verso la finestra. (*PO*, pp. 48-50)

> ['And so I survived'. Costanza smiles. 'And that's why I don't look like this anymore'. Without stopping smiling, but it is a sweet and wise smile where, against the light, it seems also to be sad, before my eyes the little girl of the past turns into the old lady she is now. She is the same person, you can see it in her eyes, lips, the irony and affectionate detachment with which she looks at me [...]. We are sitting on my sofa, Costanza brings a steaming cup of tea to her lips, we look together towards the window.]

By the end of the book, readers return to the present. Anna and Costanza smile at each other, sitting on a sofa drinking a cup of tea. They are both safe.

Constructing and Observing Cultural Memory

As in Chapters 3 to 5, the final section of this chapter is dedicated to the analysis of *Portico d'Ottavia 13* in light of cultural memory studies. As we have seen, through both editions of her book Foa reports the testimonies of those who lived in 'la Casa' on 16 October and encourages an inter- and trans-generational transmission of the round-up through the perspective of one building, via del Portico d'Ottavia 13 itself. Foa looks at the physical place of Portico d'Ottavia 13 to re-elaborate the historical facts of the round-up, but more importantly in terms of cultural memory studies she transforms it into a powerful link between past and present. The building still exists and through it readers of every age can visualise the round-up, just as Foa herself could while living in it. Portico d'Ottavia 13 is transformed into a symbolic place in which to remember the deportation, simultaneously a real and re-imagined building which becomes representative of the round-up and newly meaningful to her readers. She turns it into a place of cultural and public remembrance, where individual and personal memories become available and shareable through the processes of identification and projection that her narrative fosters, as we have seen.

    Portico d'Ottavia 13 turns into a memento, a means of not forgetting. In the preface to the adult edition, Foa notes: 'ho preferito per quanto mi è stato possibile non dimenticare nessuno: di tutti i nomi che emergevano nella ricerca ho inseguito le tracce con rigore filologico forse eccessivo e in qualche momento ossessivo' [as much as I was able, I preferred not to forget anyone: I pursued the traces of all the names that emerged in my research with perhaps excessive and sometimes obsessive philological rigour] (*PO13*, pp. xiv-xv). She goes on to refer to a commemorative plaque placed on the road surface outside 'la Casa', one of the thousands of

Stolperstein [stumbling block] memorials created by the German artist Gunter Demnig that serve to remind passers-by of the victims of the round-up by simple naming in specific places, as Foa herself does. In so doing, she clarifies the purpose of her writing, to create her own 'stumbling block' that leads to all the victims of Portico d'Ottavia 13:

> Recentemente, una pietra d'inciampo [...] è stata collocata di fronte al portone. Ricorda solo uno di quei deportati, una donna incinta di nove mesi portata via il 16 ottobre 1943. Per mettervi una pietra per ognuno dei suoi abitanti mandati a morire non basterebbe lo spazio di un lenzuolo. Che questo libro sia per *voi* come quel lenzuolo. (*PO13*, p. 15, my emphasis)

> [Recently, a stumbling block [...] was placed in front of the gate. It recalls only one of the deportees, a nine-months pregnant woman taken away on 16 October 1943. To put a stone for each of its occupants sent to die, the space of a blanket would not be enough. May this book be like that blanket *to you*.]

Foa's purpose can be accomplished only if her readers reflect on the deportation, empathise with the story, and remember it, thus she establishes a connection with them by addressing them directly as 'voi' in the hope that they will engage more easily with her story.

In terms of the five modes of writing about the past suggested by Erll and analysed in Part I, Foa's writing is highly reflexive: she scrupulously observes how the Roman round-up has been remembered in the last seventy years and tracks its scholarly discussion, she offers a new way of recollecting the round-up and so enriches the cultural memory of it.[44] The micro-histories of the dwellers of Portico d'Ottavia 13 intermingle and are connected with the macro-history of 16 October:

> La storia della casa di via del Portico d'Ottavia 13 sotto l'occupazione può essere meglio definita come una microstoria. Ho infatti cercato di illuminare, lasciando solo quelle zone d'ombra che non sono riuscita a penetrare, una realtà limitata fatta di persone e di cose, di quotidianità e di angosce, di fughe e di imprudenze, di paure e di coraggio. (*PO13*, p. 111)

> [The history of 'la Casa' in via del Portico d'Ottavia 13 under occupation can best be defined as a micro-history. Indeed, I have tried to cast light, leaving only those obscure areas that I was unable to penetrate, on a reality made up of people and things, everyday life and anguish, escapes and imprudence, fears and courage.]

She continues:

> Se le vicende della Casa [...] non ci dicono nulla che già non sapessimo, almeno a grandi linee, sulla razzia del 16 ottobre, molto ci raccontano sui nove mesi dell'occupazione di Roma e sulla vita degli ebrei del quartiere in quelle circostanze. (*PO13*, p. 114)

> [If the events of 'la Casa' [...] tell us nothing that we did not already know, at least broadly speaking, about the round-up of 16 October, they tell us much about the nine months of the occupation of Rome and about the life of the Jews of the neighbourhood under those circumstances.]

The stories of the residents of via del Portico d'Ottavia 13 constitute small but incisive tiles of the mosaic of the Roman round-up and together with the micro-histories analysed in *16 ottobre 1943*, *La Storia*, and *La parola ebreo* engender a better understanding of the event.

Portico d'Ottavia 13 can further be examined for its influence on the cultural memory of the Roman round-up, even though, given its very recent entry into the corpus, its sustained legacy is still unclear. Following Rigney's categories of literature and cultural memory analysed in Part I and for each of our other texts, *Portico d'Ottavia 13* is a 'relay station', a 'stabilizer', and an 'object of recollection'.[45] It is a 'relay station' because it transmits the unknown testimonies of ordinary people who lived in via del Portico d'Ottavia 13 and because it restricts its reconstruction of the Roman round-up to one building, 'la Casa'. Despite having been published less than ten years ago, *Portico d'Ottavia 13* is frequently cited in recent historiographical research, and so can already be defined as a 'stabilizer'.[46] It can in part be seen as an 'object of recollection' to the extent that Foa, together with Susani, re-elaborated and rewrote it in an edition for children that shields young readers from the atrocities of the deportation experience, Foa's words with Berton's images transmitting accessible and powerful awareness of the round-up to a young readership. Lastly, the children's edition is a 'calibrator', a benchmark in the historical discourse on 16 October, because, as mentioned, it is the first work about the Roman round-up written and illustrated for young readers, and it represents it, for the first time, in the tone of a fairy tale.

The two editions of the story Portico d'Ottavia 13 are closely entwined. Read together, they clarify Foa's commitment to the memory of 16 October: her need to pass on a message, to make her readers remember and reflect on the round-up as an event which exemplifies the Italian Holocaust, and her personal need to elaborate her relation to this memory and to the genocide. Together, they prompt reflection on how Foa stretched the boundaries of history to enlarge her readership and transmit historical knowledge through popular history. Both representations of 16 October are steeped in history, but they are made memorable by Foa's use of the building, the place, and the names of those who lived within it. Through both editions, Foa invites readers of all generations to follow her, up the stairs, into the apartments, into the rooms, to see the persecution and the deportation in the place where they occurred.

Notes to Chapter 6

1. The main sources I have drawn on for this account of Anna Foa's work on 16 October are: 'Anna Foa presenta *Via Portico d'Ottavia 13* alla Libreria Arion Monti' (2013) <https://www.youtube.com/watch?v=aDPobEBZwOo> [accessed 21 March 2019]; 'Anna Foa - *Portico d'Ottavia, 13*' (2014) <https://www.youtube.com/watch?v=Ms_JgmASaMk> [accessed 21 March 2019]; '16 ottobre 1943: la razzia del ghetto', *Un giorno nella storia* (Rai Radio3, 16 October 2019) <https://www.raiplaysound.it/playlist/16ottobre1943larazzianelghetto> [accessed 21 March 2020]; 'Anna Foa: la deportazione raccontata ai bambini' (Rai Scuola, 9 September 2015) <https://www.raiscuola.rai.it/tags/annafoa>[accessed 21 March 2019]; Bruno Bonomo, 'Recensione: Anna Foa, *Portico d'Ottavia 13*', *Officina della storia*, 29 April 2014 <https://www.officinadellastoria.eu/it/2014/04/29/recensione-anna-foa-portico-dottavia-13/> [accessed 21 March 2019]. I draw also

on a personal communication from Anna Foa of 4 May 2019.

2. See n. 1 above.

3. Bonomo, 'Recensione'.

4. Anna Foa, *Portico d'Ottavia 13: una casa del ghetto nel lungo inverno del '43* (Rome: Laterza, 2013), p. 43; all further Italian quotations are taken from this edition (hereafter referenced in the main text as *PO13*). English translations are my own.

5. Foa's text can be placed alongside many other works of popular, narrative, or personalised history about the Holocaust written by historians. See: Otto Dov Kulka, *Landscape of the Metropolis of Death* (London: Allen Lane, 2013); Omer Bartov, *Anatomy of a Genocide: The Life and Death of a Town Called Buczacz* (New York: Simon & Schuster, 2018). Both these author-historians have published reflections on their own works and these have been pivotal for the analysis of Foa in this chapter: Otto Dov Kulka, 'Some Reflections on History and Fiction in my *Landscape of the Metropolis of Death*: Comments on Hayden White's "The History Fiction Divide"', *Holocaust Studies*, 20.1-2 (2014), 35-44; Omer Bartov, 'Anatomy of a Genocide', *Journal of Genocide Research*, 20.4 (2018), 650-58; and Hayden White, 'The History Fiction Divide', *Holocaust Studies*, 20.1-2 (2014), 17-34.

6. See: Jurgen Habermas, *The Structural Transformation of the Public Sphere* (Cambridge: Polity Press, 1989); Nicola Gallerano, 'History and the Public Use of History', *Diogenes*, 42.168 (1994), 85-102; *L'uso pubblico della storia*, ed. by Nicola Gallerano (Milan: Franco Angeli, 1995).

7. 'Anna Foa presenta *Via Portico d'Ottavia 13* alla Libreria Arion Monti'.

8. Anna Foa, *La famiglia F.* (Rome: Laterza, 2018); Foa and Scaraffia, *Anime nere*.

9. Foa, *La famiglia F.*, p. 95.

10. '16 ottobre 1943: la razzia del ghetto'.

11. Ibid.

12. 'Anna Foa presenta *Via Portico d'Ottavia 13* alla Libreria Arion Monti' (my emphasis).

13. Email from the author, 4 May 2019.

14. 'Anna Foa - *Portico d'Ottavia, 13*'.

15. See: *La ricerca delle donne: studi femministi in Italia*, ed. by Anna Rossi Doria and Maria Cristina Marcuzzo (Turin: Rosenberg & Sellier, 1987); Anna Rossi Doria, *Memoria e storia: il caso della deportazione* (Soveria Mannelli: Rubbettino, 1998).

16. On Vittorio Foa, see for example: *Vittorio Foa e le trasformazioni della società italiana*, ed. by Amos Andreoni and Enrico Pugliese (Rome: Ediesse, 2011).

17. Email from the author, 4 May 2019.

18. Anna Foa, *Ebrei in Europa: dalla peste nera all'emancipazione XIV–XIX secolo* (Rome: Laterza, 1992), *Diaspora, Eretici: storie di streghe, ebrei e convertiti* (Bologna: Il Mulino, 2011), *Andare per ghetti e giudecche* (Bologna: Il Mulino, 2014); and Anna Foa and Francesca Rodari, *Donne e Shoah* (Milan: Mimesis, 2021); *Ebrei, minoranze, Risorgimento: storia, cultura, letteratura*, ed. by Marina Beer and Anna Foa (Rome: Viella, 2013); *Ebrei, una storia italiana: i primi mille anni*, ed. by Anna Foa, Giancarlo Lacerenza, and Daniele Jalla (Milan: Electa, 2017).

19. Foa, *Diaspora*, p. vii (hereafter referenced in the main text as *D*). English translations are my own.

20. Tim Cresswell, *Place: A Short Introduction* (Oxford: Blackwell, 2004), pp. 7-8.

21. Gaston Bachelard, *The Poetics of Space* (New York: Penguin Books, 2014), p. 35

22. See, for example, Luca Serianni, *Grammatica italiana. Italiano comune e lingua letteraria: suoni, forme, costrutti* (Turin: Utet, 1988), pp. 325-26.

23. Marianne Hirsch, *Family Frames: Photography, Narrative, and Postmemory* (Cambridge, MA: Harvard University Press, 1997), and 'Projected Memory: Holocaust Photographs in Personal and Public Fantasy', in *Acts of Memory: Cultural Recall in the Present*, ed. by Mieke Bal, Jonathan Crewe, and Leo Spitzer (Hanover, NH: University Press of New England, 1999), pp. 3-23.

24. Zeitlin, 'The Vicarious Witness', p. 19.

25. Marianne Hirsch and Leo Spitzer, 'What's Wrong with This Picture?', *Journal of Modern Jewish Studies*, 5.2 (2006), 229-52 (p. 237).

26. On this see: Susan Sontag, *On Photography* (London: Penguin, 1977); Marianne Hirsch, 'Surviving Images: Holocaust Photographs and the Work of Postmemory', *Yale Journal of*

Criticism, 14.1 (2001), 5-37; Georges Didi-Huberman, *Images malgré tout* (Paris: Minuit, 2003); Elizabeth Edwards and Janice Hart, *Photographs Objects Histories: On the Materiality of Images* (London: Routledge 2004).

27. Sontag, *On Photography*, p. 16.
28. Email from the author, 4 May 2019.
29. Carola Susani is an author of books for both children and adults; her children's books include: *Il licantropo* (Milan: Feltrinelli, 2002), *Cola Pesce* (Milan: Feltrinelli, 2004), *Susan: la piratessa* (Rome: Laterza, 2014), and *Eneide* (Rome: Laterza, 2015). Matteo Berton illustrates magazines and advertisements, as well as children's books and comics. His work 'has been awarded with a gold and a silver medal from the Society of Illustrators of New York, and selected from American Illustrator and the Children's Book Fair of Bologna' <https://matteoberton.com/> [accessed 23 March 2019].
30. Anna Foa, *Portico d'Ottavia*, illus. by Matteo Berton (Rome: Laterza, 2015) (hereafter referenced in the main text as *PO*). English translations are my own.
31. Email from the author, 4 May 2019.
32. Ibid.
33. Ibid.
34. Anne Frank, *Anne Frank: The Diary of a Young Girl*, trans. by B. M. Mooyaart-Doubleday (London: Constellation Books, 1952); John Boyne, *The Boy in the Striped Pyjamas* (London: Definitions, 2006). See: David Barnouw, *The Phenomenon of Anne Frank*, trans. by Jeannette K. Ringold (Bloomington: Indiana University Press, 2018); Adrienne Kertzer, *My Mother's Voice: Children, Literature, and the Holocaust* (Peterborough: Broadview Press, 2002); Lydia Kokkola, *Representing the Holocaust in Children's Literature* (New York: Routledge, 2003).
35. See for example Hamida Bosmajian, *Sparing the Child: Grief and the Unspeakable in Youth Literature about Nazism and the Holocaust* (New York: Routledge, 2002); Sarah D. Jordan, 'Educating Without Overwhelming: Authorial Strategies in Children's Holocaust Literature', *Children's Literature in Education*, 35.3 (September 2004), 199-218; Myrna P. Maehet, 'Authenticity in Holocaust Literature for Children', *South African Journal of Libraries and Information Science*, 66.3 (1998), 114-21; Joanne Pettitt, 'On Blends and Abstractions: Children's Literature and the Mechanisms of Holocaust Representation', *International Research in Children's Literature*, 7.2 (2014), 152-64; Walter and March, 'Juvenile Picture Books About the Holocaust'.
36. Pettitt, 'On Blends and Abstractions', p. 158.
37. Ibid.
38. 'Anna Foa: la deportazione raccontata ai bambini'.
39. Email from the author, 4 May 2019.
40. Ibid.
41. Bosmajian, *Sparing the Child*, p. 133.
42. Jordan, 'Educating Without Overwhelming', p. 214.
43. Email from the author, 4 May 2019.
44. Erll, *Memory in Culture*, pp. 158-60.
45. Rigney, 'The Dynamics of Remembrance', pp. 350-51.
46. Riccardo Calimani, *Storia degli ebrei italiani: nel XIX e nel XX secolo* (Milan: Mondadori, 2015), p. 786; Levis Sullam, *I carnefici italiani*, pp. 128 n., 138 n., 141 n.; Giuseppina Mellace, *Delitti e stragi dell'Italia fascista dal 1922 al 1945: i casi più eclatanti dell'epoca, oltre la cronaca nera* (Rome: Newton Compton, 2015), pp. 252, 255, 257; Claudio Bondì and Stefano Piperno, *Perché ci siamo salvati* (Venice: Marsilio, 2020), p. 104.

CONCLUSION

❖

It was, I think, pertinent to conclude Part II of this book with Anna Foa, a historian who repeatedly argues for the importance of literary texts in the transmission of historical knowledge into cultural memory, and for the evolution of historical understanding of the round-up of 16 October 1943. With this book, I wanted to give a sense of how *16 ottobre 1943*, *La Storia*, *La parola ebreo*, and *Portico d'Ottavia 13* have operated on the personal and on the collective level, in other words on the reader and on society. I read these texts as acts of transfer, points of memory, because they have created images which have become part of the process of creating different forms of active and passive memory of the Roman round-up; they have increased wider awareness of it and have engaged in a dialogue with historians about the interpretation of the past. I see them not only as the products of recollection or imagination, but as bearers of historical knowledge, active ingredients in the process of forging cultural memory.

Given that cultural memory is a continuing process, these concluding remarks are not intended to end the discourse but, rather, to lead to the building of alternative perceptions of the triangular relationship between history, memory, and literature. They open up the perspective to different narratives and briefly address how cinema, television, and theatre have contributed to recent popular engagement in the recollection of 16 October and strengthened understanding of the German occupation of Italy and experiences of the Holocaust. As in the case of literature, there is almost no critical research which looks specifically at the adaptation of the event of 16 October in cinema, television, and theatre.[1] Therefore, as a final point of focus, I present a sample of the contributions made to this ongoing, vital, but under-investigated field by films, television programmes, and plays since 2000.

Before 2000, a limited number of works about the Roman round-up were produced in popular media. They included two fictional films, two fictional television series, and three documentaries: *L'oro di Roma* (1961) by Carlo Lizzani; *Storia d'amore e d'amicizia* (1982) by Franco Rossi; *La Storia* (1986) by Comencini, in both television and cinema adaptations; *16 ottobre 1943* (1961) and *Memoria presente: ebrei e città di Roma durante l'occupazione nazista* (1983) by Ansano Giannarelli; and *Diario di un cronista: Piazza Giudia* (1963) by Sergio Zavoli.[2] There is no record of Italian stage plays on this subject being performed before 2009.

The turn of the century saw a slight acceleration of new works that touched on the round-up in cinema and television, and a considerable growth in theatrical productions.[3] These include three films: *Amen* (2002) by Costa-Gavras; *La finestra di fronte* (2003) by Ferzan Özpetek; and, almost twenty years later, *Freaks Out*

(2021) by Gabriele Mainetti.[4] Six documentaries appeared between 2005 and 2020: *Nata due volte: storia di Settimia ebrea romana* (2005) by Giandomenico Curi; *Nazisti a Roma* (2007) by Mary Mirka Milo; *Una storia romana* (2008) by Pupa Garibba; *Ebrei a Roma* (2012) by Gianfranco Pannone; *La razzia: Roma, 16 ottobre 1943* (2018) by Ruggero Gabbai; and *Roma e la Shoah: luoghi e storie della persecuzione* (2020) by Dario Prosperini.[5] From 2003 to 2022, five episodes of widely-known cultural television series such as *La storia siamo noi* and *Ulisse* were dedicated to the historical representation of the round-up.[6] In 2010, there was also a new, but controversial, television drama *Sotto il cielo di Roma* by the Canadian director Christian Deguay, transmitted in two episodes on Rai 1 on 31 October and 1 November.[7] Set in Rome between July 1943 and the city's liberation in June 1944, its historical inaccuracies, which included an apologetic representation of Pius XII, provoked the disapproval of the chief rabbi of Rome, Riccardo Di Segni, who felt that the programme offered distorted and distorting images of the events.[8]

Plays about 16 October have numbered fourteen. The first, *Bucefalo: il pugilatore* (2009) by Alessio De Caprio, was staged for the first time in Rome and has been repeated, almost annually, since 2009. In October 2010, two plays were staged for the sixty-seventh anniversary of the round-up: *Roma Auschwitz: andata e ritorno* by Roberto Bencivenga and *Roma, 16 ottobre 1943* by Simonetta De Nichilo and Francesca Gatto. In 2013, for the seventieth anniversary of the round-up, there were productions of two works: *Ladro di razza* by Gianni Clementi and *13419 la necessità del ritorno* by Roberto Attias. *Ladro di razza*, based on a book of the same title published by Clementi in 2010 (briefly described in Chapter 2), has been performed many times since 2013 outside Rome, in places such as Milan, Turin, Florence, Catania, and Lanciano. In 2018 it was broadcast on television by Rai 5, and in 2021 it returned to the Teatro Franco Parenti in Milan.[9] *13419 la necessità del ritorno* was staged for the first time on 16 October 2013 in Rome at the Ennio Morricone Auditorium at the University of Rome Tor Vergata; in 2014 it was performed three more times in Rome; in 2019 it was staged in Jerusalem in collaboration with the Istituto Italiano di Cultura in Tel Aviv; in 2020, for the seventy-fifth anniversary of the liberation of Auschwitz, it was included in the programme of events presented at the Istituto Italiano di Cultura in Kraków; and in 2022 it was performed at the Istituto Italiano di Cultura in Budapest for Holocaust Remembrance Day. Between 2015 and 2017, four stage plays were produced: *Esterina* by Claudia Margani in 2015; and *16 ottobre 1943* by Antonello Carpuso, *La valigia* by Corrado Plastino and *Il tema di Sara* by Loredana Ranelli in 2017. The last two were performed at secondary-school level in the provinces of Milan and Catanzaro. Finally, in 2018 no fewer than five pieces were performed for the seventy-fifth anniversary of the round-up. Two were adaptations of literary texts: *16 ottobre 1943* by Giancarlo Monticelli, which is based on Debenedetti's text, and *Quer 16 ottobbre* by Alberto Ciarafoni, which comes from the homonymous collection of poems published by Ciarafoni in 2016, as already noted in Chapter 2. The other three were original plays: *Razzia* by Amedeo Osti Guerrazzi, *Reginella* by Manuela Rossetti, and *Celeste* by Fabio Pisano.

This outline of works shows a remarkable wealth of early twenty-first-century cinematic, televisual, and theatrical re-elaborations of the Roman round-up that both indicates the coexistence of different layers of memories of the event and illustrates how the reading of history is still projected across memories and narratives of the twenty-first century, be they fictional or not. These new representations, in their efforts to share and transmit historical awareness, follow similar paths to those laid out by the literary texts explored in this book and may be subject to a similar set of theoretical questions and analysis of strategies and techniques as those elaborated throughout this volume.

Certain of these productions carry the direct marks of having been influenced by the literary works analysed here. In the last twenty years, Debenedetti's and Morante's texts in particular have been confirmed as what Ann Rigney defines as 'objects of recollection'. From the 2000s, *16 ottobre 1943* has been explicitly re-worked in at least two plays: *16 ottobre 1943* by Monticelli, and *Roma, 16 ottobre 1943* by De Nichilo and Gatto, who also included passages from *La Storia* in their play. Further analysis demonstrates that there are also other, less obvious connections, such as the films *Amen* by Costa-Gavras and *La finestra di fronte* by Ozpetek, and the latest documentary to be produced, *Roma e la Shoah* by Prosperini and Osti Guerrazzi.

Costa-Gavras's camera is like Debenedetti's eyes. They both make viewers and readers enter the ghetto in the middle of the round-up as people are trying to escape, families are herded onto trucks, children are crying, adults are speechless. In brief but powerful shots, Costa-Gavras encourages his audience to share a sense of compassion with the Jewish community, with the victims at Portico d'Ottavia. Ozpetek's *La finestra di fronte* shows the night of the round-up through a form of double anguish experienced by his protagonist Davide, who is tormented when he remembers the choice he made on the night of 16 October 1943. He has to decide whether to turn one way and warn, and thus save, his lover or to turn the other and alert his family and his community of the forthcoming round-up. He heartbreakingly decides to warn his family and his community. In this sense, the description of the round-up through Davide's emotions recalls Morante's picture of 16 and 18 October as expressed through the fears and doubts of Ida. Ozpetek also prompts reflections on the idea of memory and recollection, alterity and discrimination, and collective responsibility. The round-up is narrated through Davide's flashback memories so that the plot moves back and forth between past and present. Viewers participate in a cognitive journey to both a private and a shared past, just as Loy's readership did in *La parola ebreo*. Finally, Prosperini and Osti Guerrazzi, like Foa, represent 16 October through the description of the places connected to the deportation, showing that the history of Rome's Holocaust is engraved on stones, buildings, and archaeological sites, and on the ghetto and the intricate web of the streets of the capital.

More broadly still, we may question to what extent, as individual works or as a group of works, these twenty-first-century film, television, and theatre narratives take their place in the representation of the historical events of the round-up and in the re-elaboration of personal memories, in ways that echo the patterns we have seen in Part II of this book. We can reflect on the balance between narrative, history, and memory in films such as *La finestra di fronte* and *Freaks Out*, or in the television series *Sotto il cielo di Roma* and in the play *Ladro di razza*, for example. We can look at the focus on individual stories, which is adopted to favour a sense of identification between the audience and the characters, and the extent to which the representation of the emotions of characters fosters a sense of empathy. We can explore how such techniques trigger forms of prosthetic memories of the round-up in audiences, thus raising their sense of awareness of the past. Such a tendency is strongly evident in documentaries such as *Nata due volte* and *Una storia romana*, and in plays such as *Reginella* and *Celeste*. We can also consider attempts to not forget the round-up by establishing an inter- and trans-generational dialogue between the young and those who survived or avoided deportation, as for example in the monologue *13419 la necessità del ritorno* and in the theatrical works produced at secondary-school level, *La valigia* and *Il tema di Sara*. And many further connections and recurrent patterns of storytelling could be added to connect our literary texts to these recent representations.

This growing number of films, television programmes, and stage plays over the last two decades corresponds to a general increase in interest regarding the Holocaust, which began in the 1990s and intensified in particular after the establishment of the International Holocaust Remembrance Day, the 'Giorno della memoria', in 2001. They can be seen as an invitation to develop a sense of individual responsibility in response to the spread of nationalist parties and anti-Semitic attacks both in Italy and in Europe. These concluding remarks therefore also function as a springboard for future considerations of the willingness of directors, producers, scriptwriters, and actors to pass on memories of the Roman round-up; they are also intended to open a debate on how we might read these works as a means of reflecting on the present by looking at the past. They can be considered a starting-point for reflecting on the socio-cultural and political context in which each of the films, television programmes, and stage plays has been produced, broadcast or performed, and publicised.

The production of works and the transmission of cultural memory on the Roman round-up is thriving. Literature, cinema, television, and theatre, without even mentioning journalism, social networks, and online platforms, have contributed to a new socio-historical and cultural understanding of the Roman round-up. The trajectory of the memory of 16 October is continuously growing and these concluding remarks have opened a new field of under-explored material. But this is a matter for further research beyond the scope of this book. Cultural memory is, as noted more than once in these pages, an ongoing process and cannot be contained within the limits of a front and a back cover.

Notes to the Conclusion

1. A rare exception is Damiano Garofalo, '"Non dimenticarlo il nostro ottobre".
2. *Storia d'amore e d'amicizia*, dir. by Franco Rossi (Rai 1, Rewind, for six weeks from 24 October 1982). The series was also broadcast in Hungary in 1985 and re-transmitted in Italy twice, in the 1990s and in the 2000s. On this see, for example, Emiliano Perra, 'Buon cattolico, buon

italiano: Shoah, religione e salvataggio degli ebrei in alcune recenti miniserie', in *Televisionismo: narrazioni televisive della storia italiana negli anni della seconda Repubblica*, ed. by Monica Jansen and Maria Bonaria Urban (Venice: Edizioni Ca' Foscari, 2015), pp. 49-60 (pp. 50-51). *Diario di un cronista: Piazza Giudia*, dir. by Sergio Zavoli (Studio M.I.O., 1963); *16 ottobre 1943*, dir. by Ansano Giannarelli (REIAC Film, 1961); *Memoria presente: ebrei e città di Roma durante l'occupazione nazista*, dir. by Ansano Giannarelli (Archivio storico audiovisivo del movimento operaio, Istituto Romano per la storia d'Italia dal fascismo alla resistenza, Centro di Cultura Ebraica della Comunità israelitica di Roma, 1983).

3. A complete list, with summaries, of films, television series, and plays which deal with the round-up is to be found in the Appendix to this volume.

4. *Amen*, dir. by Costa-Gavras (Mikado Film, 2002); *La finestra di fronte*, dir. by Ferzan Özpetek (R&C Produzioni, Red Wave Films, AFS Film, 2003); *Freaks Out*, dir. by Gabriele Mainetti (Goon Films, Lucky Red, Rai Cinema, 2021).

5. *Nata due volte: storia di Settimia ebrea romana*, dir. by Giandomenico Curi (Shoah Foundation, ANED, 2005); *Nazisti a Roma*, dir. by Mary Mirka Milo (Istituto Luce, 2007); *Una storia romana*, dir. by Pupa Garibba (Europa News, 2008); *Ebrei a Roma*, dir. by Gianfranco Pannone (Blue Film, 2012); *La razzia: Roma, 16 ottobre 1943*, dir. by Ruggero Gabbai (Forma International, Fondazione Museo della Shoah, Rai Cinema, 2018); *Roma e la Shoah: luoghi e storie della persecuzione*, dir. by Dario Prosperini (Fondazione Museo della Shoah, 2020).

6. 'Il sabato nero', dir. by Gianluigi De Stefano, *La storia siamo noi* (Rai 3, 16 October 2012); '16 ottobre', *Sorgente di vita* (Rai 2, 6 October 2013); 'Una storia italiana', *Sorgente di vita* (Rai 2, 20 October 2013); '16 ottobre 1943', *Ulisse* (Rai 1, 13 October 2018); 'Viaggio senza ritorno', *Ulisse* (Rai 1, 26 January 2022).

7. *Sotto il cielo di Roma*, dir. by Christian Deguay (Lux Vide, Rai Fiction, Rai 1, 31 October and 1 November 2010). On this see Emiliano Perra, 'Good Catholics, Good Italians: Religion and Rescue in Recent Italian Holocaust Dramas', *The Italianist*, 34.2 (2014), 156-69 (pp. 161-62).

8. On this, see: Emanuel Baroz, 'Rav Riccardo Di Segni: "La fiction su Pio XII? Patacca propagandistica"', *Focus on Israel*, 1 November 2010 <http://www.focusonisrael.org/2010/11/01/pio-xii-fiction-raiuno-di-segni/> [accessed 27 October 2020]; Riccardo Bocca, 'Grandi manovre dietro a Pio XII', *L'Espresso*, 2 November 2010 <http://bocca.blogautore.espresso.repubblica.it/2010/11/02/grandi-manovre-dietro-a-pio-xii/> [accessed 27 October 2020]; Orazio La Rocca, 'Fiction Rai: l'ira degli ebrei Pio XII patacca assolutoria', *La Repubblica*, 2 November 2010 <https://ricerca.repubblica.it/repubblica/archivio/repubblica/2010/11/02/fiction-rai-ira-degli-ebrei-pio.html> [accessed 27 October 2020]; Paolo Rodari, 'Pio XII, il rabbino di Roma: "Non ci fu volontà di fermare il treno del 16 ottobre"', *La Repubblica*, 2 March 2020 <https://www.repubblica.it/vaticano/2020/03/02/news/pio_xii_il_rabbino_di_roma_non_ci_fu_volonta_di_fermare_il_treno_del_16_ottobre_-250061227/> [accessed 27 March 2020].

9. *Ladro di razza*, dir. by Gianni Clementi (Rai 5, 13 October 2018).

APPENDIX

❖

Films, Television Programmes, and Plays
Treating the Rome Round-up

13419 la necessità del ritorno (2013): a monologue by Roberto Attias. It is set in
  Rome on 1 March 1968. The round-up of 16 October 1943 is represented
  through a long flashback.
16 ottobre 1943 (1961): a documentary by Ansano Giannarelli. Debenedetti's text is
  overlaid with long shots of the ghetto in the post-war years.
16 ottobre 1943 (2018): a play by Giancarlo Monticelli. It is based on Debenedetti's
  text.
16 ottobre 1943: una storia altre storie (2017): a play by Antonello Carpuso. It recounts
  the Roman round-up through the re-elaboration of personal memories and
  diaries of the people who were in Rome on 16 October.
Amen (2002): a film by Costa-Gavras. It examines the role of the Vatican and Pius
  XII during the Holocaust. The deportation of the Jews of Rome is developed
  through long shots of the ghetto on the morning of 16 October and a close-
  up shot of the Pope who peremptorily says that the Church cannot intervene.
Bucefalo: il pugilatore (2009): a play by Alessio De Caprio. It recounts the life of
  Lazzaro Anticoli, a former boxer from the ghetto who avoided deportation
  on 16 October but was later arrested in March 1944 after Celeste Di Porto
  denounced him to the Fascists.
Celeste (2016): a play by Fabio Pisano. It narrates the story of Celeste di Porto, who
  after the round-up started to turn many Jews over to the Fascist gang Cialli-
  Mezzaroma.
Diario di un cronista: Piazza Giudia (1963): a documentary by Sergio Zavoli. It
  represents the Roman round-up through historical documents and personal
  testimonies.
Ebrei a Roma (2012): a documentary by Gianfranco Pannone. Although not
  specifically addressing the Roman round-up, it provides insights into 16
  October from the broader perspective of the second and third generations,
  the children and the grandchildren of those who lived through the war.
Freaks Out (2021): a film by Gabriele Mainetti. It is a fairy-tale with dark
  undertones, a uchronic representation of the deportation of the Roman Jews.
Esterina (2015): a play by Claudia Margani. It tells the Roman round-up through the
  friendship of two girls, a friendship which was interrupted after 16 October
  1943.

Il tema di Sara (2017): a play by Loredana Ranelli. It narrates the round-up through a combination of dialogues between people of different generations: the young discover the stories of those who lived through the round-up when they were the same age.

L'oro di Roma (1961): a film by Carlo Lizzani. Its subject is the ransom of fifty kilos of gold which happened on 26 September 1943. Only the last few scenes present the bare ghetto on the afternoon of 16 October.

La finestra di fronte (2003): a film by Ferzan Özpetek. It pictures the Roman round-up through the memory of a survivor who tells his story to a young woman.

La razzia: Roma, 16 ottobre 1943 (2018): a documentary by Ruggero Gabbai with the collaboration of Marcello Pezzetti and Liliana Picciotto. It focuses on the experiences of those Jews who avoided deportation.

La Storia (1986): an adaptation of Morante's *La Storia* both for cinema and television by Luigi Comencini. It briefly represents the departure of the Jews from Stazione Tiburtina on 18 October.

La valigia (2017): a play by Corrado Plastino. It is composed of conversations between people of different generations so that the young learn about the experiences of individuals who experienced the round-up when they were approximately the same age.

Ladro di razza (2013): a play by Gianni Clementi based on his 2010 book of the same name. The plot revolves around three main characters who are arrested by SS officers on the morning of 16 October 1943.

Memoria presente: ebrei e città di Roma durante l'occupazione nazista (1983): a documentary by Ansano Giannarelli. It depicts the relationship of the Jews with other Roman citizens and the extent to which it changed after the round-up.

Nata due volte: storia di Settimia ebrea romana (2005): a documentary by Giandomenico Curi. It is based on testimony left to the Shoah Foundation by Settimia Spizzichino, the only woman to survive deportation to Auschwitz from Rome on 16 October.

Nazisti a Roma (2007): a documentary by Mary Mirka Milo. It does not specifically focus on the Roman round-up but provides insights into 16 October within a wider history from the perspectives of the second and third generations, the children and the grandchildren of those who lived through the war.

Quer 16 ottobbre (2018): a semi-staged reading of poems about the Roman round-up directed and performed by Alberto Ciarafoni, based on his 2016 book of the same name.

Razzia (2018): a play by Amedeo Osti Guerrazzi. It consists of a series of monologues reporting the round-up from different perspectives. The event is described through the memories of some of the people who lived through it: two SS officers, two Fascists, Jews who avoided deportation, and Catholics who hid Jews.

Reginella (2018): a play by Manuela Rossetti. It is about Settimia Spizzichino, her arrest on 16 October, her deportation to Auschwitz, and her return to Rome in 1945.

Roma Auschwitz: andata e ritorno (2010): a play by Roberto Bencivenga. It narrates the arrest of Settimia Spizzichino, her experience in Auschwitz, and her return to Rome.

Roma e la Shoah: luoghi e storie della persecuzione (2020): a documentary by Dario Prosperini and written by Amedeo Osti Guerrazzi. It considers the places which are connected to the persecution of the Roman Jews. The event of 16 October is reported through the description of Portico d'Ottavia.

Roma, 16 ottobre 1943 (2010): a play by Simonetta De Nichilo and Francesca Gatto. It is a polyphonic representation of the round-up. It includes personal memories of the Jews who escaped and readings of passages from *16 ottobre 1943* by Debenedetti and *La Storia* by Morante.

Sotto il cielo di Roma (2010): a television series by Christian Deguay. It is set in Rome and reconstructs the months from the bombing of San Lorenzo in July 1943 until the liberation of the city in June 1944.

Storia d'amore e d'amicizia (1982): a television series by Franco Rossi. It is set in Rome during the war and revolves around a brotherly friendship and the love for a young Jewish woman from the ghetto who manages to avoid deportation on 16 October.

Una storia romana (2008): a documentary by Pupa Garibba. It contains the testimony left by Enrica Sermoneta Moscati, who was eleven in 1943. She avoided deportation on 16 October by going into hiding with her mother and siblings.

BIBLIOGRAPHY

❖

Archival material

Florence, Archivio contemporaneo 'Alessandro Bonsanti' — Gabinetto Vieusseux, Fondo Debenedetti, II
Rome, Biblioteca Nazionale Centrale, Vittorio Emanuele, 1618/1
Milan, Fondazione Arnoldo e Alberto Mondadori, Erich Linder Archive, 26883

Printed Sources

ACTIS-GROSSO, MAURICE, 'La colpa degli innocenti: una psicanalisi romanzesca: *Cioccolata da Hanselmann* e *La parola ebreo* di Rosetta Loy', *Narrativa*, 16 (1999), 35-62
AFFINATI, ERALDO, *Campo di sangue* (Milan: Mondadori, 1997)
ANDREONI, AMOS, and ENRICO PUGLIESE, eds, *Vittorio Foa e le trasformazioni della società italiana* (Rome: Ediesse, 2011)
ANTONUCCI, SILVIA HAIA, 'Le interviste', in *Roma, 16 ottobre 1943: anatomia di una deportazione*, ed. by Silvia Haia Antonucci and others (Milan: Guerini, 2006), pp. 96-131
ANTONUCCI, SILVIA HAIA, and CLAUDIO PROCACCIA, 'Introduzione', in *Dopo il 16 ottobre. Gli ebrei a Roma tra occupazione, resistenza, accoglienza e delazioni*, ed. by Silvia Haia Antonucci and Claudio Procaccia (Rome: Viella, 2017), pp. 7-34
ANTONUCCI, SILVIA HAIA, and CLAUDIO PROCACCIA, eds, *Dopo il 16 ottobre: gli ebrei a Roma tra occupazione, resistenza, accoglienza e delazioni* (Rome: Viella, 2017)
ANTONUCCI, SILVIA HAIA, and OTHERS, eds, *Roma, 16 ottobre 1943: anatomia di una deportazione* (Milan: Guerini, 2006)
ARENDT, HANNAH, *The Origins of Totalitarianism* (San Diego, CA: Harcourt Brace Jovanovich, 1979)
ASSMANN, ALEIDA, 'Re-framing Memory: Between Individual and Collective Forms of Constructing the Past', in *Performing the Past: Memory, History, and Identity in Modern Europe*, ed. by Karin Tilmans, Frank van Vree, and Jay M. Winter (Amsterdam: Amsterdam University Press, 2010), pp. 35-49
——'Three Stabilizers of Memory: Affect - Symbols - Trauma', in *Sites of Memory in American Literatures and Culture*, ed. by Udo J. Hebl (Heidelberg: Universitätsverlag C. Winter, 2003), pp. 15-30
ASSMANN, JAN, 'Communicative and Cultural Memory', in *A Companion to Cultural Memory Studies*, ed. by Astrid Erll, Ansgar Nünning, and Sara Young (New York: De Gruyter, 2010), pp. 109-18
BACHELARD, GASTON, *The Poetics of Space* (New York: Penguin Books, 2014)
BALESTRINI, NANNI, and OTHERS, 'Contro il romanzone della Morante', *Il Manifesto*, 18 July 1974
BARDINI, MARCO, 'Esporsi al pubblico: Elsa Morante tra occasioni mondane e impegno civile', *Status Quaestionis*, 3 (2012), 1-29
——*Morante Elsa. Italiana. Di professione, poeta* (Pisa: Nistri-Lischi, 1999)

BARNOUW, DAVID, *The Phenomenon of Anne Frank*, trans. by Jeannette K. Ringold (Bloomington: Indiana University Press, 2018)

BAROZ, EMANUEL, 'Rav Riccardo Di Segni: "La Fiction su Pio XII? Patacca propagandistica"', *Focus on Israel*, 1 November 2010 <http://www.focusonisrael.org/2010/11/01/pio-xii-fiction-raiuno-di-segni/> [accessed 27 October 2020]

BARTOV, OMER, 'Anatomy of a Genocide', *Journal of Genocide Research*, 20.4 (2018), 650-58

——*Anatomy of a Genocide: The Life and Death of a Town Called Buczacz* (New York: Simon & Schuster, 2018)

BASSANI, GIORGIO, *Il giardino dei Finzi-Contini* (Turin: Einaudi, 1962)

——'Una lapide in via Mazzini' [1952], in *Cinque storie ferraresi* (Turin: Einaudi, 1956)

BAUMEISTER, MARTIN, AMEDEO OSTI GUERRAZZI, and CLAUDIO PROCACCIA, eds, *16 ottobre 1943: la deportazione degli ebrei romani tra storia e memoria* (Rome: Viella, 2016)

BAURELLI, MAURO, 'Il dominio della Storia: intorno al romanzo di Elsa Morante', in *La memoria della politica: esperienze e autorappresentazione nel racconto di uomini e donne*, ed. by Fiamma Lussana and Lucia Motti (Rome: Ediesse, 2007), pp. 215-26

BEER, MARINA, 'Costellazioni ebraiche: note su Elsa Morante e l'ebraismo del Novecento', in *"Nacqui nell'ora amara del meriggio": scritti per Elsa Morante nel centenario della sua nascita*, ed. by Eleonora Cardinale and Giuliana Zagra (Rome: Quaderni della Biblioteca Nazionale Centrale di Roma, 2013), pp. 165-201

BEER, MARINA, and ANNA FOA, eds, *Ebrei, minoranze, Risorgimento: storia, cultura, letteratura* (Rome: Viella, 2013)

BELT, PIERRE, *Pio XII e la seconda guerra mondiale negli archivi vaticani* (Cinisello Balsamo: San Paolo, 1999)

BENSOUSSAN, GEORGE, *Histoire de la Shoah* (Paris: Presses universitaires de France, 1996)

BERGER, SARA, 'I persecutori del 16 ottobre 1943', in *16 ottobre 1943: la deportazione degli ebrei romani tra storia e memoria*, ed. by Martin Baumeister, Amedeo Osti Guerrazzi, and Claudio Procaccia (Rome: Viella, 2016), pp. 21-39

BERNABÒ, GRAZIELLA, *Come leggere 'La Storia' di Elsa Morante* (Milan: Mursia, 1991)

——*La fiaba estrema: Elsa Morante tra vita e scrittura* (Rome: Carocci, 2012)

BERNAERTS, LARS, and OTHERS, eds, *Stories and Minds: Cognitive Approaches to Literary Narrative* (Lincoln: University of Nebraska Press, 2013)

BERNARD, JACQUES, *Le Camp de la mort lente* (Paris: Arc-en-ciel, 1945)

BERTILOTTI, PAOLA, 'Contrasti e trasformazioni della memoria dello sterminio in Italia', in *Storia della Shoah in Italia: vicende, memorie, rappresentazioni*, ed. by Marcello Flores and Simon Levis Sullam, 2 vols (Turin: Utet, 2010), II, 58-114

BO, CARLO, 'I disarmati', *Corriere della sera*, 30 June 1974, p. 3

BOCCA, RICCARDO, 'Grandi manovre dietro a Pio XII', *L'Espresso*, 2 November 2010 <http://bocca.blogautore.espresso.repubblica.it/2010/11/02/grandi-manovre-dietro-a-pio-xii/> [accessed 27 October 2020]

BOMPIANI, ed., *Dizionario letterario Bompiani delle opere e dei personaggi di tutti i tempi e di tutte le letterature*, 9 vols (Milan: Bompiani, 1947-50)

BONDÌ, CLAUDIO, and STEFANO PIPERNO, *Perché ci siamo salvati* (Venice: Marsilio, 2020)

BONO, PAOLA, ed., *Questioni di teoria femminista* (Milan: La tartaruga, 1993)

BONO, PAOLA, and SANDRA KEMP, eds, *The Lonely Mirror* (London: Routledge, 1993)

BONOMO, BRUNO, 'Recensione: Anna Foa, *Portico d'Ottavia 13*', *Officina della Storia*, 29 April 2014, <https://www.officinadellastoria.eu/it/2014/04/29/recensione-anna-foa-portico-dottavia-13/> [accessed 21 March 2019]

BORGHESI, ANGELA, *L'anno della Storia 1974–1975: il dibattito politico e culturale sul romanzo di Elsa Morante* (Macerata: Quodlibet, 2019)

——*La lotta con l'angelo: Giacomo Debenedetti critico letterario* (Venice: Marsilio, 1989)

BOSMAJIAN, HAMIDA, *Sparing the Child: Grief and the Unspeakable in Youth Literature about Nazism and the Holocaust* (New York: Routledge, 2002)

BOYNE, JOHN, *The Boy in the Striped Pyjamas* (London: Definitions, 2006)

BURKE, MICHAEL, and EMILY T. TROSCIANKO, eds, *Cognitive Literary Science: Dialogues Between Literature and Cognition* (New York: Oxford University Press, 2017)

BURKE, PETER, *The French Historical Revolution: The Annales School 1929–89* (Cambridge: Polity Press, 1990)

CALIMANI, RICCARDO, *Storia degli ebrei italiani: nel XIX e nel XX secolo* (Milan: Mondadori, 2015)

CAMPUS, GIANNI, *Il treno di piazza Giudia* (Cuneo: L'arciere, 1995)

CAPOBIANCO, LAURA, ed., *Donne tra memoria e storia* (Naples: Liguori, 1993)

CAPRISTO, ANNALISA, 'La parola ebreo', *La Rassegna Mensile di Israel*, 63.3 (September 1997), 134–38

CARACCIOLO, NICOLA, *Gli ebrei e l'Italia durante la Guerra 1940–45* (Rome: Bonacci, 1986)

CAREY, SARAH, 'Elsa Morante: Envisioning History', in *Elsa Morante's Politics of Writing: Rethinking Subjectivity, History, and the Power of Art*, ed. by Stefania Lucamante (Madison, NJ: Fairleigh Dickinson University Press, 2015), pp. 69–76

CARTONI, FLAVIA, 'Narrativa e censura: *La Storia* nella prima edizione spagnola del 1976', in *Santi, Sultani e Gran Capitani in camera mia: inediti e ritrovati dall'Archivio di Elsa Morante*, ed. by Giuliana Zagra (Rome: Biblioteca Nazionale Centrale di Roma, 2012), pp. 139–48

CAVAGLION, ALBERTO, 'Il grembo della Shoah: 16 ottobre 1943 di Umberto Saba, Giacomo Debenedetti, Elsa Morante', in *Dopo i testimoni: memorie, storiografie e narrazioni della deportazione razziale*, ed. by Marta Baiardi and Alberto Cavaglion (Rome: Viella, 2014), pp. 245–61

CAVARERO, ADRIANA, 'Framing Horror', in *Concentrationary Imaginaries*, ed. by Griselda Pollock and Max Silverman (London: I. B. Tauris, 2015), pp. 47–58

CAVE, TERENCE, *Thinking with Literature: Towards a Cognitive Criticism* (Oxford: Oxford University Press, 2016)

CECCATTY, RENEDE, 'Madame della Seta aussi est juive', *Biography*, 22.3 (1999), 447

CECCHI, CARLO, and CESARE GARBOLI, 'Cronologia', in Elsa Morante, *Opere*, 2 vols (Milan: Mondadori, 1990), I, xvii–xc

CHURCHILL, WINSTON, *The Second World War*, 6 vols (Boston: Houghton Mifflin Harcourt, 1948–53)

CIARAFONI, ALBERTO, *Quer 16 de ottobre* (Padua: Il Torchio, 2016)

CINELLI, GIANLUCA, 'Silenzi e verità ne *La parola ebreo* di Rosetta Loy', *MLN*, 123.1 (2008), 8–21

CIOCCHETTI, MARCELLO, *Moravia e Piovene tra giornali e riviste del dopoguerra* (Pesaro: Metauro, 2010)

——*Prima di piantare datteri: Giacomo Debenedetti a Roma (1944–1945)* (Pesaro: Metauro, 2006)

CLEMENTI, GIANNI, *L'ebreo; Ladro di razza* (Riano: Editoria & Spettacolo, 2010)

CLIFFORD, REBECCA, *Commemorating the Holocaust: The Dilemmas of Remembrance in France and Italy* (Oxford: Oxford University Press, 2013)

COEN, FAUSTO, *16 ottobre 1943: la grande razzia degli ebrei di Roma* (Florence: Giuntina, 1994)

COLM HOGAN, PATRICK, 'Simulation and the Structure of Emotional Memory Learning from Arthur Miller's *After the Fall*', in *Cognitive Literary Science: Dialogues between Literature and Cognition,* ed. by Michael Burke and Emily T. Troscianko (New York: Oxford University Press, 2017), pp. 113–34

——'What Literature Teaches Us About Emotion: Synthesizing Affective Science and Literary Study', in *The Oxford Handbook of Cognitive Literary Studies*, ed. by Lisa Zunshine (New York: Oxford University Press, 2015), pp. 273–90

COMUNITÀ ISRAELITICA DI ROMA, ed., *Ottobre 1943: cronaca di un'infamia* (Rome: Dapco, 1961)

CONSONNI, MANUELA, 'The Impact of the "Eichmann Event" in Italy, 1961', *Journal of Israeli History*, 23.1 (2004), 91-99

CONTORBIA, FRANCO, 'Appunti per un saggio su "Mercurio"', *La Rassegna della Letteratura Italiana*, 1 (2004), 29-43

COPPA, FRANK, 'Between Morality and Diplomacy: The Vatican's "Silence" During the Holocaust', *Journal of Church and State*, 50.3 (2008), 541-68

COSTA, ANTONIO, '*Cuore, La Storia*', in *Luigi Comencini: il cinema e i film*, ed. by Adriano Aprà (Venice: Marsilio, 2007), pp. 222-30

CRESSWELL, TIM, *Place: A Short Introduction* (Oxford: Blackwell, 2004)

D'ANGELI, CONCETTA, 'Visioni di sterminio ne *La Storia*', *Cuadernos de Filología Italiana*, 21 (2014), 91-100

DE' ANGELIS, ROMANA FRANCESCA, *Per infiniti giorni* (Bagno a Ripoli: Passigli, 2014)

DEBENEDETTI, ANTONIO, *Giacomino* (Milan: Rizzoli, 1994)

DEBENEDETTI, ELISA, '16 ottobre 1943 nel ghetto di Roma rivissuto da Giacomo Debenedetti', *Strenna dei Romanisti*, 21 (2017), 159-68

DEBENEDETTI, GIACOMO, '16 ottobre 1943', *Mercurio*, 1.4 (1944), 75-97

——*16 ottobre 1943* (Rome: OET, 1945); in *Saggi* (Milan: Mondadori, 1999), pp. 25-63

——'16 ottobre 1943', *Libera stampa*, 27 April 1945

——'16 ottobre 1943', *Les Temps modernes*, 2 (August-September 1947), 305-26

——*16 ottobre 1943* (Milan: Il Saggiatore, 1959; 1961)

——*16 ottobre 1943; Otto ebrei*, ed. by Cesare Garboli, preface by Alberto Moravia (Milan: Il Saggiatore, 1973)

——*16 ottobre 1943*, ed. by Ottavio Cecchi (Rome: Riuniti, 1978)

——*16 ottobre 1943*, comm. by Natalia Ginzburg (Palermo: Sellerio, 1993)

——*October 16, 1943; Eight Jews*, trans. by Estelle Gilson (Notre Dame: University of Notre Dame press, 2001)

——*Rome 16 October 1943*, illus. and trans. by Sarah Laing (Wellington: Holocaust Centre of New Zealand, 2018)

——'L'Alfieri. "Ingegnoso nemico di se stesso"', *Poesia*, 1 (1945), 44-45; in *Saggi* (Milan: Mondadori, 1999), pp. 765-824

——*Amedeo e altri racconti* (Turin: Baretti, 1926)

——'Camilla', *Mercurio*, 2.15 (November 1945), 109-16; in *Saggi* (Milan: Mondadori, 1999), pp. 827-36

——'Campo di ebrei', *La Nuova Europa*, 1 April 1945, p. 8; in *Saggi* (Milan: Mondadori, 1999), pp. 858-65

——'Discorso sull'Alfieri', *La fiera letteraria*, 1.38 (1946), 11

——'Gide ritrovato', *La Nuova Europa*, 24 December 1944, p. 8

——'Lupi in plenilunio', *L'Epoca*, 15 March 1945, p. 3

——'Otto ebrei. 1) Ori e Settebello', *Il Tempo*, 11 October 1944, pp. 1-2

——'Otto ebrei. 2) Il Ghetto e l'Arca di Noè', *Il Tempo*, 13 October 1944, pp. 1-2

——'Otto ebrei. 3) Gli aratori del vulcano', *Il Tempo*, 15 October 1944, pp. 1-2

——*Otto ebrei* (Rome: Atlantica, 1944); in *Saggi* (Milan: Mondadori, 1999), pp. 65-91

——'Paul Valéry', *La Nuova Europa*, 29 July 1945, p. 5

——'Piantatori di datteri', *L'Epoca*, 1 January 1946, p. 1

——*Saggi* (Milan: Mondadori, 1999)

——*Saggi critici* (Florence: Solaria, 1929)

——*Saggi critici: terza serie* (Milan: Il Sagiattore, 1959)

——'Il silenzio del mare', *La Nuova Europa*, 28 January 1945, p. 6

——'Lo stile del Croce', in *L'opera filosofica storica e letteraria di Benedetto Croce: saggi di scrittori italiani e stranieri e bibliografia dal 1922 al 1941*, ed. by Edmondo Cione (Rome: Laterza, 1942), pp. 264-74

——'Testimonianza di gratitudine', in *La piccola patria: cronache della guerra in un comune toscano giugno-luglio 1944*, ed. by Pietro Pancrazi (Florence: Le Monnier, 1946), pp. 135-40

——'Trincea degli ebrei', *L'Epoca*, 8 May 1945, pp. 1-2

——*Vocazione di Vittorio Alfieri* (Rome: Riuniti, 1977)

DEBENEDETTI, GIACOMO [WRITING AS 'g. d.'], 'Contrabbandi alla storia', *La Nuova Europa*, 31 December 1944, p. 8

——'Febbre a 40', *L'Epoca*, 12 February 1945, p. 1

——'Libertà dalla paura', *L'Epoca*, 13 April 1945, p. 1

DEBENEDETTI, GIACOMO [WRITING AS RENATA ORENGO], 'Nascita del D'Annunzio. Ritratto di Gabriele D'Annunzio come poeta: "Intermezzo"', *Argomenti*, 1.7-8 (September-October 1941), 55-62

DEBENEDETTI, MARCO EDOARDO, 'Cronologia', in Giacomo Debenedetti, *Saggi* (Milan: Mondadori, 1999), pp. lxix-lvxx

DE FELICE, RENZO, *Storia degli ebrei italiani sotto il fascismo* (Turin: Einaudi, 1961)

DELLA COLLETTA, CRISTINA, *Plotting the Past: Metamorphoses of Historical Narrative in Modern Italian Fiction* (West Lafayette, IN: Purdue University Press, 1994), pp. 117-51

DEMARIA, CRISTINA, *Il trauma, l'archivio e il testimone: la semiotica, il documentario e la rappresentazione del reale* (Bologna: Bononia University Press, 2012)

DE ROGATIS, TIZIANA, 'Elsa Morante's *History: A Novel* and Svetlana Alexievich's *The Unwomanly Face of War*: Traumatic Realism, *Archives du Mal* and Female Pathos', in *Trauma Narratives in Italian and Transnational Women's Writing*, ed. by Tiziana de Rogatis and Katrin Wehling-Giorgi (Rome: Sapienza Università Editrice, 2022), pp. 79-111

DE ROGATIS, TIZIANA, and KATRIN WEHLING GIORGI, 'Traumatic Realism and the Poetics of Trauma in Elsa Morante's Works', *Allegoria*, 83 (2021), 169-83

DE SIMONE, CESARE, *Roma città prigioniera: i 271 giorni dell'occupazione nazista (8 settembre '43-4 giugno '44)* (Milan: Mursia, 1994)

DEL BOCA, ANGELO, *Italiani, brava gente? Un mito duro a morire* (Vicenza: Neri Pozza, 2005)

DIDI-HUBERMAN, GEORGES, *Images malgré tout* (Paris: Minuit 2003)

DI NICOLA, LAURA, *Mercurio: storia di una rivista 1944-1948* (Milan: Il Saggiatore, 2012)

——'Il progetto "Mercurio" negli anni del dopoguerra', *Rivista di Letteratura Italiana*, 1-2 (2005), 407-12

DOV KULKA, OTTO, *Landscape of the Metropolis of Death* (London: Allen Lane, 2013)

——'Some Reflections on History and Fiction in my *Landscape of the Metropolis of Death*: Comments on Hayden White's "The History Fiction Divide"', *Holocaust Studies*, 20.1-2 (2014), 35-44

EDWARDS, ELIZABETH, and JANICE HART, *Photographs Objects Histories: On the Materiality of Images* (London: Routledge 2004)

ELIOT, GEORGE, *Il mulino sulla Floss*, trans. by Giacomo Debenedetti (Milan: Mondadori, 1940)

ELKANN ALAIN, and ALBERTO MORAVIA, *Vita di Moravia* (Milan: Bompiani, 1990)

ELLI, ENRICO, 'Storia e memoria nella narrativa di Rosetta Loy', *Vita e Pensiero*, 2 (1996), 135-44

ERLL, ASTRID, 'Cultural Memory Studies: An Introduction', in *A Companion to Cultural Memory Studies*, ed. by Astrid Erll, Ansgar Nünning, and Sara Young (New York: De Gruyter, 2010), pp. 1-17

——*Memory in Culture* (New York: Palgrave Macmillan, 2011)

——'Narratology and Cultural Memory Studies', in *Narratology in the Age of Cross-*

disciplinary Narrative Research, ed. by Sandra Heinen and Roy Sommer (Berlin: De Gruyter, 2009), pp. 212-27

—— 'Re-writing as Re-visioning: Modes of Representing the "Indian Mutiny" in British Novels, 1857 to 2000', *European Journal of English Studies*, 10.2 (2006), 163-85

ERLL, ASTRID, and ANN RIGNEY, 'Literature and the Production of Cultural Memory', *European Journal of English Studies*, 10.2 (2006), 11-115

ERLL, ASTRID, ANSGAR NÜNNING, and SARA YOUNG, eds, *A Companion to Cultural Memory Studies* (New York: De Gruyter, 2010)

ESPOSITO, ELENA, 'Social Forgetting: A Systems-theory Approach', in *A Companion to Cultural Memory Studies*, ed. by Astrid Erll, Ansgar Nünning, and Sara Young (New York: De Gruyter, 2010), pp. 181-89

FANNING, URSULA, *Italian Women's Autobiographical Writings in the Twentieth Century* (Madison, NJ: Fairleigh Dickinson University Press, 2017)

FEINSTEIN, WILEY, *The Civilization of the Holocaust in Italy: Poets, Artists, Saints, Anti-Semites* (Madison, NJ: Fairleigh Dickinson University Press, 2003)

FOA, ANNA, *Andare per ghetti e giudecche* (Bologna: Il Mulino, 2014)

—— *Diaspora: storia degli ebrei nel Novecento* (Rome: Laterza, 2009)

—— *Ebrei in Europa: dalla peste nera all'emancipazione XIV–XIX secolo* (Rome: Laterza, 1992)

—— *Eretici: storie di streghe, ebrei e convertiti* (Bologna: Il Mulino, 2011)

—— *La famiglia F.* (Rome: Laterza, 2018)

—— *Portico d'Ottavia 13: una casa del ghetto nel lungo inverno del '43* (Rome: Laterza, 2013)

—— *Portico d'Ottavia*, illus. by Matteo Berton (Rome: Laterza, 2015)

FOA, ANNA, and LUCETTA SCARAFFIA, *Anime nere: due donne e due destini nella Roma nazista* (Venice: Marsilio, 2021)

FOA, ANNA, and FRANCESCA RODARI, *Donne e Shoah* (Milan: Mimesis, 2021)

FOA, ANNA, GIANCARLO LACERENZA, and DANIELE JALLA, eds, *Ebrei, una storia italiana: i primi mille anni* (Milan: Electa, 2017)

FOA, PAOLO, and GUIDO VALABREGA, eds, *Gli ebrei in Italia durante il fascismo*, 3 vols (Milan: CDEC, 1961-63)

FOÀ, UGO, 'Relazione del Presidente della Comunità Israelitica di Roma Ugo Foà circa le misure razziali adottate in Roma dopo l'8 settembre (data dell'armistizio Badoglio) a diretta opera delle Autorità Tedesche di occupazione', in *Ottobre 1943: cronaca di un'infamia*, ed. by Comunità Israelitica di Roma (Rome: Dapco, 1961), pp. 9-29

FOCARDI, FILIPPO, *Il cattivo tedesco e il bravo italiano: la rimozione delle colpe della Seconda guerra mondiale* (Rome: Laterza, 2013)

—— 'La memoria della guerra e il mito del "bravo italiano": origine e affermazione di un autoritratto collettivo', *Italia contemporanea*, 220.21 (2000), 93-99

—— *Nel cantiere della memoria: fascismo, resistenza, Shoah, foibe* (Rome: Viella, 2020)

FONTANA, LUCA, 'Elsa Morante: A Personal Remembrance', *Poetry Nation Review*, 14.6 (1988), 20

FOOT, JOHN, *Italy's Divided Memory* (New York: Palgrave, 2009)

—— 'Via Rasella, 1944: Memory, Truth, and History', *Historical Journal*, 43.4 (2000), 1173-80

FORCELLA, ENZO, *La resistenza in convento* (Turin: Einaudi, 1999)

FORLENZA, ROSARIO, 'Sacrificial Memory and Political Legitimacy in Postwar Italy: Reliving and Remembering World War II', *History and Memory*, 24.2 (2012), 73-116

FORTES, SUSANA, *Esperando a Robert Capa* (Barcelona: Planeta, 2009)

FRANDINI, PAOLA, *Il teatro della memoria: Giacomo Debenedetti dalle opere ai documenti* (Lecce: Manni, 2001)

FRANK, ANNE, *Anne Frank: The Diary of a Young Girl*, trans. by B. M. Mooyaart-Doubleday (London: Constellation Books, 1952)

GALLERANO, NICOLA, 'History and the Public Use of History', *Diogenes*, 42.168 (1994), 85-102

——, ed., *L'uso pubblico della storia* (Milan: Franco Angeli, 1995)

GARBOLI, CESARE, *Il gioco segreto: nove immagini di Elsa Morante* (Milan: Adelphi, 1995)

——'Un crocicchio di esistenze', *Corriere della sera*, 30 June 1974, p. 3

——, ed., *Giacomo Debenedetti 1901–1967* (Milan: Il Saggiatore 1968)

GAROFALO, DAMIANO, '"Non dimenticarlo il nostro ottobre": la retata del 16 ottobre 1943 sullo schermo', in *16 ottobre 1943: la deportazione degli ebrei romani tra storia e memoria*, ed. by Martin Baumeister, Amedeo Osti Guerrazzi, and Claudio Procaccia (Rome: Viella, 2016), pp. 151-68

GATHERCOLE, PATRICIA M., '*La parola ebreo*', *World Literature Today*, 72.2 (January 1998), 351

GIMENEZ CAVALLO, MARIA, 'Elsa Morante's "La Storia": A Posthumanist, Feminist, Anarchist Response to Power', *Annali d'Italianistica*, 34 (2016), 425-47

GINZBURG, NATALIA, 'Elzeviri: "La Storia"', *Corriere della sera*, 30 June 1974, p. 3

——*Lessico famigliare* (Turin: Einaudi, 1963)

GORDON, ROBERT S. C., *An Introduction to Twentieth-century Italian Literature: A Difficult Modernity* (London: Duckworth, 2005)

——'The Holocaust in Italian Collective Memory. "Il giorno della memoria", 27 January 2001', *Modern Italy*, 2:2 (2006), 167-188

—— *The Holocaust in Italian Culture, 1944–2010* (Stanford, CA: Stanford University Press, 2012)

——'Postmodernism and the Holocaust', in *Postmodern Impegno: Ethics and Commitment in Contemporary Italian Culture*, ed. by Pierpaolo Antonello and Florian Mussgnug (Bern: Peter Lang, 2009), pp. 167-88

——'Which Holocaust? Primo Levi and the Field of Holocaust Memory in Post-war Italy', *Italian Studies*, 61.1 (2006), 85-113

GOSETTI, GIORGIO, *Luigi Comencini* (Milan: Il Castoro Cinema, 1988)

GRAHAM, ROBERT A., *Il Vaticano e il nazismo* (Rome: Cinque Lune, 1975)

GRECO, SILVANA, 'Liliana Segre, or the Courageous Struggle against "Indifference" and for Social Recognition', *Academicus*, 19 (2019), 9-31

GREMOLI, SABRINA, and KETI LELO, 'La localizzazione della popolazione ebraica romana arrestata e deportata nell'ottobre del 1943', in *Roma, 16 ottobre 1943: anatomia di una deportazione*, ed. by Silvia Haia Antonucci and others (Milan: Guerini, 2006), pp. 89-94

GUIDOTTI, GLORIA, 'L'intraducibile della *Storia* di Elsa Morante nella Spagna del 1976', *Cuadernos de Filología Italiana*, 11 (2004), 167-76

HABERMAS, JURGEN, *The Structural Transformation of the Public Sphere* (Cambridge: Polity Press, 1989)

HALBWACHS, MAURICE, *Les Cadres sociaux de la mémoire* (Paris: Alcan, 1925)

—— *On Collective Memory*, trans. by Lewis A. Coser (Chicago: Chicago University Press, 1980)

HERMAN, DAVID, ed., *Narrative Theory and the Cognitive Sciences* (Stanford, CA: CSLI Publications, 2005)

HERUBEL, JEAN-PIERRE V. M., 'Historiography's Horizon and Imperative: Febvrian Annales Legacy and Library History as Cultural History', *Libraries & Culture*, 39.3 (2004), 293-312

HILBERG, RAUL, *The Destruction of the European Jews* (New Haven, CT: Yale University Press, 1961)

HIRSCH, MARIANNE, *Family Frames: Photography, Narrative, and Postmemory* (Cambridge, MA: Harvard University Press, 1997)

——'The Generation of Postmemory', *Poetics Today*, 29.1 (2008), 103-28

——'Projected Memory: Holocaust Photographs in Personal and Public Fantasy', in *Acts of*

Memory: Cultural Recall in the Present, ed. by Mieke Bal, Jonathan Crewe, and Leo Spitzer (Hanover, NH: University Press of New England, 1999), pp. 3-23

—— 'Surviving Images: Holocaust Photographs and the Work of Postmemory', *Yale Journal of Criticism*, 14.1 (2001), 5-37

HIRSCH, MARIANNE, and LEO SPITZER, 'Testimonial Objects: Memory, Gender and Transmission', *Poetic Today*, 27.2 (2006), 353-83

—— 'What's Wrong with This Picture?', *Journal of Modern Jewish Studies*, 5.2 (2006), 229-52

HUTCHEON, LINDA, *A Poetics of Postmodernism: History, Theory and Fiction* (New York: Routledge 1988)

IBSCH, ERLUD, 'Memory, History, Imagination: How Time Affects the Perspective on Holocaust Literature', in *Contemporary Jewish Writers in Italy: A Generational Approach*, ed. by Raniero Speelman, Monica Jansen, and Silvia Gaiga (Utrecht: Igitur, 2007), pp. 1-13

JACOPONI, TIZIANA, '*La Storia*: un libro, un film', *Narrativa*, 17 (2000), 117-22

JANECZEK, HELENA, *Lezioni di tenebra* (Milan: Mondadori, 1997)

—— *La ragazza con la Leica* (Parma: Guanda, 2017)

JONA, EMILIO, and VANNI SCHEIWILLER, *Giacomo Debenedetti: l'arte del leggere* (Milan: Libri Scheiwiller, 2001)

JORDAN, SARAH D., 'Educating Without Overwhelming: Authorial Strategies in Children's Holocaust Literature', *Children's Literature in Education*, 35.3 (September 2004), 199-218

JOSI, MARA, 'Civil Disobedience: Elsa Morante, the Student Movement and the Years of Lead', in *The Winter of Italy's Discontent*, ed. by Maurizio Rebaudengo and Dagmar Reichdart (Oxford: Peter Lang, forthcoming)

—— 'From Book to Screen: Images of the Fascist Dictatorship in Elsa Morante's *La Storia*', *Annali d'italianistica*, 41 (forthcoming)

KANSTEINER, WULF, 'Finding Meaning in Memory: A Methodological Critique of Collective Memory Studies', *History and Theory*, 41.2 (2002), 179-97

KATZ, ROBERT, *Black Sabbath* (London: Barker, 1969)

—— *Sabato Nero*, trans. by Enrica Labò (Bologna: Rizzoli, 1973)

—— *Death in Rome* (London: Cape, 1967)

KERTZER, ADRIENNE, *My Mother's Voice: Children, Literature, and the Holocaust* (Peterborough: Broadview Press, 2002)

KLINKHAMMER, LUTZ, *L'occupazione tedesca in Italia 1943-1945* (Turin: Bollati Boringhieri, 1993)

—— *Stragi naziste in Italia: la guerra contro i civili 1943-1944* (Rome: Donzelli, 2006)

KOCH, FRANCESCA, and SIMONA LUNADEI, 'Il 16 ottobre nella memoria cittadina', in *La memoria della legislazione e della persecuzione antiebraica nella storia dell'Italia Repubblichina*, ed. by the Istituto romano per la storia dell'Italia republicana (Milan: Franco Angeli, 1999)

KOKKOLA, LYDIA, *Representing the Holocaust in Children's Literature* (New York: Routledge, 2003)

KRAUSNICK, HELMUT, and OTHERS, *Anatomy of the SS State*, trans. by Richard Barry and others (London: Collins, 1968)

KRUPP, GARY L., *Pope Pius XII and World War II: The Documents of Truth* (London: Xlibris, 2012)

LA ROCCA, ORAZIO, 'Fiction Rai: l'ira degli ebrei Pio XII patacca assolutoria', *La Repubblica*, 2 November 2010 <https://ricerca.repubblica.it/repubblica/archivio/repubblica/2010/11/02/fiction-rai-ira-degli-ebrei-pio.html> [accessed 27 October 2020]

LACHMANN, RENATE, 'Cultural Memory and the Role of Literature', *European Review*, 12.2 (2004), 165-78

—— *Memory and Literature* (Minneapolis: University of Minnesota Press, 1997)

LANDSBERG, ALISON, 'Memory, Empathy, and the Politics of Identification', *International Journal of Politics, Culture and Society*, 22.2 (2009), 221-29

——*Prosthetic Memory: The Transformation of American Remembrance in the Age of Mass Culture* (New York: Columbia University Press, 2004)

LANG, BEREL, 'Holocaust Genres and the Turn to History', in *The Holocaust and the Text: Speaking the Unspeakable*, ed. by Andrew Leak and George Paizis (Basingstoke: Macmillan, 2000), pp. 17-31

LANGER, LAWRENCE, *Holocaust Testimonies. The Ruins of Memory* (New Haven, CT: Yale University Press, 1991)

LAZZARO-WEISS, CAROL, *From Margins to Mainstream: Feminism and Fictional Modes in Italian Women's Writing* (Philadelphia: University of Pennsylvania Press, 1993)

LERNER, GAD, 'Quel normale antisemitismo', *La Repubblica*, 12 February 2020 <https://www.repubblica.it/commenti/2020/02/12/news/quel_normale_antisemitismo-300805182/> [accessed 12 February 2020]

LEVI, LIA, *Una bambina e basta* (Rome: E/O, 1994)

LEVI, PRIMO, *Se questo è un uomo* (Turin: De Silva, 1947)

——*La tregua* (Turin: Einaudi, 1963)

LEVI CAVAGLIONE, PINO, *Guerriglia nei castelli romani* (Florence: La Nuova Italia, 1971)

LEVIS SULLAM, SIMON, *I carnefici italiani: scene dal genocidio degli ebrei, 1943–1945* (Milan: Feltrinelli, 2015)

LIMENTANI, GIACOMA, *In contumacia* (Milan: Adelphi, 1967)

LINDENBERG, JUDITH, 'La Religion juive ou la découverte de l'altérité dans *La parola ebreo* de Rosetta Loy', *Cahiers d'études italiennes*, 7 (2008), 45-51

LOY, ROSETTA, *La bicicletta* (Turin: Einaudi, 1974)

——'Confessione d'autore', *Paragone*, 39.12 (1988), 116-21

——*Cioccolata da Hanselmann* (Milan: Rizzoli, 1995)

——*La parola ebreo* (Turin: Einaudi, 1997)

——*First Words: A Childhood in Fascist Italy*, trans. by Gregory Conti (New York: Metropolitan Books/Henry Holt, 2000)

——*La porta dell'acqua* (Turin: Einaudi, 1976)

——*La porta dell'acqua* (Milan: Rizzoli, 2000)

——'La Tentation autobiographique', *Magazine littéraire*, 404 (2001), 98-103

LUCAMANTE, STEFANIA, *Forging Shoah Memories: Italian Women Writers, Jewish Identity, and the Holocaust* (New York: Palgrave MacMillan, 2014)

——'The "Indispensable" Legacy of Primo Levi: From Eraldo Affinati to Rosetta Loy Between History and Fiction', *Quaderni d'Italianistica*, 24.2 (2003), 87-104

——*Quella difficile identità: ebraismo e rappresentazioni letterarie della Shoah* (Rome: Iacobelli, 2012)

——'The World Must Be the Writer's Concern', in *Elsa Morante's Politics of Writing: Rethinking Subjectivity, History, and the Power of Art*, ed. by Stefania Lucamante (Madison, NJ: Fairleigh Dickinson University Press, 2015), pp. 88-111

LUCENTE, GREGORY L., *Beautiful Fables: Self-consciousness in Italian Narrative from Manzoni to Calvino* (Baltimore, MD: Johns Hopkins University Press, 1986)

——'Scrivere o fare... o altro: Social Commitment and Ideologies of Representation in the Debates over Lampedusa's *Il Gattopardo* and Morante's *La Storia*', *Italica*, 61.3 (1984), 220-51

MAEHET, MYRNA P., 'Authenticity in Holocaust Literature for Children', *South African Journal of Libraries and Information Science*, 66.3 (1998), 114-21

MAFFEY, ALDO, 'Quando venne a trovarci in via del Tritone', *Il Messaggero*, 24 November 1986, p. 5

MANACORDA, GIULIANO, 'Giacomo Debenedetti: *16 ottobre 1943* e *Otto ebrei*', in *Il Novecento di Debenedetti*, ed. by Rosita Tordi (Milan: Mondadori, 1991), pp. 303-11

MANSFIELD, KATHERINE, *Il libro degli appunti*, trans. by Elsa Morante (Milan: Longanesi, 1941)

MARCHETTI, SILVIA, 'Private Memory, Public History, and Testimony in Rosetta Loy's *La parola ebreo*', in *Memoria collettiva e memoria privata: il ricordo della Shoah come politica sociale*, ed. by Stefania Lucamante and others (Utrecht: Utrecht Publishing and Archiving Services, 2008), pp. 111-22

MARCUS, MILLICENT, *Italian Film in the Shadow of Auschwitz* (Toronto: University of Toronto Press, 2007)

MAROTTI, MARIA ORNELLA, 'Feminist Historians/ Historical Fictions', *Italian Culture*, 14 (1996), 147-60

——'Introduction', in *Gendering Italian Fiction: Feminist Revisions of Italian History*, ed. by Maria Ornella Marotti and Gabriella Brooke (Madison, NJ: Fairleigh Dickson University Press, 1999), pp. 15-27

——'Literary Historicism and Women's Tradition', *Italian Culture*, 13 (1995), 261-72

——'Revisiting the Past: Feminist Historians/ Historical Fictions', in *Gendering Italian Fiction: Feminist Revisions of Italian History*, ed. by Maria Ornella Marotti and Gabriella Brooke (Madison, NJ: Fairleigh Dickson University Press, 1999), pp. 41-70

MARTINELLI, ELEONORA, 'E la parola "ebreo" divenne insulto: dialogo sulla memoria con Vittorio Foa', *L'Unità*, 10 June 1997, p. 4

MATTESINI, FRANCESCO, *La critica letteraria di Giacomo Debenedetti* (Milan: Garzanti, 1994)

MELLACE, GIUSEPPINA, *Delitti e stragi dell'Italia fascista dal 1922 al 1945: i casi più eclatanti dell'epoca, oltre la cronaca nera* (Rome: Newton Compton, 2015)

MICCOLI, GIOVANNI, *I dilemmi e i silenzi di Pio XII* (Bologna: Rizzoli, 2000)

MILLU, LIANA, *Il fumo di Birkenau* (Milan: La Prora, 1947)

MINGHELLI, GIULIANA, 'What's in a Word? Rosetta Loy's Search of History in Childhood', *MLN*, 116.1 (2001), 162-76

MODIANO, RENZO, *Di razza ebraica* (Milan: Scheiwiller, 2005)

MOLINARI, MAURIZIO, and AMEDEO OSTI GUERRAZZI, *Duello nel ghetto: la sfida di un ebreo contro le bande nazifasciste nella Roma occupata* (Milan: Rizzoli, 2017)

MORANTE, ELSA, 'Il 19 luglio 1943', *Il Messaggero*, 16 June 1974, p. 3

——*Algo en la Historia*, trans. by Juan Moreno (Barcelona: Plaza & Janés, 1976)

——*L'amata: lettere a e di Elsa Morante*, ed. by Marcello Morante and Giuliana Zagra (Turin: Einaudi, 2012)

——'Il beato propagandista del paradiso', in *Pro o contro la bomba atomica*, in *Opere*, 2 vols (Milan: Mondadori, 1990), II, 1555-69

——*Le bellissime avventure di Caterì dalla trecciolina* (Turin: Einaudi, 1942)

——'La censura in Spagna', *L'Unità*, 15 May 1976, p. 3

——*Il gioco segreto* (Milan: Garzanti,1941)

——*Opere*, 2 vols (Milan: Mondadori, 1990)

——*Lo scialle andaluso* (Turin: Einaudi, 1963); in *Opere*, 2 vols (Milan: Mondadori, 1990), I, 1405-80

——'Il soldato siciliano', *L'Europeo*, 1.6 (December 1945); in *Opere* (Milan: Mondadori, 1990), I, 1509-15

——*La Storia: Romanzo* (Turin: Einaudi, 1974); in *Opere*, 2 vols (Milan: Mondadori, 1990), II, 255-1036

——*History: A Novel*, trans. by William Weaver (New York: Aventura, 1984)

MORANTE, MARCELLO, *Maledetta benedetta* (Milan: Garzanti, 1986)

MORAVIA, ALBERTO, *La ciociara* (Milan: Bompiani, 1957)

NEUMANN, BRIGIT, 'The Literary Representation of Memory', in *A Companion to Cultural Memory Studies*, ed. by Astrid Erll, Ansgar Nünning, and Sara Young (New York: De Gruyter, 2010), pp. 333-43

NEZRI-DUFOUR, SOPHIE, 'La Figure du juif dans *La Storia* d'Elsa Morante', *Cahiers d'études italiennes*, 7 (2008), 65-74

NOBÉCOURT, JACQUES, 'Il silenzio di Pio XII', in *Dizionario storico del papato*, ed. by Philippe Levillain (Milan: Bompiani, 1996), pp. 1883-89

OLICK, JEFFREY K., 'Collective Memory: The Two Cultures', *Sociological Theory*, 173 (1999), 333-48

OLICK, JEFFREY K., and DANIEL LEVY, 'Collective Memory and Cultural Constraint: Holocaust Myth and Rationality in German Politics', *American Sociological Review*, 62.6 (1997), 921-36

ORAM, LYDIA M., 'Rape, Rapture and Revision: Visionary Imagery and Historical Reconstruction in Elsa Morante's *La Storia*', *Forum Italicum*, 37.2 (2003), 409-35

ORENGO, RENATA, *Diario del Cegliolo: cronaca della guerra in un comune toscano, giugno-luglio 1944* (Milan: Scheiwiller, 1965)

ORTENER, JESSICA, TEA SINDBÆK ANDERSEN, and FEDJA WIERØD BORČAK, '"Fiction Keeps Memory About the War Alive": Mnemonic Migration and Literary Representations of the War in Bosnia', *Memory Studies*, 15.4 (2022), 918-34

OSTI GUERRAZZI, AMEDEO, *Caino a Roma* (Rome: Cooper, 2005)

PALAZZESCHI, ALDO, *I fratelli Cuccoli* (Florence: Vallecchi, 1948)

PANNOCCHIA, FEDERICA, *Quando dal cielo cadevano le stelle* (Trento: Eden, 2016)

PARISI, LUCIANO, 'I collage di Rosetta Loy', *Romance Studies*, 22.1 (2004), 75-82

PARRI, MARIA GRAZIA, 'La parola ebreo', *Rivista di Studi Politici Internazionali*, 65.1 (January 1998), 156

PAVAN, ILARIA, and GURI SCHWARZ, eds, *Gli ebrei in Italia tra persecuzione fascista e reintegrazione postbellica* (Florence: Giuntina, 2001)

PEDERIALI, GIUSEPPE, *Stella di Piazza Giudìa* (Florence: Giunti, 1995)

PEDULLÀ, WALTER, *Il Novecento segreto di Giacomo Debenedetti* (Milan: Rizzoli, 2004)

PELLIZZARI, MARIA ROSARIA, ed., *Le donne e la storia: problemi di metodo e confronti storiografici* (Naples: Edizioni Scientifiche Italiane, 1995)

PERRA, EMILIANO, 'Buon cattolico, buon italiano: Shoah, religione e salvataggio degli ebrei in alcune recenti miniserie', in *Televisionismo: narrazioni televisive della storia italiana negli anni della seconda Repubblica*, ed. by Monica Jansen and Maria Bonaria Urban (Venice: Edizioni Ca' Foscari, 2015), pp. 49-60

—— 'Good Catholics, Good Italians: Religion and Rescue in Recent Italian Holocaust Dramas', *The Italianist*, 34.2 (2014), 156-69

PETRAGLIA, GAETANO, *La matta di piazza Giudia: storia e memoria dell'ebrea romana Elena di Porto* (Florence: Giuntina, 2022)

PETTITT, JOANNE, 'On Blends and Abstractions: Children's Literature and the Mechanisms of Holocaust Representation', *International Research in Children's Literature*, 7.2 (2014), 152-64

PEZZETTI, MARCELLO, *16 ottobre 1943: la razzia degli ebrei di Roma* (Rome: Gameni, 2013)

—— *Il libro della Shoah italiana: i racconti di chi è sopravvissuto* (Turin: Einaudi, 2009)

PIAZZA, BRUNO, *Perchè gli altri dimenticano* (Milan: Feltrinelli, 1959)

PICCIOTTO, LILIANA, 'The Decision-making Process of the Roundup of the Jews of Rome (October 1943): A Historiographic Revisitation Based on OSS (Office of Strategic Services) Documents', *Yad Vashem Studies*, 48.1-2 (2020), 1-36

PICCIOTTO FARGION, LILIANA, *Il libro della memoria: gli ebrei deportati dall'Italia (1943-1945)* (Milan: Mursia, 2002)

——, ed., *L'occupazione tedesca e gli ebrei di Roma: documenti e fatti* (Rome: Carocci, 1979)

PIETRAFESA, LUCA, *16 ottobre 1943. Viaggio nella memoria: voci, testimonianze e immagini del rastrellamento e della deportazione degli ebrei di Roma* (Rome: Reality Book, 2014)

PIRLET, CAROLINE, and ANDREAS WIRAG, 'Towards a "Natural" Bond of Cognitive and Affective Narratology', in *Cognitive Literary Science: Dialogues Between Literature and Cognition,* ed. by Michael Burke and Emily T. Troscianko (New York: Oxford University Press, 2017), pp. 35–53

PLASTINO, CORRADO, *La valigia* (Milan: StreetLib, 2017)

POPOFF, GABRIELLE ELISSA, '"Once Upon a Time there was an S.S. Officer": The Holocaust between History and Fiction in Elsa Morante's *La Storia*', *Journal of Modern Jewish Studies,* 11.1 (2012), 25–38

PORCELLI, STEFANIA '"As If He Wanted to Murder Her": Fear, Disgust and Anger in *La Storia*'s Rape Scene', *Close Encounters in War Journals,* 1 (2018), 65–81

PORTELLI, ALESSANDRO, *L'ordine è già stato eseguito: Roma, le Fosse Ardeatine, la memoria* (Rome: Donzelli, 1999)

PROCACCIA, CLAUDIO, and GIANCARLO SPIZZICHINO, 'I sommersi e la città', in *Roma, 16 ottobre 1943: anatomia di una deportazione,* ed. by Silvia Haia Antonucci and others (Milan: Guerini, 2006), pp. 75–88

PUGLIESE, STANISLAO G., 'Bloodless Torture: The Books of the Roman Ghetto under the Nazi Occupation', *Libraries and Culture,* 34.3 (1999), 241–53

RANCATI, ELENA, '*La Storia*: il "caso Morante"', in *Libri e scrittori di via Biancamano: casi editoriali in 75 anni di Einaudi,* ed. by Roberto Cicala and Velania La Mendola (Milan: EDUCatt, 2009), pp. 339–446

RANZATO, GABRIELE, *La liberazione di Roma: alleati e resistenza (8 Settembre 1943–4 Giugno 1944)* (Bari: Laterza, 2019)

RE, LUCIA, 'Utopian Longing and the Constraints of Racial and Sexual Difference in Elsa Morante's *La Storia*', *Italica,* 70.3 (1993), 361–75

RÉPACI, LEONIDA, *Taccuino segreto: prima serie (1938–1950)* (Lucca: Fazi, 1967)

REVELLI, NUTO, *La strada del Davai* (Turin: Einaudi, 1966)

——*L'ultimo fronte: lettere di soldati caduti o dispersi nella seconda guerra mondiale* (Turin: Einaudi, 1971)

RICCARDI, ANDREA, *L'inverno più lungo: 1943–44. Pio XII, gli ebrei e i nazisti a Roma* (Rome: Laterza, 2008)

RIGANO, GABRIELE, '16 ottobre 1943: accadono a Roma cose incredibili', in *Roma, 16 ottobre 1943: anatomia di una deportazione,* ed. by Silvia Haia Antonucci and others (Milan: Guerini, 2006), pp. 19–74

——'Appendice', in *Roma, 16 ottobre 1943: anatomia di una deportazione,* ed. by Silvia Haia Antonucci and others (Milan: Guerini, 2006), pp. 147–200

——*Il caso Zolli: l'itinerario di un intellettuale in bilico tra fedi, culture e nazioni* (Milan: Guerini e Associati, 2006)

——*L'interprete di Auschwitz: Arminio Wachsberger, un testimone d'eccezione della deportazione degli ebrei di Roma* (Milan: Guerini, 2015)

——'Pio XII e il 16 ottobre: note sul dibattito storiografico', *Rivista di Storia della Chiesa in Italia,* 68.1 (2014), 165–86

——'Il Vaticano e la razzia del 16 ottobre 1943', in *16 ottobre 1943: la deportazione degli ebrei romani tra storia e memoria,* ed. by Martin Baumeister, Amedeo Osti Guerrazzi, and Claudio Procaccia (Rome: Viella, 2016), pp. 63–85

RIGNEY, ANN, 'All This Happened, More or Less: What a Novelist Made of the Bombing of Dresden', *History and Theory,* 47 (2009), 5–24

——'Cultural Memory Studies: Mediation, Narrative, and the Aesthetic', in *Routledge International Handbook of Memory Studies,* ed. by Anna Lisa Tota and Trever Hagen (London: Routledge, 2015), pp. 65–75

——'The Dynamics of Remembrance: Texts Between Monumentality and Morphing', in

A Companion to Cultural Memory Studies, ed. by Astrid Erll, Ansgar Nünning, and Sara Young (New York: De Gruyter, 2010), pp. 345-56

——*Imperfect Histories. The Elusive Past and the Legacy of Romantic Historicism* (Ithaca, NY: Cornell University Press, 2001)

——'Portable Monuments: Literature, Cultural Memory and the Case of Jeanie Deans', *Poetics Today*, 25.2 (2004), 361-96

RITTNER, CAROL, and JOHN K. ROTH, eds, *Pope Pius XII and the Holocaust* (London: Bloomsbury, 2016)

RODARI, PAOLO, 'Pio XII, il rabbino di Roma: "Non ci fu volontà di fermare il treno del 16 ottobre"', *La Repubblica*, 2 November 2010 <https://www.repubblica. it/vaticano/2020/03/02/news/pio_xii_il_rabbino_di_roma_non_ci_fu_volonta_di_ fermare_il_treno_del_16_ottobre_-250061227/> [accessed 27 October 2020]

ROGOYSKA, JANE, *Gerda Taro: Inventing Robert Capa* (London: Jonathan Cape, 2013)

ROSSI DORIA, ANNA, *Memoria e storia: il caso della deportazione* (Soveria Mannelli: Rubbettino, 1998)

ROSSI DORIA, ANNA, and MARIA CRISTINA MARCUZZO, eds, *La ricerca delle donne: studi femministi in Italia* (Turin: Rosenberg & Sellier, 1987)

SABA, UMBERTO, *Scorciatoie e raccontini*, in *Tutte le prose* (Milan: Mondadori, 2001), pp. 3-106

SALVATORELLI, LUIGI, 'Come faccio il mio giornale', *Cosmopolita*, 17 May 1945, p. 4

SARFATTI, MICHELE, *Gli ebrei nell'Italia fascista: vicende, identità, persecuzione* (Turin: Einaudi, 2000)

SCHABER, IRME, *Gerda Taro: With Robert Capa as Photojournalist in the Spanish Civil War* (Stuttgart: Axel Menges, 2019)

SCHIFANO, JEAN-NOËL, and TJUNA NOTARBARTOLO, *Cahiers Elsa Morante* (Naples: Edizioni Scientifiche Italiane, 1993)

SCHUMAN, HOWARD, ROBERT F. BELLI, and KATHERINE BISCHOPING, 'The Generational Basis of Historical Knowledge', in *Collective Memory of Political Events: Social Psychological Perspectives*, ed. by James W. Pennebaker, Darío Paez, and Bernard Rimé (Mahwah, NJ: Lawrence Erlbaum Associates, 1997), pp. 47-77

SCHWARZ, GURI, and ARTURO MARZANO, *Attentato alla sinagoga: Roma, 9 ottobre 1982, il conflitto israelo-palestinese e l'Italia* (Rome: Viella, 2013)

SEGRE, CESARE, *Tempo di bilanci* (Turin: Einaudi, 2005)

SEGRE, LILIANA, 'Siate farfalle che volano sopra i fili spinati', *La Repubblica*, 29 January 2020 <https://www.repubblica.it/politica/2020/01/29/news/siate_farfalle_che_volano_ sopra_i_fili_spinati-247109535/> [accessed 29 January 2020]

SERIANNI, LUCA, *Grammatica italiana. Italiano comune e lingua letteraria: suoni, forme, costrutti* (Turin: Utet, 1988)

SERKOWSKA, HANNA, 'About One of the Most Disputed Literary Cases of the Seventies: Elsa Morante's *La Storia*', *Italianistica Ultraiectina*, 1 (2006), 372-86

——'La Storia morantiana sullo schermo', *Cuadernos de Filología Italiana*, 21 (2014), 173-83

SGAVICCHIA, SIRIANA, 'Fonti storiche e filosofiche nell'invenzione narrativa della *Storia*', in *'La Storia' di Elsa Morante*, ed. by Siriana Sgavicchia (Pisa: ETS, 2012), pp. 101-24

SICILIANO, ENZO, *Alberto Moravia* (Milan: Bompiani, 1982)

SOCIETÀ ITALIANA DELLE STORICHE, ed., *Discutendo di storia: soggettività, ricerca, biografia* (Turin: Rosemberg & Sellier, 1990)

——*Generazioni: trasmissione della storia e tradizione delle donne* (Turin: Rosemberg & Sellier, 1993)

SODI, RISA, *Narrative and Imperative: The First Fifty Years of Italian Holocaust Writing 1944–1994* (New York: Peter Lang, 2007)

——'Whose Story? Literary Borrowings by Elsa Morante's *La Storia*', *Lingua e Stile*, 33.1 (1998), 141-53

SONTAG, SUSAN, *On Photography* (London: Penguin, 1977)

SORANI, ROSINA, 'Dal diario di Rosina Sorani impiegata della Comunità di Roma nel periodo dell'occupazione tedesca', in *Ottobre 1943: cronaca di un'infamia*, ed. by Comunità Israelitica di Roma (Rome: Dapco, 1961), pp. 35-43

SPINAZZOLA, VITTORIO, *L'egemonia del romanzo* (Milan: Il Saggiatore, 2007)

SPIZZICHINO, SETTIMIA, and ISA DI NEPRI OLPER, *Gli anni rubati: le memorie di Settimia Spizzichino, reduce dai Lager di Auschwitz e Bergen-Belsen* (Cava de' Tirreni: Comune di Cava de' Tirreni, 1996)

STEARNS, PETER N., and CAROL Z. STEARNS, 'Emotionology: Clarifying the History of Emotions and Emotional Standards', *The American Historical Review*, 90.4 (1985), 813-36

STEUR, CLAUDIA, *Theodor Dannecker: ein Funktionär der Endlösung* (Essen: Klartext, 1997)

STILLER, ALEXANDER, *Benevolence and Betrayal: Five Italian Jewish Families under Fascism* (New York: Summit Books, 1991)

SULLAM CALIMANI, ANNA VERA, 'A Name for Extermination (Hurban, Auschwitz, Genocide, Holocaust, Shoah)', *Modern Language Review*, 94:4 (1999), pp. 978–999

——*I nomi dello sterminio* (Turin: Einaudi, 2001)

SUSANI, CAROLA, *Cola Pesce* (Milan: Feltrinelli, 2004)

——*Eneide* (Rome: Laterza, 2015)

——*Il licantropo* (Milan: Feltrinelli, 2002)

——*Susan: la piratessa* (Rome: Laterza, 2014)

TAGLIACOZZO, LIA, *La generazione del deserto: storie di famiglia, di giusti e di infami durante le persecuzioni razziali in Italia* (Lecce: Manni, 2020)

TAGLIACOZZO, MICHAEL, 'La comunità di Roma sotto l'incubo della svastica: la grande razzia del 16 ottobre 1943', in *Gli ebrei in Italia durante il fascismo*, ed. by Paolo Foa and Guido Valabrega, 3 vols (Milan: CDEC, 1961-63), III, 8-38

TERDIMAN, RICHARD, *Present Past: Modernity and the Memory Crisis* (Ithaca, NY: Cornell University Press, 1993)

THOMAS, GORDON, *The Pope's Jews: The Vatican's Secret Plan to Save the Jews from the Nazis* (New York: Thomas Dunne Books, 2012)

TORDI, ROSITA, ed., *Il Novecento di Debenedetti* (Milan: Mondadori, 1991)

TORNIELLI, ANDREA, *Pio XII: Eugenio Pacelli, un uomo sul trono di Pietro* (Milan: Mondadori, 2007)

TOSCANO, MARIO, '16 ottobre 1943. La costituzione della memoria: i difficili inizi', in *16 ottobre 1943: la deportazione degli ebrei romani tra storia e memoria*, ed. by Martin Baumeister, Amedeo Osti Guerrazzi, and Claudio Procaccia (Rome: Viella, 2016), pp. 109-33

VERDELLI, CARLO, 'Indagine Eurispes: il 15,6% crede che la Shoah non sia mai esistita, erano 2,7% nel 2004', *La Repubblica*, 30 January 2020 <https://www.repubblica.it/cronaca/2020/01/30/news/indagine_eurispes_il_15_6_crede_che_la_shoah_non_e_mai_esistita_erano_il_2_7_nel_2004-247140837/> [accessed 8 Febraury 2020]

WACHSBERGER, ARMINIO, 'Testimonianza di un deportato da Roma', in *L'occupazione tedesca e gli ebrei di Roma: documenti e fatti*, ed. by Liliana Picciotto Fargion (Rome: Carocci, 1979), pp. 173-207

WALKER, REBECCA M., 'Bringing Up the Bodies: Material Encounters in Elsa Morante's *La Storia*', *Italian Studies*, 76.1 (2021), 82–95

WALTER, VIRGINIA A., and SUSAN F. MARCH, 'Juvenile Picture Books About the Holocaust: Extending the Definitions of Children's Literature', *Publishing Research Quarterly*, 9.3 (1993), 36-51

WEHLING GIORGI, KATRIN, '"Come un fotogramma spezzato": Traumatic Images and Multistable Visions in Elsa Morante's *History: A Novel*', in *Trauma Narratives in Italian and Transnational Women's Writing*, ed. by Tiziana de Rogatis and Katrin Wehling-Giorgi (Rome: Sapienza Università Editrice, 2022), pp. 55-78

WHITE, HAYDEN, 'The History Fiction Divide', *Holocaust Studies*, 20.1-2 (2014), 17-34

——*Metahistory: The Historical Imagination in Nineteenth-century Europe* (Baltimore, MD: Johns Hopkins University Press, 1973)

WISTRICH, ROBERT S., *Who's Who in Nazi Germany* (London: Weidenfeld & Nicolson, 1982)

WOOD, SHARON, 'Excursus as Narrative Technique in *La Storia*', in *Elsa Morante's Politics of Writing: Rethinking Subjectivity, History, and the Power of Art*, ed. by Stefania Lucamante (Madison, NJ: Fairleigh Dickinson University Press, 2015), pp. 77-87

——'Rosetta Loy: The Paradox of the Past', in *The New Italian Novel*, ed. by Zygmunt Baranski and Lino Pertile (Edinburgh: Edinburgh University Press, 1993), pp. 121-38

YOUNG, JAMES E., *The Texture of Memory* (New Haven, CT: Yale University Press, 1993)

ZANARDO, MONICA, 'La biblioteca della Storia attraverso lo studio dei manoscritti: alcuni esempi di utilizzo delle fonti', in *Le fonti di Elsa Morante*, ed. by Enrico Palandri and Hanna Serkowska (Venice: Edizioni Ca' Foscari, 2015), pp. 111-19

——*Il poeta e la grazia: una lettura dei manoscritti della* Storia *di Elsa Morante* (Rome: Edizioni di storia e letteratura, 2017)

ZEITLIN, FROMA, 'The Vicarious Witness: Belated Memory and Authorial Presence in Recent Holocaust Literature', *History and Memory*, 10.2 (1998), 5-42

ZILLMANN, DOLF, 'Mechanisms of Emotional Involvement with Drama', *Poetics*, 23 (1994), 33-51

ZIMMERMAN, JOSHUA D., ed., *Jews in Italy under Fascist and Nazi Rule, 1922–1945* (Cambridge: Cambridge University Press, 2005)

ZOLLI, EUGENIO, *Prima dell'alba: autobiografia autorizzata* (Cinisello Balsamo: San Paolo, 2004)

ZUCCOTTI, SUSAN, *The Italians and the Holocaust: Persecution, Rescue, and Survival* (London: Halban, 1987)

——*Under His Very Windows. The Vatican and the Holocaust in Italy* (New Haven, CT: Yale University Press, 2000)

ZUNSHINE, LISA, 'What is Cognitive Cultural Studies?', in *Introduction to Cognitive Cultural Studies*, ed. by Lisa Zunshine (Baltimore, MD: Johns Hopkins University Press, 2010), pp. 1-33

——, ed., *The Oxford Handbook of Cognitive Literary Studies* (New York: Oxford University Press, 2015)

Audiovisual Sources

'16 ottobre', *Sorgente di vita* (Rai 2, 6 October 2013)

'16 ottobre 1943', *Ulisse* (Rai 1, 13 October 2018)

16 ottobre 1943, dir. by Ansano Giannarelli (REIAC Film, 1961)

'16 ottobre 1943: la razzia del ghetto', *Un giorno nella storia* (Rai Radio3, 16 October 2019) <https://www.raiplaysound.it/playlist/16ottobre1943larazzianelghetto> [accessed 21 March 2020]

Amen, dir. by Costa-Gavras (Mikado Film, 2002)

'Anna Foa: la deportazione raccontata ai bambini' (Rai Scuola, 9 September 2015) <https://www.raiscuola.rai.it/tags/annafoa> [accessed 21 March 2019]

'Anna Foa presenta *Via Portico d'Ottavia 13* alla Libreria Arion Monti' (2013) <https://www.youtube.com/watch?v=aDPobEBZwO0> [accessed 21 March 2019]

'Anna Foa — *Portico d'Ottavia, 13*' (2014) <https://www.youtube.com/watch?v=Ms_JgmASaMk> [accessed 21 March 2019]

Le avventure di Pinocchio, dir. by Luigi Comencini (Rai 1, April 1972)

Diario di un cronista: Piazza Giudia, dir. by Sergio Zavoli (Studio M.I.O., 1963)

Ebrei a Roma, dir. by Gianfranco Pannone (Blue Film, 2012)

La finestra di fronte, dir. by Ferzan Özpetek (R&C Produzioni, Red Wave Films, AFS Film, 2003)

Freaks Out, dir. by Gabriele Mainetti (Goon Films, Lucky Red, Rai Cinema, 2021)

Ladro di razza, dir. by Gianni Clementi (Rai 5, 13 October 2018)

Memoria presente: ebrei e città di Roma durante l'occupazione nazista, dir. by Ansano Giannarelli (Archivio storico audiovisivo del movimento operaio, Istituto Romano per la storia d'Italia dal fascismo alla resistenza, Centro di Cultura Ebraica della Comunità israelitica di Roma, 1983)

Nata due volte: storia di Settimia ebrea romana, dir. by Giandomenico Curi (Shoah Foundation, ANED, 2005)

Nazisti a Roma, dir. by Mary Mirka Milo (Istituto Luce, 2007)

L'oro di Roma, dir. by Carlo Lizzani (Ager Film, Sancro Film, C.I.R.A.C., Contact Organisation, Lux Film, 1961)

La razzia: Roma, 16 ottobre 1943, dir. by Ruggero Gabbai (Forma International, Fondazione Museo della Shoah, Rai Cinema, 2018)

Roma e la Shoah: luoghi e storie della persecuzione, dir. by Dario Prosperini (Fondazione Museo della Shoah, 2020)

'Il sabato nero', dir. by Gianluigi De Stefano, *La storia siamo noi* (Rai 3, 16 October 2012)

Sotto il cielo di Roma, dir. by Christian Deguay (Lux Vide, Rai Fiction, Rai 1, 31 October and 1 November 2010)

La Storia, dir. by Luigi Comencini (Rai 2, Antenne 2, SACIS, 1986)

La Storia, dir. by Luigi Comencini (Rai 2, December 1986)

Storia d'amore e d'amicizia, dir. by Franco Rossi (Rai 1, Rewind, for six weeks from 24 October 1982)

La tregua, dir. by Francesco Rosi (3 Emme Cinematografica, Stephan Films, UCG Images, Dazu film, 1997)

'Una storia italiana', *Sorgente di vita* (Rai 2, 20 October 2013)

Una storia romana, dir. by Pupa Garibba (Europa News, 2008)

'Viaggio senza ritorno', *Ulisse* (Rai 1, 26 January 2022)

La vita è bella, dir. by Roberto Benigni (Cecchi Gori Group, Melampo Cinematografica, 1997)

INDEX

❖

www.ingramcontent.com/pod-product-compliance
Lightning Source LLC
Chambersburg PA
CBHW050658110426
42739CB00035B/3445